Migrants in Translation

Migrants in Translation

*Caring and the Logics of Difference in
Contemporary Italy*

Cristiana Giordano

UNIVERSITY OF CALIFORNIA PRESS

University of California Press, one of the most
distinguished university presses in the United States,
enriches lives around the world by advancing scholarship
in the humanities, social sciences, and natural sciences. Its
activities are supported by the UC Press Foundation and
by philanthropic contributions from individuals and
institutions. For more information, visit www.ucpress.edu.

University of California Press
Oakland, California

Library of Congress Cataloging-in-Publication Data

Giordano, Cristiana, 1971–
    Migrants in translation: caring and the logics of
difference in contemporary Italy / Cristiana Giordano.
        pages cm
    Includes bibliographical references and index.
    ISBN 978-0-520-27665-9 (hardback)
    ISBN 978-0-520-27666-6 (paper)
    ISBN 978-0-520-95866-9 (e-book)
    1. Ethnopsychology—Italy. 2. Immigrants—Cultural
assimilation—Italy. 3. Immigrants—Mental health—
Italy. 4. Assimilation (Sociology)—Psychological aspects.
I. Title.
    GN502.G56 2014
    155.8 20945—dc23
                                        2014006526

Manufactured in the United States of America
23   22   21   20   19   18   17   16   15   14
10   9   8   7   6   5   4   3   2   1

In keeping with a commitment to support
environmentally responsible and sustainable printing
practices, UC Press has printed this book on Natures
Natural, a fiber that contains 30% post-consumer waste
and meets the minimum requirements of ANSI/NISO
Z39.48-1992 (R 1997) (Permanence of Paper).

A mio padre,
in memoriam

Contents

Illustrations

Acknowledgments

I am deeply grateful to Roberto Beneduce, who opened the doors of the Centro Frantz Fanon to me and allowed me to learn about the complexities of ethno-psychiatry and the political project behind the Centro. Without his generosity and openness this project never would have happened. My special thanks also go to Simona Taliani, Francesco Vacchiano, and Paola Spadafina, who were always generous with their time in conversing with and teaching me about their work and clinical cases. At the Centro, I am also indebted to the trainees and other mental health professionals for sharing with me thought-provoking conversations about clinical work and its political implications. Among the cultural mediators, I am most grateful to Lahcen Aalla for letting me follow him in the many institutional settings where he trained cultural mediators. Most important, I am indebted to all the patients at the Centro for allowing me to be part of their therapeutic sessions. To them I give my deepest thanks.

I thank the Catholic nuns who welcomed my presence as a volunteer and researcher at the shelters. I owe particular gratitude to the women who lived at the shelters for sharing their frustrations and hopes with me and for teaching me about their lives and homes. Special thanks go to the director and staff at the Catholic nonprofit association that supports foreign women as they file criminal charges. They gave me full access to documents and helped me learn about the practice of *denuncia,* which became a central question of this book. Most of all, I owe my deepest gratitude to Elisabeth Aguebor Attila, who showed me the intricacies of what it means to be a cultural mediator in various institutional settings and to translate women's stories of prostitution and migration. She became a great friend and teacher to me.

This book emerges out of research that I conducted for my PhD at the University of California, Berkeley. My deepest thanks go to Stefania Pandolfo for her capacity to understand my strengths and weaknesses, for pushing me to dare and think fully, and for her friendship. She has taught me integrity and passion for the careful work of accounting for the complexities and contradictions of the world. Lawrence Cohen's unlimited knowledge, kind mentorship, and capacity to tell stories— even the most tragic ones—with a sense of poetry and irony have made him a very important presence as a mentor and a friend. William Hanks has taught me to think through some very challenging material on linguistics and the anthropology of language. Our conversations about translation have pushed me in inspiring directions. His wisdom has been an important gift in moments of discouragement. Mia Fuller patiently prepared me for fieldwork in Italy, a country I began learning about after leaving it. Her incredible scholarship and kindness of heart make her a wonderful teacher. Also at UC Berkeley, I would like to extend my gratitude to Alexei Yurchaik, Mariane Ferme, Nancy Scheper-Hughes, and Paul Rabinow. They have been inspiring interlocutors from whom I have learned a lot. The Institute of European Studies, the Department of Italian Studies, the Graduate Division, and the Department of Anthropology at UC Berkeley; the Woodrow Wilson National Fellowship Foundation; and the Hellman Fellowship from the University of California, Davis (UC Davis), all granted institutional and material support for this project.

As a postdoctoral fellow at the McGill Division for Social and Transcultural Psychiatry, I met a wonderful community of scholars and mental health practitioners. Laurence Kirmayer and Allan Young provided precious intellectual engagement and kindness and helped me deepen my understanding of transcultural psychiatry and its political entanglements. I feel particularly grateful to have met Kelly McKinney, Alessandra Miklavcic, Vincenzo Spigonardo, Eugene Raikhel, and Suparna Choudhury; writing and thinking with them has provided me with a great example of a supportive and inspiring intellectual community. Their comments on my work are interwoven throughout this book. Kelly McKinney has always gone the extra mile to encourage me to believe in my work; her friendship and honesty are great gifts to me.

At UC Davis, I have found a rich intellectual home in which to flourish. I have benefited greatly from my colleagues in the anthropology department, who engaged in this project with generosity and helped me sharpen the book's argument; they include Joe Dumit, Li Zhang, Suzana Sawyer, Tim Choy, Don Donham, Suad Joseph, Alan Klima, Smriti Srinivas, Janet Shibamoto-Smith, and James Smith. I owe deep gratitude to Marisol de la Cadena, who has put special care into reading chapters of this book and whose openness, courage and intelligence have taught me more than I can express. Other colleagues, students, and friends at UC Davis have offered precious feedback and support: Josh Breslau, Nickolas D'Avella, Stefanie Greater, Ladson Hinton, Ingrid Lagos, Laura Meek, Lena Mehari, Julia Morales Fontanilla, Rossio Motta, Ayesha Nibbe, Aaron Norton, Jorge Nunez Vega, Mar-Y-Sol Pasquiers, Camilo Sanz, Sylvia Sensiper, Eric Taggart, and Adrian Yen. In particular, I thank my research assistants, Vivian Choi and Matthew Nesvet, for their patient work and careful reading, and Manuela Boucher-de la Cadena, for helping me with the bibliography.

Thanks to all the students in my psychological and medical anthropology classes at UC Davis from 2010 to 2013 who helped me develop some of the material in this book. I also thank the participants in Lisa Stevenson's "Violence and Subjectivity" seminar at McGill University who read an early draft of this book in spring 2013; they were generous and astute readers who pushed me in some very productive ways.

I feel very fortunate to be part of a large community of colleagues and friends around the world who have read parts of this work and have deeply influenced my way of thinking: Damir Arsenijevic, Ellen Corin, Veena Das, Elisabeth Davis, Aurora Donzelli, Tarek Elhaik, Ugo Fabietti, Didier Fassin, Paul Ginsborg, Eric Glassgold, Deborah Gordon, John Hill, Saida Hodzic, Laura Hubbard, Marco Jacquemet, Kevin Karpiak, Eduardo Kohn, Tatyana Mamut, Pompeo Martelli, Shaylih Muelhmann, Mary Murrell, Valentina Napolitano, Mariella Pandolfi, Rachel Prentice, Tamar Rapoport, Elisabeth Roberts, Timoteo Rodriguez, Chris Roebuck, Natasha Schull, Pino Schirripa, Fouzieyha Towghi, Mauro Van Haken, Ken Varcoe, and Ian Whitmarsh. I especially thank Fiamma Montezemolo for showing me how ethnography can be conveyed through art and for the generous gift of one of the images that appears in this book.

At UC Press, I thank Reed Malcolm for believing in this book. The three reviewers' comments guided my revision of the text in ways that have made it stronger and more compelling. I am grateful to Anitra

Grisales, who copyedited the manuscript and helped me restructure the book at a very crucial stage of its production.

I am profoundly grateful for those friends and colleagues who have read the whole manuscript in great detail, sometimes more than once. In particular, I thank Lisa Stevenson for reading this work with wonderful sensitivity, loyalty, and taste for the nuances; Rima Praliauskiene for her depth of perception, honesty, and solidarity; Rhiannon Welch for her careful reading, editing, and enthusiasm for the material; Lucinda Ramberg for her smart comments, generosity, and endless support; Luca D'Isanto for being an important interlocutor at different stages of this project and for reading and commenting on this text with great care, helping me make it a better book. I also thank Patricia Speier who, over the course of years, has taught me how to listen and speak differently and who has helped me find a voice.

Finally, my sisters, Antonella, Romana, and Paola, and my mother, Rosanna Colonna, were part of this project in many different ways: they provided love and solidarity, helped me get access to institutional places and people, and engaged me in smart conversations on the topics of this book and beyond. My nephews Emanuele Negro and Davide Besuschio were great research assistants for two summers.

I dedicate this book to the memory of my father, Alessandro Giordano, who passed away as I finished writing it. His intelligence, warmth, and sense of humor have accompanied me throughout this project, and always will.

Prior versions of some of the material in this book appeared in the following articles: "Practices of Translation and the Making of Migrant Subjectivities in Contemporary Italy," *American Ethnologist* 35, no. 4 (November 2008): 588–606; and "Translating Fanon in the Italian Context: Rethinking the Ethics of Treatment in Psychiatry," *Transcultural Psychiatry* 48, no. 3 (2011): 228–56.

Introduction

In 2002 I went to the region of Piedmont, northern Italy, to conduct an ethnography of Italian ethno-psychiatry. This emerging therapeutic approach to foreign patients creates a space—both therapeutic and political—to incorporate cultural and experiential difference into its work. While in this book I analyze the specific therapeutic practices of clinical ethno-psychiatry in Italy, I also document its political impact on other Italian institutions (the Catholic Church, the police, and social services) involved in aid and recovery programs for, as the state calls them, "victims of human trafficking." At the time of my research, these institutions were increasingly turning to ethno-psychiatrists for help shaping culturally and psychologically appropriate interventions for foreigners, many of whom were women who had gotten involved in prostitution after migrating to Italy. Ethno-psychiatry became central to challenging the way the state recognized these women and how it identified which foreign "victims" were worthy of receiving legal rights.

In observing how each institutional setting worked with the ethno-psychiatrists and their patients, I realized that each actor engaged in practices of translation to produce an intelligible account of the other, or to relate to difference. Each, in its own way, has its own scripts, roles, and stories that represent the foreigner and translate her alterity into its own language. In other words, difference poses the issue of alternative forms of life, of radically heterogeneous worlds that the state must reduce to recognizable categories, thus depriving them of their otherness. In my own rendering of the landscape of these various institutions, I approach ethno-psychiatry as a practice that creates epistemological breaks in the discourses of psychiatry and critiques how the state reduces the other to familiar categories in order to, paradoxically, identify her as an outsider.

In my case, doing fieldwork meant going back "home," where I was born and where I spent the first twenty-five years of my life. I had to relearn and gain a new understanding of many of the familiar categories I had been raised with. I based my research in Novara, my hometown, and in Turin, one hour away by train. This was not my first venture into the topic. In the early 1990s, while an undergraduate in philosophy at the University of Pavia (fifteen miles south of Milan), and together with other students, I volunteered at shelters for foreigners. Italy had not yet passed a comprehensive immigration law—the Martelli Law was approved in 1998—and thus was an easy entry point to Europe for migrants from northern and sub-Saharan Africa. Many of these shelters for documented and undocumented foreigners depended on lay and religious volunteers to keep them open and running properly. Of course, what qualified as "proper" differed from one group of volunteers to another. For instance, there were long discussions between members of my group—mostly of left-wing philosophy and anthropology majors— and volunteers from Catholic nongovernmental organizations (NGOs) about how foreigners and volunteers should behave at the table. When the men from Senegal cooked *mafe* (a peanut butter–based vegetable and rice dish) we enjoyed eating with our hands from a common bowl, as was their practice. The Catholic volunteers thought it was unhygienic, so they introduced silverware and plates, to our dismay. We tried to practice what we learned in anthropology classes about colonialism and the work of Frantz Fanon and thus objected to the images of Jesus and Mary that other volunteers placed on the nightstands of the Tunisian and Senegalese men living at the shelter. What forms of recognition of the other were at play there? Was it recognition, or was it conversion? The different ways volunteers approached this question pointed to the complex and contradictory overlapping of religious and secular logics at the heart of practices of integration in Italy.

Ten years later, when I decided to conduct fieldwork in Italy, I was reminded of these experiences at the shelter, and of the conundrum embedded in institutional logics and projects of integration. While lecturing in cultural anthropology at a school for social work, I met the group of ethno-psychiatrists and cultural mediators that inspired this book. Not only were they seriously engaged in extending psychosocial support to documented and undocumented foreigners, but they also shared my background in medical anthropology, which they applied to their clinical work. In the mid-1990s they opened the Centro Frantz Fanon in Turin, an ethno-psychiatric clinic that, as an alternative to public mental health services, offers psychological support to asylum seekers and victims of torture and trafficking. They also advise Italian social workers, educators, volunteers, state bureaucrats, and mental health practitioners who work with migrant populations. In Italy, this kind of culturally competent service lacks any institutional or economic support. Therefore, at the time of my research, the Centro was funded mostly through projects sponsored by the region, the municipality, and, occasionally, the European Union (EU).

The work of this group of practitioners intrigued me for several reasons. First of all, the mental health of foreigners in most European countries and in North America raises unresolved questions about psychiatry, a critical frame for exploring the legacies of colonial violence and postcolonial transition (Santiago-Irizarry 2001; Beneduce 2007; Keller 2007). In Italy, ethno-psychiatry and its objects of inquiry offer privileged windows into the migration experiences of postcolonial populations and their effects on the ethics and politics of therapeutic work. Second, their clinical practice and political engagement provide a critique of the politics of recognition and cohabitation. Their approach to cultural difference within and outside the clinic challenges mainstream therapeutic and state apparatuses, showing the arbitrariness of psychiatric categories and the strategy of embracing "multiculturalism" to deal with difference. And thus, curious about the questions ethno-psychiatry posed, between June 2002 and July 2004 I followed these practitioners as they worked inside and outside of the clinical space.

One hot afternoon in late May 2003, I went to the Centro Frantz Fanon to assist with a therapy session that Dr. F had scheduled with a young woman from Nigeria. The Centro is well known in Turin and the rest of the country for combining healing practices from patients' backgrounds with Western psychological theories, as well as a critique of mainstream biomedical approaches to mental health. Since patients and therapists do not typically share the same therapeutic and epistemological frame, the Centro provides a "space of mediation" in which a shared frame might be negotiated. Cultural mediators fluent in the patient's language are usually present in the therapeutic setting to provide cultural and linguistic translation, but on that day no Nigerian mediator was available. The patient, Favor,[1] was twenty-five years old and was brought to the clinic by Maria, a woman in her late fifties who volunteered at a Catholic shelter for foreigners in Turin. Favor had experienced several crises at the shelter, during which she would convulse, fall to the ground, and nearly faint. According to Maria, these events looked like epileptic seizures. The doctor at the public hospital diagnosed them as, possibly, psychotic episodes. The priests and nuns in charge of the shelter approached the problem differently: they put a rosary around her neck to calm her down. As a result, Favor became even more agitated. When she had yet another crisis, they decided to take her to the Centro Fanon.

Dr. F welcomed Favor in the consultation room and had her sit on a chair between us. He had warned me that, according to what Maria had told him about Favor, she was in a lot of pain. He started by asking her about her life in Nigeria. She told us about her Catholic upbringing and wealthy family background. She had a degree in management, and she had never thought about traveling abroad until she met an older woman in Lagos named Edith, who encouraged her to go to Italy to continue her studies. This woman invited her to visit her in Benin City, where she initiated her into a spiritual practice that involved wearing all white, using perfume, and putting incense on her forehead during rituals. Favor became fascinated with Edith and followed all her instructions, even when her parents disapproved. Indeed, they grew very suspicious of the woman from Benin City. When one of Favor's sisters died in an accident, her father accused Favor of causing it by being involved in evil rituals that cast a spell on the family. Her relationship with her family became very tense.

One day Edith took her to a voodoo ceremony in Benin City, where they took some of her hair and blood. Dr. F asked her whether she knew what the ritual was about. Favor said she did not know; she never asked. They told her only that the ceremony could either cure her or make her crazy. Dr. F was very familiar with the rituals women performed before and after leaving Nigeria to protect their journeys, seal alliances between people and with spirits, and, often, create ties and debts. He asked Favor which spirit was present during the ritual, and she responded that it was a "spiritual husband." "Do you mean the ritual was a marriage to Mami Wata, the goddess of the waters?" he asked. Over the years he had treated many women who were devotees of the goddess and was familiar with the symptoms that indicated a disturbed relationship to the deity. Favor laughed and replied, "No, he was just a spiritual husband."

After the ritual, Edith convinced Favor to leave for Italy, a journey Favor paid for with her father's money. Once in Italy, she got involved in prostitution networks, and her madam (another woman from Nigeria) did another voodoo ritual using her nails and pubic hair. Favor was told that if she did not abide by the madam's rules she would go mad. When Favor abandoned the street and her madam to enter the state's rehabilitation program for victims of human trafficking, she started having crises. Dr. F asked her whether she could relate some of her current experiences to what happened in Nigeria before she left. She replied that she often felt that the spiritual husband to whom she was married during the rituals in Benin City was making love to her. It happened in her sleep. Also, before meeting Edith she used to pray to Jesus and see his heart; now, every time she tried to pray her mind wandered endlessly, and she would feel dizzy. At one point I noticed that she stopped answering the doctor's questions and had an inquisitive look on her face. Then she said, "I know voodoo works in Nigeria, but does it work here, too, even if we are far away and there is a sea in between? I am worried about what is happening to me; I want to know whether it is true here as it was in Nigeria." Dr. F asked her whether she remembered the crises she had at the shelter, but she did not. He touched her head and asked where they touched her during the voodoo rituals. He knew that was part of the process. He made another appointment with her and reassured her that we would talk more about it all. We then met with Maria separately. Dr. F told her that Favor was a bright woman who wanted to feel better, and there were just a few issues to work on. We made a follow-up appointment for the next week.

Later that day, as Dr. F and I were closing the Center and discussing the session with Favor, he explained to me that it was not his job to produce a biomedical diagnosis for the symptoms she presented. The hospital had already done that and decided she was experiencing psychotic episodes. But, he argued, this kind of diagnostic category does not take into account the sociocultural and historical contexts that are often at the root of patients' symptoms. Favor, for example, was presenting a body caught in a complex history of overlapping practices and discourses: voodoo rituals, a spiritual husband, exorcism, Catholicism and the rosary, and crossing borders. Her symptoms were both an individual expression and a political and historical commentary on what crossing borders does to the psyche and the body. They told a story of multiple alliances, of betrayal and debts, and of spirits that may or may not cross borders with the bodies they once inhabited. In order to listen to the complexity of her experiences, Dr. F argued, we have to suspend the use of psychiatric diagnoses that are like other medical practices we call "traditional"; they are the products of a specific historical and cultural context. They translate suffering into medical codes that are believed to be universally true without paying attention to the larger cultural contexts in which the individual's experience is shaped. He added that social workers and doctors often assume women like Favor, whom the law considers "victims of human trafficking,"[2] are traumatized by the experience of prostitution. But Dr. F argued that their malaise often came from farther away, from home countries devastated by war, poverty, and long histories of colonization and violence. In other words, patients' stories and their symptoms were more complex than what a psychiatric diagnosis ("psychotic episode") or state's category ("victim") could contain and explain.

THE DOUBLE BIND OF RECOGNITION

Through a case study of new forms of therapy emerging in Italy, this book looks at how difference is translated and recognized in the political context of modern nation-states. This book is about the paradoxes that arise from the overlapping projects of liberal inclusion, postcolonial violence, and the politics of difference. The larger context for this work is contemporary Europe, where cultural and political identities are being negotiated between a presumed cultural affinity among European countries and an increasingly multicultural and multiracial society forming within Europe itself. In this context, legal and illegal foreigners—mostly from Eastern Europe and northern and sub-Saharan Africa—are often portrayed as a "threat" to national and supranational identities, security, and cultural and religious values. Contemporary Italy is struggling to conceive of a new European multicultural society, on the one hand, and to deal with its own internal fragmented identities, on the other. This book is an ethnographic reflection on the legal, therapeutic, and moral techniques of integration and cultural translation that have emerged in response to the increasing numbers of documented and undocumented others, among them stateless people, refugees, and victims of abuse, torture, and trafficking. In my research, I have found that the Italian state reveals its political, legal, and moral frameworks particularly in the way it approaches the issue of foreign prostitution as a modern form of slavery.

In 2000 Pia Covre, an Italian sex worker and a cofounder of the Italian Committee for the Civil Rights of Prostitutes, gave the opening speech at an international seminar on social exclusion in Geneva. There she referred to the foreign prostitute[3] as "an emblematic figure of singularity" for the state that confers rights. Covre emphasized that the foreign prostitute "embodies something extra, which is indigestible, an immeasurable difference which no prostitution policy wants to remove or mitigate."[4] This book is precisely about this "indigestibility" of the foreign other and the mechanisms of translation that various institutions use to make her recognizable, includable, and thus digestible. I unveil the mechanism of exclusion/inclusion embedded in the state's categories of recognition that, in the case of victims of human trafficking, only function through the binary structure victim/agent; but I also indicate how a new politics is possible beyond the binary opposition of the state and beyond psychiatric classifications of pathology and normality.

Cultural difference often gets portrayed as and reduced to an issue of migration: migrants exist because there are borders. Indeed, we could claim that contemporary notions of "migration" only make sense in the context of the nation-state. While I look at different projects of recognition that emerge in response to what the state portrays as the "threat" of foreign migration, I also argue that the issue of difference exceeds the politics of migration. This excess is acknowledged in emerging therapeutic spaces that respond to foreign others' needs by including healing techniques from their home countries and by questioning the host society's techniques of inclusion. In Italy, legal and moral techniques of integration/recognition use a combined language of therapeutics and of cultural difference, which then intersect in complex ways with religious logics of confession and redemption.

"Recognition" has become a keyword for anthropologists, political theorists, and philosophers interested in contemporary forms of the state and its techniques for addressing issues of identity and difference. A central category in Hegel's understanding of the master-slave dialectic, "recognition" today captures the moral stakes of many kinds of conflicts. Whether the issue is Muslim minorities in Europe (Asad 2003), indigenous land claims in Australia (Povinelli 2002), the coexistence of different temporalities in various archives in Peru (De la Cadena 2010), or immigration policies in Italy, the term *recognition* seems to capture both the normative basis of political claims and the violence embedded in them.

Recognition can only come from an "other." In Fanon's reflections (1967 [1952]), the gaze of the colonizer fixes the colonized in an image of inferiority that the colonized internalizes. The gaze produces mimesis through *imagos*. Unlike the work of the imagination, imagos are projections imposed on the other. Lacan (1966) describes the mirror stage as the moment in a child's development when, by standing in front of the mirror, the child perceives itself for the first time as other than the mother. In psychoanalytic terms, the subject emerges as the nexus of projections that come from elsewhere, in an intersubjective play of reflections and appropriations. Thus, recognition is predicated upon an experience of fundamental alienation and misrecognition.

In liberal nation-states, recognition is often described in the language of tolerance, inclusion, and multiculturalism (Taylor 1994; Brown 1995; Povinelli 2002). It comprises techniques that aim to make the social world intelligible to the state. The act of recognition can be a way to *disclose* or *reveal* the other's foreignness, but it can also work to *appropriate* and *reduce* difference, or at least make it identifiable or recognizable to the state.[5] In this book, however, I want to show the broader implications of recognition as a political practice often grounded in power asymmetries and structures of subordination that have an impact on the lives of citizens and, most important, those who will never achieve this status.

At its best, the politics of recognition aims to fight deep-seated forms of social injustice in relations of identity and difference (Merkell 2003, 17). In the early 1980s, this kind of politics emerged as central to liberal democracy in demanding more justice with regard to issues of ethnicity and race. It was framed as an alternative response to practices of assimilation and as a human right (Taylor 1994). The politics of recognition is articulated through categories that sustain the identities of socially and historically situated subjects understood as members of specific communities and bearers of particular identities (Merkell 2003, 11). The question of identity is central to recognition, which grounds sovereignty in the knowledge of who one is and where one belongs in the larger communities. On the one hand, difference ultimately needs to be translated into categories of identity that the state can know, manage, and, to some extent, protect. On the other hand, because recognition is also driven by the desire for democratic equality, it can propose a relationship to difference aimed at overcoming it and thus reducing it to sameness. What started as an alternative proposal to assimilation has turned into the performance of identity as a fixed category that translates the other into what is familiar.

What if the other cannot be known? What if difference cannot be recognized? What other languages could we use to talk about cohabitation and the multiple temporalities of modernity? Would *acknowledgment*, rather than recognition, allow for a different politics of life, beyond the logics of understanding and sovereignty? I understand "acknowledgment" as the political and ethical act of surrendering the desire to know through already established categories and of accepting the challenges of difference and the possibility of not knowing, not understanding, and thus embracing uncertainty. Acknowledgment calls for a coming to terms with the fact that difference exceeds categories; the other cannot be assigned a fixed identity, only an opaque and shifting sense of belonging. This kind of relation to difference requires struggling with categories of recognition, undoing them in order to realize that there is no identity contained in them. I thus see acknowledgment as a space for what Jacques Rancière (1999) calls politics, where the other's difference introduces change in established discourses and thus discards preexisting identities.

To understand what constitutes political action for Rancière, let me turn to the distinction he makes between "policing" and "politics." For him, political action is about changing the social order, creating a form of *dissensus* (disagreement) that changes the meaning of political engagement and redefines what is sayable and visible within a given community. He distinguishes between political acts and policing practices: the former refer to those engagements that transform preexisting shared assumptions and create new possibilities of social existence; the latter concern the management of given social roles and places that are left unchanged though rearranged (Rancière 1999). In light of this distinction, I make a parallel between policing and politics of recognition, on the one hand, and politics and acknowledgment, on the other. While recognition presumes an object—the other—that can be known and translated into an identity category, acknowledgment is not about knowing the other but about the possible relations and encounters in which forms of life are made and boundaries between individuals and communities are blurred.

This book approaches Italian ethno-psychiatry as a practice that models acknowledgment through a type of clinical listening that is political and therefore in disagreement with the policing mechanisms of the state, which claims to know foreign others through categories such as victim, migrant, and political refugee. I focus on this therapeutic practice as an alternative technique—and relation to difference— that provides culturally sensitive therapeutic services to foreigners, political refugees, and victims of torture and trafficking, in addition to supervising the work of social workers, health practitioners, and volunteers who work with them.[6] I argue that while ethno-psychiatry's use of cultural material as therapeutic can reify the other's difference for therapeutic reasons, it also provides a radical critique of psychiatric, legal, and moral categories of inclusion, thus allowing for a rethinking of the politics of difference and recognition. Ethno-psychiatrists' practical approaches to cultural difference can serve as a model for letting difference exceed and remake those fixed categories. When Dr. F met Favor for the first time, his questions attempted to locate her symptoms in her larger political and cultural context, not to translate them into a diagnostic category. To translate her experiences into a biomedical category would imply making it commensurate with a known entity, the diagnosis. In this sense it would be in line with a mechanism of recognition that reduces difference to the familiar. Dr. F, on the contrary, listened to the different languages Favor used. He engaged her own disconcertment vis-à-vis her symptoms and the efficacy of voodoo at a distance. As I will show through other clinical cases in the book (in chapters 1, 2, and 6), this therapeutic approach allows for different understandings of health and illness not only to emerge but also to question the receiving country's hegemonic medical model and patients' other models of health.

Outside of the clinic, Catholic groups, the Immigration Office, and social services often enlisted ethno-psychiatrists' expertise to shape appropriate interventions for foreigners. Translation is key to these collaborations with institutions and their languages. Through conceptual acts of translation, a complex interplay of therapeutic, bureaucratic, and religious apparatuses transforms foreign others into political categories—the "migrant," "refugee," and "victim"—that the state can recognize and use to legitimize their difference. Simultaneously, this translation gives foreigners access to services and rights. I thus argue that projects of recognition of foreign others are articulated through various techniques of translation that can either acknowledge the incommensurability of difference or attempt to domesticate it within familiar categories. In other words, translation is a mechanism that can create either opacity or transparency. This is the double bind of multiculturalism, as Étienne Balibar has argued:

> Institutions reduce the multiplicity or complexity of identifications. But do they suppress that multiplicity in such a way as to constitute one single identity? . . . [T]his is "normally" *impossible*, even though it is, just as "normally," *required*. There is a *double*-bind here. This is where the basis of the

problem of "multicultural" society lies: not simply in the plurality of the state, but in the oscillation for each individual between the two equally impossible extremes of absolutely simple identity and the infinite dispersal of identities across multiple social relationships. (Balibar 2002, 67; original emphasis)

Ethno-psychiatry aims to inhabit and loosen this double bind and thus challenge multicultural projects of inclusion. This means struggling with the categories of recognition provided by both psychiatry and the state.

The point I make throughout this book is that all the agents involved in the integration of foreign others into Italian society, from state bureaucrats to cultural mediators, from Catholic nuns to ethno-psychiatrists, adopt a model of translation to be able to understand and relate to the other's difference. The state enacts a violent translation: it does not see the foreigner as an individual with rights and privileges but rather as a univocal autobiographical narrative that is applied to every migrant. This process involves an act of misrecognition, since the other is often irreducible to the stories that the state expects to hear. The Catholic nuns and state bureaucrats attempt to engage in alternative forms of translation to mitigate the violent effects of misrecognition, so they turn to ethno-psychiatrists for advice on how to be culturally sensitive in their efforts to reintegrate victims of human trafficking. However, they often translate what they learn from ethno-psychiatry into yet other categories of recognition that reduce the other to a familiar presence. Ethno-psychiatry, on the contrary, uses different mechanisms of translation to make sure that the foreigner's story and language is translated in its unique, singular difference. For ethno-psychiatry, this means that it needs to suspend the state's category of the victim of human trafficking, for example, as well as the psychiatric diagnoses that practitioners and social services assign to patients at local hospitals. Ethno-psychiatry introduces an interruption in the discourses of the state and thus produces a new politics of difference that I understand as a kind of acknowledgment of difference rather than a recognition. All the mechanisms of translation that I document in these different institutional settings (the clinic, the Immigration Office, the police station, and the shelter) involve theatrical elements that point to the performative power of these places and their discourses, and to the kind of politics or policing they produce as well, which at some level mirror the theater of the state. There is an unavoidable violence implicit in any cultural act of translation, whether acknowledged or not. It is the price one pays for any discourse of integration and inclusion in a multicultural society; it is, precisely, the double bind of multiculturalism.

IN THE CLINIC AND BEYOND

Let me pause and explain the specificity of ethno-psychiatric practice vis-à-vis psychiatry. As a branch of biomedicine, psychiatry interprets mental experiences as pathologies that can be observed in the same way that a natural scientist observes the structure of a cell or forms of cancers. Psychiatrists use diagnoses as literal translations of "natural" disorders. Psychiatric diagnostic categories provide a universal language to describe what occurs in the mind and to match it with specific treatment, either pharmaceutical or psychodynamic, or both (Kleinman 1988; Luhrmann 2000). However, as phenomenological psychiatrists have pointed out, the problem with psychiatric diagnoses is that through claims of scientific validity and evidence, they erase the unique and diverse experience of the individual.[7]

In Italy in the 1960s, Franco Basaglia founded his "democratic psychiatry" on the idea that diagnoses express the hegemonic institutional power that prevents a broader understanding of madness. He noted how the misery of the asylum intersects with the misery of society (Scheper-Hughes and Lovell 1987; Giordano 2011) and argued that the diagnostic apparatus conceals suffering behind categories. He believed that a real encounter between doctor and patient must occur independently of psychiatry's labels. Italian ethno-psychiatry follows this tradition of politically engaged clinical practice and furthers Basaglia's contributions by including cultural difference in the domain of therapy. By integrating foreign patients' etiologies and healing practices within the therapeutic space and by suspending psychiatric diagnoses, ethno-psychiatry turns psychiatry inside out by questioning its universal truth (Beneduce and Taliani 2006; Beneduce 2007). We could thus see ethno-psychiatry as a way to provincialize psychiatry (Chakrabarty 2000). In this clinical context, symptoms find different and competing explanations and multiple therapeutic languages circulate. Here, we can think about translation as a process that enables a different listening to and acknowledgment of otherness, as opposed to trying to make it commensurate with the language of psychiatry.

Throughout this book I approach the field of ethno-psychiatry (originally associated with colonial psychiatry and the study of indigenous pathologies) as both an ethnographic site and a theoretical frame. As an ethnographic site, I follow ethno-psychiatry as it is practiced both inside and outside the Centro Fanon. In clinical practice, it challenges the hegemonic discourse of psychiatry by locating patients' symptoms in larger political, cultural, and historical contexts of colonial and postcolonial domination. Ethno-psychiatrists use a similar approach when they consult for state agencies and religious groups. Thus, they influence legal and religious practices of social integration by questioning their ethnocentrism. As a theoretical frame, I use the work of Frantz Fanon, Franco Basaglia, Ernesto de Martino, and Tobie Nathan. These authors developed a critique of Western hegemonic representations of difference that I take up, in part, to decolonize epistemic relations with foreign others. Ethno-psychiatry also offers critical commentary on Italian colonization and the unresolved definitions of national identity that resurface today and shape Italian institutions' response to new waves of foreign migration.

By the time I conducted my research, approximately seven hundred foreign clients had been referred to the Centro, a good number of whom had gone through psychotherapy (Beneduce and Martelli 2005).[8] Between 2002 and 2004, the group of ethno-psychiatrists at the clinic was composed of two psychiatrists (one of whom is also a medical anthropologist), two psychologists also trained in anthropology, one psychologist, four cultural mediators, and about ten trainees who had just graduated in psychology. Collectively, this group of therapists inhabits multiple professional positions—from clinical and academic work to psychological and anthropological training—and is fluent in a range of disciplinary debates, from psychoanalysis and other psychological approaches to anthropology. Some are full-time mental health practitioners; others also hold faculty positions at the university in anthropology and psychology departments; some hold PhDs in anthropology and are involved in field research in some of the patients' countries of origin (Morocco, Mali, Cameroon, Nigeria); finally, trainees usually have a degree in psychology and while in training are exposed to anthropological literature and controversies about culture, healing, selfhood, and what counts as normality and pathology in different medical traditions, among other issues.

While doing research at the Centro, I sat in on therapy sessions with fifteen patients. They ranged in age from twenty to thirty-five years old, with some older and some younger. Only five came regularly to the clinic for periods ranging from a few months to two years. I should note that the Centro often confronts the problems of working with a population that frequently cannot afford regular treatment, either because they are in transition or because their precarious conditions do not allow for consistency. As some practitioners explained, this limits the kind of therapeutic treatment they can provide. I got to know some female patients who had been involved in prostitution and who, at the time of my research, were in a rehabilitation program for victims of human trafficking. Usually they had been referred to the Centro by social services or the associations in charge of them. The stories that emerged in this setting alluded to other institutional contexts that these women had to pass through as "victims" in order to fulfill the state's requirements for rehabilitation. I followed their footsteps through the various phases of the program (filing criminal charges at the police station, life at a shelter) tracing the logics, languages, and techniques that converted them first into "illegal migrants," then into "victims," and finally into "rehabilitated subjects." Like actors in a play moving from one scene to the next, each institution prescribed them specific roles, languages, and behaviors.

Following this group of women led me to conduct ethnographic and archival research in two additional institutional settings involved in implementing a program of social protection for victims: a Catholic legal aid, nonprofit organization for former victims of human trafficking and a Catholic shelter. These sites work in conjunction with various aid projects for foreigners. The Catholic legal aid association helps women who want to leave prostitution file criminal charges against their exploiters. In this context, I learned how one drafts the text of a *denuncia* (the act of filing criminal charges) with the help of a cultural mediator who translates between foreign women, Italian volunteers, and/or police officers. This text is later sent to the police station for approval. I spent countless hours listening to these interviews, which were usually conducted at the association's office and occasionally at the police station itself. At the shelter Catholic nuns turn to ethno-psychiatrists for advice on how to work with foreign women victims of trafficking. In this way, the nuns adjust their universal moral mission to the language of cultural sensitivity as therapy—a sort of act of translation in and of itself—which they also use to negotiate the women's responses and ideas of freedom. Thus, three layers of translation intersect in these processes: the foreigner's complex experiences, the languages of therapy, and the translation of therapy into religious, legal, and moral rehabilitation.

The Catholic associations accepted that I devoted some of my time to "accompanying" women through different steps of the program, such as going to the police station to apply for documents, to the hospital for medical checks, to the office of employment, and to social services to look for housing. In fact, the practice of *accompagnamento*, accompanying women in their institutional trajectories, is central to the work of Italian associations involved in integration projects for foreigners. The idea that former female prostitutes need to be guided, accompanied, and assisted in the process of becoming legal subjects is at the core of social policies of victim rehabilitation and fundamentally shapes the practices of Italian volunteers, bureaucrats, and therapists helping the migrant through the process of becoming legal. Accompagnamento evokes the image of the child who needs to be sustained and contained in order to achieve autonomy. Similarly, foreign women "victims" are portrayed as subjects in need of guidance and protection, unable to function independently in the world.

Thus, I participated in this practice, and spent long hours waiting in various institutional settings with these women to obtain documents, see a doctor, and be interviewed for jobs. Waiting often provided an occasion for conversations. At other times, it offered the women an opportunity to share their feelings of frustration. When women assigned me the role of volunteer (rather than of researcher), I would find myself caught in the very complexities of the encounters between foreigners and Italians that I was attempting to understand.

THE CONUNDRUMS OF TRANSLATION

In this book, I engage both philosophical and anthropological reflections on translation. I use the term *translation* both literally—as the process through which one language is rendered into another—and as a theoretical metaphor through which to think about difference. In fact, the issue of translation is central not only to hermeneutic philosophy but also to anthropology because it questions alterity and its commensurability or incommensurability: Given the multiplicity of languages, what makes them translatable into another? Can translation reach and convey the other's difference?

It is precisely around these questions that various contemporary hermeneutic approaches confront one another, explicitly or implicitly. On the one hand, by privileging communication and relation between languages, some philosophers emphasize the translatability and transparency of a community of communication (Gadamer 1975; Apel 1980; Habermas 2000). Their theories suggest that it is possible to achieve intelligibility between languages, but they conceive of "community" and "language" as too stable to provide a subtle understanding of the complexity of dialogues (Crapanzano 1992). The process is aimed at coming to a compromise and making translation "clearer and flatter than the original" (Gadamer 1975, 348). On the other hand, philosophers such as Benjamin (1968), Heidegger (1975), Derrida (Derrida, McDonald, and Levesque 1985), and Blanchot (Blanchot and Rottenberg 1997) emphasize distance and the irreducible difference of the other. Here, translation is a leap into the unknown of language and is impossible to shed light on. Every translation is an attempt to take this leap and to translate one side of the abyss that separates languages without effacing it (Heidegger 1975, 19). The act of translating becomes a form of listening and poses a fundamental epistemological question about what is knowable of the other language and what remains untranslatable (and unknown). It evokes opacity rather than transparency, and points to the impossibility of translating what in language is destined to be silent and intractable (Resta 1988). According to this position, translation is not flatter than the original but instead produces an "epiphany." Walter Benjamin (1968, 73) referred to this characteristic of translation when he described it as the literary form that is "charged with the special mission of watching over the maturing process of the original language and the birth pangs of its own." Anthropologists have added the fundamental question of power relations to this debate. When we translate, we also confront the inequality of power embedded in different languages: some prevail; others are erased (Asad 1986; Maranhão 2003; Cohen 2005). Translation can domesticate and annihilate difference (Heeschen 2003); in so doing, it has the capacity to liberate difference (Münzel 2003).

In this scenario, it is a matter of deciding where the truth of the other resides: if translation produces transparency, then the truth lies in that which can be translated in language; if translation shows the opacity of languages, otherness lies in that which remains untranslatable. The paradox of the latter position is that the relationship with the other is figured as a relationship of separation. How can we think about difference as a distance that *creates* a relation, which binds by way of separation? In my work, I believe that the task of the anthropologist becomes very similar to the task of the translator, in Benjamin's terms. And so does the task of the clinician in the ethno-psychiatric setting, where all participants in the therapeutic consultation (mental health practitioners, cultural mediators, anthropologists, patients) are called on to inhabit the position of the translator, becoming foreign to themselves and within their mother tongues, so that another account about suffering can emerge and be heard, in its difference and intractability.

Being caught in webs of translation was a quotidian experience for me and for the people I worked with—foreigners and Italians alike. Moreover, translation as a long-standing philosophical and anthropological question points to the complexities of what it means to live together in a society that figures the presence of foreign others as a "threat" and is obsessed with making the other understandable by translating difference into more familiar terms, often uttered in institutional languages. I see this process of translation as deeply ambivalent and fraught with paradoxes. On the one hand, translating can be an act of power and erasure that makes the inequalities of languages evident (Asad 1986). On the other hand, Benjamin (1968, 75) has taught us that the task of the translator is to accept the difference and multiplicity of languages and find "a somewhat provisional way of coming to terms with the foreignness of languages." In this sense, translating is not an exact transposition of meaning from one linguistic system into another but rather a process of transformation that both languages (the original and the target language) undergo. The paradoxes lie in the fact that each practice of translation, while erasing, also transforms both foreigners and Italians. Through an act of effacement, translation also constitutes new subjectivities.

In my ethnographic research, I observed different practices of translation that resonated with both these traditions of thought. The tension between them opens a productive space within which we may examine the forms of recognition that are produced through translation. By rendering the foreign prostitute's story into the bureaucratic language of denuncia, for example, women enter the realm of a rehabilitation program that aims to emancipate them from exploitation and transform them into autonomous subjects. Catholic nuns who run shelters for foreign ex-prostitutes also take part in this process. These mechanisms of translation always move across dangerous polarities: it invokes the infinite singularity of the other; and it renders singularity into a story that makes the other knowable/recognizable for state bureaucracy and the law at large. In ethno-psychiatry, on the contrary, I believe collecting stories in patients' own mother tongues is an important and powerful practice with which to approach difference. Nevertheless, here, too, translation works across different bridges: the ethno-psychiatrists suspend biomedical forms of translation (diagnoses and the pathologization of difference) for the sake of another kind of translation that attempts to acknowledge the uniqueness of the other's predicament. This mechanism of translation clashes with the state's politics of recognition and the law's demand to standardize the foreigner as a victim, a refugee, a prostitute, rather than a legitimate recipient of rights. A central theme in this book is how the state and religious groups use confessional logics to make foreigners resemble the "average" Italian. Ethno-psychiatry, on the other hand, highlights the backgrounds and complex histories of the patients, providing a different kind of listening that, although framed in the register of the therapeutic, approaches difference as a distance that creates a relation, that binds by way of separation. Said otherwise, ethno-psychiatry posits a new kind of therapeutics and politics.

To conclude, I frame ethno-psychiatry both as a therapeutic technique and as a theory of alterity that is similar to a critical medical anthropology. I compare the relationship of the medical anthropologist to medicine to that of the ethno-psychiatrist to psychiatry. Both anthropologists and ethno-psychiatrists attend to the predicament of the patient in a different way than the doctor and the psychiatrist. The difference between these two forms of listening is a question of translation. Medicine and psychiatry take translation as transparent. Symptoms can be translated into pathologies, and pathologies into forms of treatment. For the anthropologist and the ethno-psychiatrist, on the other hand, symptoms can also be the language of dissent and critique; they speak of a larger history and are always inscribed in a cultural and political context. In line with a critical medical anthropology, ethno-psychiatry offers a way of encountering the other that acknowledges the limitations of medical knowledge, engages the epistemic breaks produced by other discourses and experiences of suffering, and uses the clinical setting as a locus of social change (Scheper-Hughes 1990).

MIGRATION AND CITIZENSHIP IN POSTWAR ITALY

In this book, I engage the issue of social change through the lens of foreign migration to Italy and how it intersects with different institutions and their discourses. Contemporary experiences of migration stem from a larger set of problems that have characterized Italy's relationship to capitalist nation-statehood since the eighteenth century. Late-nineteenth- and early-twentieth-century debates about Italian national identity have a discursive afterlife in current projects of "making Italians." To be sure, contemporary practices of making citizens out of foreign others may be read in relation to the famous and often misquoted declaration by the fin-de-siècle Italian nationalist Massimo D'Azeglio, "We have made Italy, now we must make Italians" (quoted in Steinberg 2007; Welch 2008). Far from a steady march of rationalism and capital across the peninsula, Italy's entrance into modern nationhood revealed what is often glossed as "fragmentation" (Allen and Russo 1997; Piattoni 1998). Many writers analyzed these forces through such dichotomies as tradition/modernity, agriculture/industrialization, and popular religion/ Catholicism (Ginzburg 1980; Holmes 1989; Yanagisako 2002). These oppositions—dear as they were to liberal-democratic policy makers— were mapped onto geographic space. Italy's relatively late and turbulent entrance into nationhood was attributed to a deep fracture (socioeconomic at best, racial at worst) between north and south (Gramsci 1978).[9] Official discourse identified the southern regions and their diverse populations as "backward," in contrast to an industrially advanced north (Banfield 1965; Schneider 1998). Anthropologists have shown that the south's asymmetrical relations with the north cannot be reduced to a culture of poverty (Banfield 1965; Putman 1993; de Martino 2000 [1948]; Belmonte 2005). Instead, the north has legitimized its political control through an Orientalist discourse that reifies the many regions of southern Italy into a univocal "question." Nicola Mai (2002) has demonstrated how, in contemporary Italy and post-Maastricht Europe,[10] old representations of southerners are now translated onto migrants—the other against which to define a new EU-compatible Italian identity. The "southern question" is thus resuscitated today as a way to talk about foreign others and the danger they pose to national cohesion.

While the "southern question" was feverishly debated in public discourse just after unification, two additional and related problem sets emerged: (1) increasing numbers of impoverished Italians (primarily southern) left Italy definitively to find work in northern Europe and the Americas; (2) Italy struggled to enter the colonial contest with schemes for "demographic" colonization in the Horn of Africa (Ginsborg 1990; Del Boca 1992; Labanca 2002; Ben-Ghiat and Fuller 2005).[11] Each of these related processes were tied in the late nineteenth century to Italy's attempts to secure a role among the great Western powers; at the heart of these preoccupations was the question of crafting national subjects who would be capable of carrying Italy toward the modernity it so longed for.

These discussions about the propriety of Italian citizens were inevitably marked by understandings about race (*razza* or *stirpe*) and culture (*civiltà*) that would reemerge during Liberal Italy's invasion of Libya (1911–12) and the fascist invasion of Ethiopia and Cyrenaica (1934–36). In 1912, Italy passed the first law that granted Italian citizenship on the basis of *jus sanguinis*—bloodline and inheritance—in contrast to the territorially based *jus soli*. For example, if someone who is not of Italian descent is born in Italy, he is not automatically granted citizenship; however, if someone of Italian origin is born outside of Italy, he is considered an Italian citizen because of his bloodline. Such regulation endorsed a notion of nationality as a tenacious bond that can endure emigration and be passed down to descendants in the diaspora (Ballinger 2007).

Questions of citizenship and recognition cropped up again after World War II, when Italy experienced a series of "internal" migrations: the repatriation of Italian nationals from former possessions, the management of non-Italian displaced persons seeking refuge, and another exodus of laborers from rural southern areas to northern Italian cities. Between the fall of Mussolini and the 1980s, what distinguished Italian citizens from other residents of the lost possessions who wanted to return to Italy was their *lingua d'uso* (language of use) (Brettell 2003; Ballinger 2007).[12]

The emphasis on blood and ancestry profoundly influenced the subsequent citizenship law (Law 91, 1992), which still regulates issues of residency and naturalization today (Calavita 2005). While Italian law resorts to the language of blood and ancestry, in practice immigrants who have been residents for an uninterrupted period and prove to be fluent in Italian and integrated into various aspects of "Italian life" can be granted citizenship. The cultural dimension of Italianness could be interpreted as a contradiction to the law—based on jus sanguinis—and as a way of fostering both cultural assimilation and a more racialized discourse on blood.

Qualifying as a "political refugee" or as a "victim of human trafficking" is often the last resort for non-European migrants who want to live in Italy legally. Although in Europe the institution of a Schengen Area[13] and the post-Maastricht European Union facilitated the circulation of goods and people, they also increased constraints on external migrations. Thus, while the new Europe emerged as a supernational entity freed of internal borders, with respect to Europe's outside, the nation-state has gained power and force. The state creates illegal migrants by making and enforcing laws whose infraction constitutes illegal residence. For instance, in France, Miriam Ticktin (2011) found that those who can prove they have an illness that cannot be treated in their home country are more easily granted documents under humanitarian clauses than those who migrate for economic reasons: illness travels better than poverty. So does victimization.

In 1998, Italy passed a law allowing "victims of human trafficking" the right to temporary and renewable residence permits in order to escape from situations of violence and abuse, but on the condition that they participate in a rehabilitation program. These programs are fully funded by the state, but they are implemented mostly by Catholic groups engaged in fighting criminality and foreign prostitution.[14] For a woman seeking a residency permit in Italy under Article 18, the first step of rehabilitation requires filing criminal charges against her traffickers. Other steps involve living in a shelter (usually run by Catholic nuns), professional training in Italian language and in cooking and housekeeping "Italian style," elderly care, and receiving medical examinations. Women are sometimes referred to the hospital and/or the ethno-psychiatric clinic for psychological support. Nuns, psychiatrists, ethno-psychiatrists, and cultural mediators collaborate in rehabilitation programs and often share the fragments of women's stories that each is able to collect in an effort to understand the larger context of their lives. On the other hand, foreign women often have to navigate the complex discourses and divergent social projects that portray them as subjects that must be "rehabilitated," "autonomous," and "emancipated."

We see, then, that today's attempts by Italian institutions to manage these newest foreigners are at least as old as the nation-state itself. Since the 1990s, anthropologists writing for an English public have paid attention to the phenomenon of migration to Italy[15] and to the new forms of integralism (Holmes 2000), intolerance, and racism (Cole 1997; Sniderman 2000; Cole and Booth 2007) that have emerged in response to the increasing presence of foreign populations. This book builds on these studies by showing how the encounter between foreign others and Italians addresses the broader question of European identities after Maastricht and the imperative to negotiate between cultural affinity and a multicultural and multiracial Europe (Belier and Wilson 2000; Holmes 2009).

THE FRAME OF THE BOOK: A THEATER OF THE MIGRANT

As I started writing this book, I realized that my ethnographic material and the field sites where I conducted my research had a "theatrical" structure. I was in part reminded of what Victor Turner (1982, 9) called the "theatrical" potential of social life, even though this book is not about, strictly speaking, the structures of specific performances and rituals. I am concerned here with the theatricality of institutions and the roles and subjectivities they enable. In particular, I approach each institutional site—the clinic, the police station, the Immigration Office, and the shelter—as a theatrical scene that stages specific ways of portraying, understanding, and including the other. These scenes articulate and display the receiving country's relationship to the foreigner. In a way, this book addresses the theatricality of the state and the rituals and processes it sets in motion through various institutions in order to incorporate and recognize the other. By highlighting this performative aspect of the state, I want to draw attention to the illusions of inclusion and rehabilitation that the state creates and the kinds of images of alterity that are projected onto the other. The state stages its own authority through categories of recognition and inclusion that institutions make available, such as the migrant, victim, asylum seeker, and prostitute. In this way, a great public play based on the ambiguous figure/character of the other is staged, and confrontations between medicine and religion, techniques of conversion and healing, practices of state recognition, and stories of identity erasure and rewriting are performed. Moreover, the state's aid and integration policies for victims resemble rituals of passage (Van Gennep 1960; Turner 1967)—punctuated by the confessional logics I discuss in chapters 4 and 5—that are marked by liminal transitory states that transform the identity of the foreign prostitute into an illegal victim to be reappropriated later as a rehabilitated legal self.

Some chapters are preceded by a short section titled "Entering the Scene" that introduces the various settings of my research: the ethnopsychiatric clinic, the Immigration Office, the police station, the shelter, and then back in the clinic. The scenes are not fixed, and the script is not immutable. There are moments of improvisation, and moments when an external voice interjects to question the script itself. I see ethnopsychiatry as the knowledge that challenges state and religious practices of integration and introduces a way of acknowledging the other's difference that undoes preexisting categories. While ethno-psychiatry and its therapeutic techniques represent a central scene of this book, they also enter all the others to disrupt and rearticulate the script in relation to the foreign other.

This book is populated by many voices. I begin with those of Italian ethno-psychiatrists, my central interlocutors, who agreed to my partici-

FIGURE 1. Turin, Italy, 2005. Photo by Elena Perlino.

pation in clinical consultations and discussed with me the challenges of their practice, as well as the complex legacy (of Italian and colonial psychiatries, psychoanalysis, and medical anthropology) that informs their work. Next are the voices of foreign women (mostly from Nigeria, Albania, and Romania) I met at the ethno-psychiatric clinic, the police station, and shelters, as well as outside of these institutional settings. They explain stories of migration, suffering, and desire; how they relate to different institutional figures; and their own understandings of freedom and emancipation. In addition, we hear the voices of bureaucrats and social workers questioning their own practices of inclusion and turning to ethno-psychiatry in an attempt to be more "culturally sensitive." Finally, there are the voices of Catholic nuns who reformulate their universalizing mission and the meaning of conversion in a secular vernacular language while engaging in the rehabilitation programs for victims.

In chapter 1, we enter the ethno-psychiatric clinic, the Centro Frantz Fanon. I draw from clinical encounters with Nigerian patients (former victims) in order to trace the ways in which cultural material provides therapists with a framework for developing a new practice of listening wherein the patient's relationship to the magical and the supernatural—

as constitutive orders of subjectivity—are taken seriously and are put in dialogue with the language of psychiatry and psychoanalysis. To listen outside of the structure of psychiatric diagnoses is a form of acknowledgment that, I argue, counters the modality of recognition that biomedical diagnostic criteria provide and that the state offers through integration projects. What is important in ethno-psychiatry is how it recuperates the concept of culture within therapy differently from colonial ethno-psychiatry, which used it to explain colonized behaviors and psychic life with no attention to their political valence, and politicizes culture by showing its potential to create another discourse on difference inside and outside of psychiatry.

The work of the Centro's ethno-psychiatrists can only be understood within the larger landscapes of Italian psychiatry and medical anthropology. In chapter 2, I thus turn to the work of the psychiatrist Franco Basaglia and the philosopher and anthropologist Ernesto de Martino to provide a genealogy of Italian ethno-psychiatry. To the same ends, I discuss the theories of domination and culture developed by Frantz Fanon and Tobie Nathan that have influenced practitioners' clinical approach at the Centro. This chapter also offers an occasion to reflect upon ethno-psychiatry as a contested field that raises questions about mental health, citizenship, and identity and thus allows for a rethinking of clinical work as a mode of politics, for foreign and Italian patients alike.

The difference in approaches between ethno-psychiatry's politics of alterity and the state's politics of recognition emerges clearly when ethno-psychiatrists exit the clinical space to consult with state bureaucrats, social workers, and volunteers involved in integration projects for foreigners. Chapter 3 introduces us to the Immigration Office at Turin's Town Hall, where I follow Dr. R in his role as a consultant for an aid program for victims of human trafficking sponsored by the Ministry of Equal Opportunities and by the municipality of Turin. Here, my focus turns to Article 18 of the Immigration Law that grants "victims of human trafficking" legal status and provides support for them to leave prostitution networks. By examining meetings at which social workers, educators, and Catholic nuns turn to the ethno-psychiatrist for advice on how to implement this law in a "culturally competent" way, I analyze the intersections of the bureaucratic, religious, and therapeutic discourses that frame the relationship of the state vis-à-vis the foreign prostitute. How the state translates the ethno-psychiatric approach into its own categories of difference shows that although ethno-psychiatry provides a radical critique of psychiatric, legal, and moral categories of inclusion, the state often reduces its political potential to yet other categories of recognition.

Chapter 4 takes us to yet another setting, the police station. Following the previous chapter's introduction to the rehabilitation program for victims, here I focus on the first step of the program, the act of denuncia against exploiters, and the various layers of translation that produce it. In the denuncia, a translation of the invisible illegal self into the recognized legal self occurs through an act of rendering—and ventriloquizing—women's stories into juridical language. Women often repeat the stories of denuncia in the ethno-psychiatric clinic where clinical work seeks to recuperate a more "authentic" speech that can legitimate patients as political subjects. Women's stories often appear discrepant, depending on the institutional setting in which they tell them. In contexts such as the police station, the courtroom, or the Immigration Office, women's testimonies are sometimes perceived as lies. What if the discrepancies of women's accounts could count in these contexts as a complex testimony—the result of several regimes of truth intersecting with each other? How might the state and its legal system converse with a different regime of truth—a testimony that does not qualify as truthful but is nevertheless not a lie? These are some of the questions that ethno-psychiatry and its intersection with state policies of integration invite us to pose. After discussing the social and legal implications of constructing the foreign woman as a "victim," I argue that the question of redemption and expiation is not only a crucial issue for Catholic groups involved in aid programs, but is also central to integration policies promoted by the state. In this chapter, I show how the logics of the victim rehabilitation program mirrors the Catholic logics of confession, thus revealing how juridical norms are deeply influenced by the vocabulary of religious morality. The different logics at play in these programs question the secularity of the state and show how intricate and often unsolvable cohabitation is (Asad 2003; Bowen 2007).

I further explore the relations between religious and juridical logics in rehabilitation programs in chapter 5, where I introduce the scene of a Catholic shelter for "victims." After addressing the question of freedom as a core issue for both the law that grants legal status to victims and the Catholic groups involved in its application, I show how women's self-stated projects of emancipation often contrast with the nuns' conception of autonomy. While nuns, bureaucrats, and social workers see living at the shelter as a way to become free—and to translate a socially unacceptable identity into a commensurable subjectivity—the women often refer to it as "being in prison." Divergent and overlapping logics coexist. While the nuns claim that we are all "God's children" and therefore share a common humanity, they also recognize the women's cultural difference and turn to ethno-psychiatrists for advice. In an attempt to question their project of conversion, the nuns develop an understanding of redemption as a secular project of saving lives in line with state projects of recognition. Just as in the case of the meetings at the Immigration Office that I describe in chapter 3, nuns tend to translate ethno-psychiatry's approach to difference into other categories of recognition, thus missing out on ethno-psychiatry's challenge to acknowledge difference rather than reduce it to the familiar.

Chapter 6 loops back to the Centro Fanon, where I reflect on the clinical story of an Albanian woman named Afërdita. I draw from therapeutic consultations, discussions among ethno-psychiatrists, and meetings with Catholic nuns in charge of the shelter where she resided. Multiple institutional logics produce different narratives about Afërdita that are cumulative, and they produce written accounts and spoken assessments of her that have the power to fix her in the temporalities of institutional bureaucracy and to represent her through different classifications. Here we see the logics of the institutions' recognition through the lens of an individual story. The fragmented memories, retelling of dreams, and missed narratives that emerged in the ethno-psychiatric setting show how Afërdita spoke from a space of loss that other institutional languages could not recognize. In this case, ethno-psychiatrists approached Afërdita's experience from a phenomenological perspective that listened to her difference outside of the debates on culture and recognition.

After mapping the different ways in which ethno-psychiatry provides a clinical alternative space to acknowledge foreigners' suffering and a therapeutic language for the state and Catholic groups to understand otherness, I conclude that difference exceeds the normative realm of the law, psychiatry, and religion. I thus turn to other scenes outside of institutions and ask what kind of life is invented in those interstices.

PART ONE

Entering the Scene

The Walls

"I think these walls need to be repainted soon," said one of the young psychologists the day the Centro Fanon moved to a different location in Turin. "These images of exotic people are not very appropriate in an ethno-psychiatric center for immigrants, are they?" he added. And indeed, the walls made me consider how uncanny this institutional space was as the new location for the Centro. "I agree," I responded. "They make me feel a bit uncomfortable, and I wonder how patients would feel about them."

It was a few months into my fieldwork when the Centro Fanon's old lease expired. The new location was in the basement of one of the state's mental health departments, in the southwest part of town. A psychiatrist who was sympathetic to the group's work had offered a space in his department in exchange for training his clinical staff in medical anthropology and ethno-psychiatry. To enter the basement we went through a small metallic red door facing a secondary street. After a dozen steps down, a long corridor in front and one to the left led to the different rooms. There were three in total, plus a big kitchen where the outpatients from the mental health department upstairs cooked their meals during the week. The walls in the corridors were covered in paintings done during an art workshop for patients a couple of years before. The illustrations were of iconic characters from different parts of the world; they seemed to be standing next to each other at the front of the stage after just having performed a play, waiting to be applauded or booed. The characters, in scattered order, ranged from representations of an Egyptian man to an American Indian, a Brazilian dancer, an unspecific African savage, a Bedouin, a Japanese martial artist, a Chinese man, an Inuit, a clown with no specific nationality, and some human silhouettes that were outlined in a single color, waiting to take on a specific persona from the imagination of the temporary artist assigned to the task. These persona-less shapes showed that the work had been abandoned before its completion; they were left suspended, like ghosts waiting to be assigned a definitive shape.

The Egyptian man had a naked torso and wore tight green pants; the Nile ran across his body diagonally—from the right shoulder to his left toe—and on its shores a pyramid and a sphinx filled in the character's torso. Scattered on other parts of the body were inscriptions and hieroglyphics. His head was portrayed in profile, with his eye defined by heavy black pencil, and he wore a crown in the shape of a snake. Next to him, the Inuit wore a parka with a hood covering her head. She had rosy cheeks and the Canadian flag drawn on her chest. In one hand she held a bunch of fish threaded on a fishing line, and the other hand patted a baby seal. In the background, there was an igloo. The Inuit and the Chinese man held hands. The latter wore a loose garment the color of the blue sky with a red belt, from which a panda's smiling face popped out. The artist had sketched the Chinese flag and a bowl of rice on the garment. As a last touch, a naked Buddha sitting in the lotus position on a bed of flower petals looked over the Chinese character from above his right shoulder (fig. 2). On the opposite wall, the Japanese martial artist looked straight into the eyes of the Inuit and Chinese characters, as if vying for the best visibility in the Center's corridors. The martial artist stood on one leg, with the other bent, almost forming a right angle with his hip. He had a bandana on his head, the Japanese flag on his right shoulder, and a rising sun on the other as antonomasia for the Far East. A pagoda was sketched at his feet, while eucalyptus trees adorned his tight pants (fig. 3).

Another wall featured the American Indian standing alone, with braided black hair and red feathers sticking out. His arms were up, in sign of surrender; in one hand he had a hatchet, and on his back he carried a quiver. His trousers featured drawings of an Indian tent, a fire, and a big pipe for smoking. A totem pole stood next to him. Yet another wall hosted other darker-skinned characters, including a Brazilian woman with big red lips, pineapples, and the national flag drawn on her blouse, with exotic fish and birds on her miniskirt; and an African man

FIGURE 2. Centro Frantz Fanon: Paintings on the walls, No. 1, Turin, 2003. Photo by author.

FIGURE 3. Centro Frantz Fanon: Paintings on the walls, No. 2, Turin, 2003. Photo by author.

of unspecified nationality with a naked torso, dressed in a sarong, a lance in his hand, and a tattoo of a big elephant on his arm. A big red African continent was drawn on his sarong, at the level of his genitals, reminiscent of a fig leaf belonging to another story and another time. Finally, a generic Arab man with a beard and mustache wore a turban and a long orange dress and held a saber on one hand; in the background palm trees, camels, and an oil rig were randomly distributed in the landscape.

Here and there, the featureless shapes seemed to wander aimlessly among the rest of the cast. It seemed that at any time they could swallow the other characters up or bring them back to an undefined stage of their existence, confuse their particular characteristics, mix them all up so that it would be impossible to distinguish the Inuit from the Brazilian, the African from the Indian. And so it happened when the staff painted over these life-size images: they all disappeared under the coat of white paint.

When I first walked into this place, I was stunned by the figures. I spent a long time observing and photographing them as they so perfectly captured a stereotyped way of representing difference. I was never able to learn who thought up the idea of the workshop, nor was I able to ascertain the inspiration behind the drawings. After a few attempts to find out, I gave up and surrendered to the uncanniness of this particular clinical space for foreign patients. It was something Michel de Certeau would refer to as the "strangeness circulating underground" (1996, 1). In his recounting of the events surrounding the diabolic possession of a group of Ursuline nuns in Loudun, a seventeenth-century French provincial town, de Certeau interprets the possession as the return of former unresolved societal, political, and religious conflicts. The possession rekindled and transposed these conflicts onto a different scene— the convent—offering them a different range of expressions and languages. For de Certeau, this return of the past is a consequence of the strangeness circulating underground, of the uncanny of history that repeats and re-presents itself under different disguises.

Many months later, as I was preparing to leave Italy and return to the United States to write this book, I remembered those figures; they appeared to me like "the strangeness circulating underground." Without my realizing it, they had accompanied my experience in and through the different institutional settings that I researched. I helped the staff paint the walls white, but no matter how many layers of paint we added, the strong-colored silhouettes of the original drawings still created a shadow effect. Their vague contours remained visible. Not even time could make the walls completely absorb the white paint. This gave them a ghostly feeling, and the characters underneath the white paint seemed to retain a life of their own or, at the very least, residues of a previous vitality. To me, they came to represent both a reminder and a risk. Or, better yet, the reminder of a risk. Something was being whitewashed—a stereotyped way of imagining difference that has the performative power to reduce it to its simulacrum. The staff and I agreed that we were dealing with strange simulacra of otherness, which ethno-psychiatry struggled with in its efforts to problematize difference in the clinical setting and make it a productive tool for therapy. Ethno-psychiatrists often worked with Italian social workers, mental health practitioners, and volunteers involved in aid programs for foreigners—all of whom could have very stereotyped views of the foreigner, if not very discriminatory approaches to what cultural and social integration meant. Therefore, to me, the images on the walls stood for the material repressed under layers of whiteness that could later resurface in the form of unresolved and simplistic ways of thinking about the other. They were also a reminder of a colonial past that had culturalized the other and pathologized culture. In other words, they represented the haunting of history that could creep into practices of inclusion, recognition, and healing of the foreign other, at any moment, in unexpected places, and for various purposes.

CHAPTER I

On the Tightrope of Culture

The potential [of ethno-psychiatry] lies in the possibility of
getting closer to the experience of the other, . . . not with the
aim to "understand" . . . him, but to recognize his discourse
. . . as irreducible to dominant paradigms, something that
clinical work with the local population rarely shows; the risk
lies in potentially encouraging projective mechanisms of
representation where the pain of the other appears as
circumscribed and distant and the suffering of the migrant as
exotic and culturalized.

—Simona Taliani and Francesco Vacchiano, *Altri corpi*

Mary was in her early thirties when social services referred her to the
Centro Fanon. She wore an open expression on her face, often smiling
and always willing to talk about her experiences and concerns, but she
also looked sad. I met her on a late November afternoon at the Centro.
She had migrated from Nigeria approximately three years before we
met, and she was still undocumented. Over this period, she had gone
back to Nigeria once. When she returned to Italy, she was pregnant and
had just lost her husband in a car accident in Nigeria. She went to the
hospital for a prenatal visit, where she was diagnosed as HIV-positive.
Social services subsequently placed her in a locally funded program for
pregnant HIV-positive foreigners. She lived with her sister in what
social workers described as very precarious economic conditions, in a
small, dark apartment where a lot of people of all ages, mostly Nigerians, cycled in and out. Her sister was probably involved in prostitution,
but it was unclear whether Mary was as well. She gave birth to an HIV-
positive son who became negative after several months of retroviral
treatment. A year after giving birth, the social workers thought that she

was "depressed"; she was crying a lot and felt guilty about her health and her son's future. They referred her to the ethno-psychiatric center, where the doctors knew, as one social worker put it, "how to deal with cultural difference."

A short time after the initial referral, Mary became one of Dr. L's patients. I sat in on her therapy sessions for several months, often conversed with the practitioners in charge of her case at the Centro, and spent some time with her outside the clinic, at the apartment she shared with her sister. Three people participated in Mary's sessions: Dr. L, a trainee, and me. In this case, no Nigerian mediator was available to assist in the consultation, but Mary spoke enough Italian and the doctor enough English for them to understand each other. In general, ethno-psychiatrists at the Centro would meet patients together with a cultural mediator who helped with issues of translation or cultural interpretation when necessary. Dr. L had a lot of experience working with Nigerian patients and had conducted several years of ethnographic research in West Africa on curing techniques, childhood, and witchcraft. Like other practitioners at the Centro, she held degrees in both psychology and anthropology and was committed to bridging the practices of both in her clinical work.

Over the course of several consultations, Mary spoke of her difficulties in Italy: she did not have a residence permit; she was afraid of getting caught by the police and sent back to Nigeria; she feared for her life and her son's future; and she was terrified at the idea that other Nigerians in Italy might find out about her HIV status, which felt like a death sentence to her. She was haunted by dreams about her dead husband and could not talk about him without ending in a desperate cry. The threat of death was a refrain in her stories. Although Dr. L explained to her that her illness did not mean imminent death and that retroviral treatments could make a great difference, her fears persisted. She once said, "If I take the medicines here, I will heal, but if the police send me back there, I will die." Because she referenced death in different ways, I wondered whether she was alluding to different kinds of death, not just corporeal. In this clinical context, patients often voice or express through symptoms the fear of social death (both in Italy and back home), the shame of returning home without proof of success, concern about family members' jealousy and envy, and the threat of revenge. Death also speaks to ruptured relationships, to symbols that no longer grant meaning to experience, and to the failure of her migratory process.

We spent a lot of time speaking about which social program could grant her a residency permit. Because she was the mother of a minor who was born HIV-positive in Italy, she could qualify for the "health reasons" that the state uses to recognize parents of offspring affected by life-threatening conditions. At first, the stories that emerged in our discussions were mostly about Mary's life in Italy and the pressing concerns she had about her health and legal status. As another ethno-psychiatrist pointed out to me:

> It is easier to collect accounts of migrants' lives in Italy than to find out about their lives before they migrated; when you try to get to those stories, they are often impenetrable. In these cases, you gently try to reorient them to their cultural background by establishing connections with family members, practices, and rituals, so that slowly another story can be told.

People's premigration stories are impenetrable for various reasons. Many patients who are referred to the Center have experienced different forms of violence and abuse. Some have been persecuted and tortured in their countries, have experienced war, and have sought political asylum elsewhere. Stories about "home" often resist narration because they recall an inhospitable place, one that is impossible to reinhabit, both physically and symbolically. At other times, "home" is an opaque reality that has been overshadowed by the urge to assimilate, integrate, and become other in ways that live up to the receiving society's standards of behaviors and of desiring. Italian institutions that grant legal status to foreigners often require clear narrations of their migration trajectories and countries of origin. Such pressure often results in confused accounts that are symptomatic of an impossible encounter between bureaucratic language and the complexity of people's histories. For instance, how does one translate the desire to escape from poverty by accepting prostitution as a lucrative activity? Or understand the desire to use the body as a powerful tool that brings wealth outside of the discourse of trafficking? "Home" can also become an object of impossible desire that exile has turned into a fantasy. There is often a gap in patients' language that points to an impossibility to remember and to speak. It can be understood as the response to trauma that disrupts language and consciousness. In all these cases, the accounts concerning life before migration take time to shape in the clinical encounter, which thus becomes the scene where experiences that cannot be communicated in language are nonetheless forced into the open.

During one consultation, Mary recounted a dream. Her husband had come to see her to tell her that he had died because his family had done voodoo on them and that she and their son were in danger. She had to go back to their house in Benin City, Nigeria, to find a wire and then return to Italy. If she could not find it, something bad might happen to them. On this occasion, Dr. L told Mary not to fear her husband's visits at night: "If he comes back in your dreams, talk to him, try to find out why his family turned their backs to you." Later, when we were alone, the therapist commented, "In her context, dead people are not just memories or dreams, they are real." She further explained that dreams were "an instrument of the present," an experience that provided memories from the past and reworked them in light of the present.

To me, the doctor's reflection was an invitation to the participant to take her dreams seriously and address them in their ghostly reality. I was also reminded of the fact that dreams can offer a space of doubling, where people who are dead in life are alive in dreams, where the boundaries between life and death are blurred. Dreaming of a dead person may signify that her influence in the dreamer's life is still present or that her death is real only in waking life. In this sense, the therapist was not just alluding to Mary's experience in which dead people could come back to life in dreams, but also to a quality of dreams that makes them not only a screen onto which images and symbols are projected but a moment in which existence is articulated in different forms (Binswanger and Foucault 1986). Or so I interpreted it. The clinical encounter provided a space for her memory, where past and present, death and life became blurred in dreams and where the impossibility to remember could be faced so that the subject may access a different kind of speech.

Mary's dream brought up other stories. Her husband's family was, in her words, from a village where "they did a lot of voodoo." His family was very envious of the couple because they did well financially and were able to buy a house in Nigeria and emigrate to Europe. Moreover, they imagined she had made a fortune during her time in Italy, and now her son would inherit all his father's money and the house. She was afraid of them and the harm they could do. She said they killed her husband, or that they did not protect him enough—"They did voodoo on him"—and that her HIV was the consequence of a spell. She also spoke about the bad worms inhabiting her body. They were red because they sucked her blood. She got them because "bad people had cast a spell" on her when she was pregnant. She almost died, but then she saw a native doctor in Nigeria who helped her; even so, the worms were still in her body. She also heard an ongoing echo in her ears and head that caused her a lot of pain.

She wanted some drugs because she had problems sleeping, which was why she had agreed to come to the Center in the first place. Dr. L, however, did not prescribe any medicine. First, she listened to the other symptoms that Mary presented: she had a strong pain in her ears, and the worms went from her head to her feet, through her shoulders and breast, and then all the way down her spine. Her knees were hurting, too. Mary had seen her cousin, a healer, who poured a powder made of pepper and other things from Nigeria into her ear. Along with suggesting that she undergo further medical tests, Dr. L attempted to go beyond the initial diagnosis of depression. She asked Mary if she could speak to the spirits who were causing her and her family pain. She also inquired if the presence of worms in Mary's body resulted from a failure to perform some rituals as part of her worship of gods and goddesses. In this way, the therapist was letting the patient know that she was familiar with and understood that rituals had powerful meanings and that spirits could speak and be spoken to. Mary explained that the pain had to do with something else. The doctor then asked Mary about her family back in Nigeria: "Do they know about your medical problems? What do they make of them?" Her mother knew, and her father died after she told him about it. She felt tremendous guilt.

Mary referred to her husband by his African name, Osaliato. Dr. L asked Mary what her other name was, and what it meant. "Osatuame," she replied. "It means 'God has pity on me.'" Prompted by Dr. L's questions, Mary said that her father had given her the name. When Mary's mother was pregnant with her, a woman from their village did voodoo, putting her at risk of losing the child. But Mary was nonetheless born healthy, and thus her father named her "God has pity on me." When Dr. L heard this story, she reformulated it by saying, "Your father was right because you are strong, otherwise you would not have been born. You are still strong now." As she later explained to the trainee and me, asking about the name in Edo—Mary's mother tongue—was a way to create a relationship of trust in which Mary could feel comfortable evoking parts of her life in Nigeria and know that the therapist could attend to it. She specified that it was important to know when to ask these types of questions; the purpose is to let the patient express herself in her own terms and let her know that her references are not completely foreign to us and that she can bring them to the therapeutic space.

A couple of months into therapy, Dr. L asked whether Mary talked to her son about his dead father. No, she responded, not without falling into despair. She feared that her son might be doomed to a similar tragic destiny. While discussing the case with me, Dr. L had admitted that it was difficult for her to deal with how the memory of Mary's dead husband played out in the therapy sessions. We knew Mary's sister had gotten rid of any objects related to him in order to protect Mary from her sadness. But he appeared in her dreams and claimed that his family remembered and sometimes helped or protected him. "Why don't you put a picture of him in a corner of the house and build an altar to him?" asked Dr. L. Mary started crying. She felt unable to do it. The therapist reassured her she did not need to rush it but insisted that it would be beneficial to her and to her son. Maybe she could also recite a prayer in Edo, she added. Mary asked if she should light a candle and suggested that maybe it should be white. Sure, the therapist replied, as long as she did it. Mary cried hard but said she would do it and thanked us.

At the end of the same consultation, in a therapeutic/pedagogic way, Dr. L suggested that Mary go to the exhibition of African art currently showing at a museum in town, as a way to reconstitute some connections with "home." Mary answered with some hesitation, asking, "What is an art exhibit?" Dr. L explained that there were life-sized statues from Nigeria and other parts of Africa that represented kings and queens of ancient times. "I don't want to see other people from Nigeria. I don't want them to find out about my illness," Mary replied. Dr. L explained that the statues were not human beings but a kind of object that resembled kings and queens and other humans. I added that she did not need to talk to anyone at the museum; it was a space just meant to exhibit objects. Later I asked myself whether this was an instance of the misunderstandings that could lead to a comedy of errors, where each group's uncertainty about the other confirms preexisting anxieties and misconceptions (Obeyesekere 2005). When Mary said she did not want to see other Nigerians, did she mean other Nigerians visiting the museum? Did Dr. L, and I along with her, instead assume that she did not know what an exhibit or a museum is based on the understanding that they are a Western construction? Perhaps Mary truly did not know what an art exhibit was; or maybe statues are more than mere museum artifacts and can act upon us and see through us, like the gods, goddesses, kings, and queens that they stand for. It is hard to know.

In the context of ethno-psychiatric clinical work, practitioners are engaged in finding an "intermediate space"—a space of mediation—between the therapist's theories and techniques and the patient's ways of expressing suffering in an attempt to avoid reducing symptoms to biomedical diagnostic criteria. At the same time, they encourage patients to maintain relations with their respective backgrounds in forms that range from being in contact with family members, performing rituals, or speaking their mother tongue to attending groups or churches with their fellow nationals.

This intermediate space can also be understood as a space of transference. In psychoanalytic treatment, *transference* is the term used to describe how the relationship between the analyst and the analysand is translated by and through the lens of the analysand's past relational experience. In the therapeutic setting, old memories and experiences are reenacted and emotions are projected onto the analyst. Through the process of unconscious reenactment, the patient assigns the analyst specific roles that resemble relationships in the patient's life. For example, the patient may transfer feelings of hate and frustration onto the therapist in ways that resonate or coincide with the feelings she may have toward a parent. The setting thus becomes a theater of the unconscious where the patient can act out past traumatic experiences and, with the analyst's support, work through past traumas by revisiting the relationship that caused it. In other words, if the patient had experienced an abusive relationship with the mother, through transference that relationship might be reconstituted to such an extent that its effects can be worked through differently. Thus, transference is a form of mediation— a space of translation—that rearticulates intersubjective relations and the meanings attached to them. Although the ethno-psychiatric setting is not a psychoanalytic one, when ethno-psychiatrists talk about the clinic as a "space of mediation," they are alluding to the process whereby the patient's painful motives and affects are transformed into publicly accepted symbols and meanings. Obeyesekere (1990) called this process "the work of culture," and Winnicott (1967) spoke of cultural experience as that third area between the inner or personal psychic life and the world in which the individual lives as a space of creation.[1]

Through Mary's case I became interested in the question of when and how cultural material opens up, or closes down, the space of therapy. In many ways, I had to shift my focus to approach the issue of culture from a clinical/therapeutic angle and to ask what work "culture" does in this context. In the discussion that follows, I trace some of the ways in which "culture" is identified, at different moments in the therapeutic space, through diverse symbols, practices, words, and techniques. The contours of what counts as the patient's cultural background are in flux; they take shape as the result of a set of relationships the clinical context enables. I, for example, was curious about the ways in which Dr. L evoked Mary's "culture" in relation to the African art exhibition, or to praying in Edo, or to referring to her African name. What counts as her "culture," and in relationship to what? My anthropological desires to understand what mattered as cultural often coincided with those of the ethno-psychiatrists, trained in both anthropology and psychology or psychiatry. I shared with the ethno-psychiatrists the sense that this latter angle was sometimes at odds with the anthropological discussions on culture as a construction with indefinite boundaries. As I show in the rest of the chapter, in clinical work the anthropological and therapeutic takes on culture can become incommensurable, and yet it is precisely this untranslatability that produces encounters and spaces where categories are undone and a different listening can take place. This way of listening is a response to the new speech that emerges in the discourse of patients. As Dr. L suggested, the purpose of evoking cultural identifications was not to identify the patients' cultural background but to enable them to find a language and a memory that was lost in the process of migrating. I also began to understand the clinical use of cultural material as a way to reintroduce the political dimension of suffering, not just in the language of psychiatry, but also, more broadly, in the state's politics of recognition and integration of foreign others.

WALKING THE TIGHTROPE

The process of naming cultural material as part of therapy was in part inspired by Tobie Nathan's clinical work with foreigners in the outskirts of Paris. In 1979, Nathan, a psychologist and psychoanalyst of Jewish Egyptian descent, opened the first ethno-psychiatric clinic and designed new treatment techniques for foreign patients that included healing practices from the patients' background and used cultural material as a therapeutic tool. In his early work, Nathan (1996) used the metaphor of the womb to refer to a reassuring and structuring envelope framed by culture that provided holding and healing within the ethno-psychiatric setting.[2] He assumed that the structure that culture provided could get lost in the experience of migration, and that therapy could help reconstitute it. Both Nathan and ethno-psychiatrists at the Centro often refer to culture as a "therapeutic lever." When the term *lever* is applied to culture one is apt to think about an actual object or a series of identifiable symbols that stand as cultural references and that have an effect on the patient's state. In this sense, cultural identifications are conceived of as tools to lessen pain, to lift the weight of suffering by activating a mechanism of healing that can only be triggered through certain words, allusions, and gestures. The image of the lever thus evokes something in and of itself simultaneously static and transformative.

The therapeutic process designed by Nathan is ambivalent and complex, as I learned through the ethno-psychiatrists' work at the Centro. Practitioners there have rearticulated Nathan's early influence and departed from it. They do not assume culture to be an original set of meanings and practices left untouched and protected by the membrane of the maternal womb. Rather, they understand it as both a reassuring and violent set of symbols, simultaneously providing coherent and incoherent meaning to patients' experiences; for them, "culture" can be a tool in flux, a set of antagonistic and threatening practices.

It was never clear from Mary's accounts whether the people she feared seeing belonged to a prostitution network or whether she had ever worked in the sex industry at all, and if so, for how long, even though she once said she worked in the streets for a short period but never declared it to the institutions. Her account was opaque. What made it even more elusive was the layered process of translation at play in the therapeutic setting. In order to understand the nature of her symptoms and start a quest for a cure, Dr. L referred to the possibility that Mary was a devotee of Mami Wata, goddess of the waters, dispenser of wealth and abundance, to whom many Nigerian women are tied by promises of loyalty and worship and to whom they are offered as brides before migration. Failure to fulfill the duties of devotion may result in the goddess taking revenge and in the manifestation of bodily symptoms, like strong headaches or the worms inhabiting Mary's body. Nigerian women in Italy often talk about the difficulties of maintaining worship of the goddess. For some of them, resuming their devotion to her has led to feeling better. Ethno-psychiatrists may suggest this return to a form of devotion as a therapeutic strategy, to observe whether the patient benefits from it. In the cases I observed, acknowledging the existence of the goddess on the part of the therapists made women feel acknowledged, or even validated to a certain extent, in a sphere of their lives that other institutions (e.g., the state, the hospital, Catholic NGOs) classified as superstition. This acknowledgement was effective in reducing some of the symptoms they experienced.

If we understand symptoms not just as an index that signals the existence of an illness or disturbance but rather as a sign or a symbol formed in the interface between the unconscious and the conscious, and in which something of the illness is incarnated and manifested—the anger of the goddess, or the sense of guilt of the devotee—then the therapeutic work revolves around interpretation, not decoding symptoms into diagnostic categories.[3] This process of interpretation is a form of translation that I understand through Benjamin's (1968) idea of translation as a way to abide and provisionally come to terms with the difference and multiplicity of languages. The symptom is in and of itself a translation of sorts. In the context of ethno-psychiatry—a practice and theory positioned at the thresholds of different knowledges (psychiatry, psychoanalysis, anthropology, philosophy)—various forms of translation are at work. Patients and doctors translate between their different understandings of suffering and cure; doctors translate between various medical languages (psychiatry, ethno-psychiatry, spirit possession, magic) and what may count as healing at different moments in the clinical work. Misunderstandings—like the one about the African art exhibition—are produced by complex encounters and negotiations (translations) and are themselves forms of understanding.

The misunderstanding occurring in this clinical context—just as in translation—can be a productive moment. In the relationship between therapist and patient (and in translation between one language and another), misunderstanding can help the therapeutic process and produce new meaning in language. The French psychoanalyst Jacques André has argued, "Agreement and understanding of the protagonists in the analytic situation . . . [signal] more of a hindrance to the analytic process than the mark of its dynamic" (2006, 567). This can be said of both the clinical and the ethnographic encounters, where various forms of foreignness meet. To reach an exhaustive understanding of the other implies having reduced difference to sameness. In translation, this would suggest that it is possible to achieve transparency of meaning through exact equivalents of words in every language. Yet Benjamin points to the fact that transparency is not the ultimate goal of translation. For him, that which resists literal transposition produces an epiphany in both languages. Translation thus creates newness. To translate is simultaneously to betray and to be faithful to an original meaning; it produces both understanding and misunderstanding. I interpret the processes of translation at work within the ethno-psychiatric setting as forms of acknowledgment that have surrendered the certainty of diagnostic categories as tools of recognition and can pay attention to the interruptions and enigmas of the patient's speech. Translation, here, does not produce agreement but rather dis-agreement (Rancière 1999).

In Mary's case, it was clear that what the doctor presented as a source of support and reconnection to a familiar context was only sometimes perceived as reassuring. When I later conversed with Dr. L, I discovered that she herself was ambivalent about her suggestion that Mary visit the African art exhibition. This instance created a conundrum, or at least I saw it as such. How patients respond to references to cultural material can vary greatly. In some cases, it proved effective. Other patients at the Centro responded very well when ghosts and spirits, djinns, and gods and goddesses were evoked and invited in the clinic. The vocabulary of "magic" and "witchcraft" is translated into superstition and belief in the public hospital, where biomedicine translates symptoms into psychiatric diagnoses regardless of the patients' backgrounds. For instance, practitioners at the Centro usually do not assign the diagnosis of schizophrenia or depression unless they are dealing with patients who have previously received such diagnoses from clinicians at the public hospitals before being referred to them. In these cases, they may refer to psychiatric diagnoses to question them or to continue the pharmaceutical treatments associated with them. Or they may use diagnoses instrumentally when they write psychological assessments for asylum seekers or victims of torture or trafficking (knowing that some psychiatric categories speed up the bureaucratic processes of obtaining documents). In the ethno-psychiatric setting, on the contrary, at any given time the ambivalent ways in which patients—and therapists—position themselves with regard to homes, mother tongues, techniques of cure, and what counts as "cultural material" can be expressed. In trying to recuperate what psychiatry excluded from its field of understanding, ethno-psychiatry creates a space—both therapeutic and political—that aims to include difference (cultural and experiential) as a fundamental variable in therapeutic work. In so doing, one of the ways in which ethno-psychiatrists work is by translating practices, experiences, ways of expressing suffering, rituals of cure, and symptoms into the language of culture. Instead of a fixed notion, "culture" is a vehicle of translation, a concept that enables different types of interpretation in the clinical encounter. In this context, culture also takes on a political meaning, because it introduces a difference that the state (in its various forms) can only recognize as belief and thus classify as unreal or untrue (Farquhar 2013).

Writing about his clinical practice, Roberto Beneduce (2007), founder of the Centro Fanon and leading figure in the contemporary field of clinical intervention with foreign patients in Italy, has defined ethno-psychiatry as a "clinic of ambivalence."[4] I read this as referring to different layers of ambivalence: on the one hand, the patients' ambivalent positions with regard to their cultural identifications that shift in the course of life and migration; on the other, the ambivalence of the ethno-psychiatric practice itself, which emerges at the juncture of different—and often contradictory—etiologies and ways of conceiving what counts as normal, pathological, and, ultimately, as human.[5]

After this consultation, I asked Dr. L why she suggested that Mary go to the museum: "What do you mean by 'culture' when you evoke the African art?" With other Nigerian patients I had heard therapists suggest that they attend Pentecostal churches if that could provide them with a network on which to rely. I was also curious about how Dr. L would go about assessing whether patients perceived cultural references as either persecutory or therapeutic. Her response captured the complexity of her position and the challenges inherent in it:

> Sometimes in the clinical encounter we present patients with pieces of their culture. At times, you have to reify culture to make things happen. By using a certain reified idea of culture, you can see how patients respond to it and how they themselves use it. In this way, we understand better what culture means to them. One strategy is to reimmerse patients in what is persecutory in order to become stronger. In the clinic, you use culture as if you were a tightrope walker: you reify [it] without mummifying it. It is a fine balance, and you create a dialectic among the participants.[6]

She continued, explaining that a complex process of reification, manipulation, creation, and simplification of what comes to be seen as culture takes place in the therapeutic space. There are moments during treatment when it is important to essentialize and present patients with a possibly homogenized idea of culture, followed by other moments in which that same idea is questioned, deconstructed, and further manipulated. This is a complex process, "something that can slip from your grasp," Dr. L added, if you do not know how to handle all the different phases of therapy and the various configurations that cultural references can take in the course of therapy. The idea here is not to reconnect patients to their cultural backgrounds but rather to produce the conditions for the subject to speak and find ways to be in the world.

For now, I want to reflect on the process of reifying culture that Dr. L mentioned as the actualization of a means of communication that is identified as "culture"—or our understanding of "their culture"—and that has the potential to become a shared field of understanding between patients and doctors. Her words reminded me of the experience of transference in the psychoanalytic setting that I mentioned earlier. For the therapist, the patient's transference of old patterns onto the therapeutic relationship is a way to get a better feel for the patient's experience and to relive certain memories with the patient. For the patient, transference provides a space where the play of the unconscious can be acted out differently. Similarly, in ethno-psychiatry we can understand culture as a transitional space wherein patients and therapists negotiate their positions vis-à-vis symbols and practices (Winnicott 1967). As Dr. L explained, by using certain ideas of culture and observing patients' responses, we learn about their experience of the world. Transference can thus be understood as a controlled misunderstanding wherein roles and meanings are unconsciously assigned and produce self-knowledge. In this sense, misunderstanding is not the sign of failed therapy but quite the opposite. It allows an encounter that occurs through various detours and crossings wherein subjectivity is produced and cure unfolds.

In regard to the art exhibition, Dr. L was aware that a misunderstanding may have taken place; she had wanted to evoke Africa as a geographic space, not as a cultural one, she explained to me. Her intention was to create an occasion for Mary to remember where she came from and to start putting together different pieces of her story, before and after migration. She agreed that at that moment she had taken on a more pedagogical position vis-à-vis Mary, a role she played with some discomfort. She herself was voicing and struggling with one of the dilemmas inherent in evoking cultural material in this setting. She pondered what other therapeutic strategies she could have used, what other ways could have served the purpose of creating a supportive space for Mary, who was experiencing a strong sense of alienation and fear.

The ethno-psychiatrists' strategy of relying on cultural material and/ or practices that they understand as familiar to the patient in order to create a sense of belonging and recognition leaves room for a series of questions about the status of what is therapeutic. Is there persecutory potential in this approach, and can it influence therapy's outcome? Or, as Dr. L suggested, can being reimmersed in what the patient perceives as threatening, and reexperiencing haunting presences within this setting, fulfill a therapeutic promise? What counts as therapeutic in such a clinical ethos? Why does culture matter?

Allowing for words from patients' different contexts to circulate in the clinical setting, to talk about symptoms, to name suffering, is a way of creating a space of mediation and translation (or transference) where the unsaid of the patient's story can be articulated, or at least can be heard as silence or seen as bodily signs. Within this practice, acknowledging the legitimacy of cultural interpretations seems to unblock both the patient's and the family's speech (in those cases when family members are present in the consultations or contacted by patients to discuss symptoms) and to release associative chains that resituate symptoms within a personal and collective history (Corin 1997). I understand this form of acknowledgment as therapeutic. This framework prevents the patient from getting caught in one hegemonic discourse of suffering and enables a different kind of listening on the part of the doctors. The cultural approach provides a space of critique of dominant techniques in clinical work and repoliticizes the issue of difference. For instance, I began to understand Dr. L's suggestions to pray in Edo and her listening to Mary's references to voodoo and native doctors not only as part of a therapeutic approach but also as a political gesture that creates dissonance with the apparatus of biomedicine and the state, which relegate cultural, historical, and economic difference outside of its purview.

A MATTER OF INVENTION: CONUNDRUMS OF CULTURE

"But what happens if and when the tightrope walker falls from the rope?" I later asked myself. I was struck by how well the image of the tightrope walker captured the tensions that therapists see in their work. What happens in the clinical setting when what figures as culture fails, is ineffective, or gets contested? Do these moments count as therapeutic as much as those in which patients identify with and respond positively to what Dr. L referred to as a "reified idea of culture"? Put otherwise, what practices of making, remaking, translating, recognizing, and undoing the temporary and fleeting object of "culture" are at play in this clinical space? Moreover, who is the tightrope walker? Is it the therapist, the patient, or the cultural mediator who translates for them? Or does everyone share equally the challenges of falling and remaining in balance while walking on a tight rope of culture, anthropologist included?

This clinical moment showed me one of ethno-psychiatry's conundrums, and my own conundrum as an anthropologist. At stake here are not only the different layers of translation embedded in this therapeutic practice and in my task as an anthropologist (also a sort of translator) but also the various meanings—concrete, elusive, and shifting—of what, through processes of translation, is identified and invented as "culture" or "cultural material" at different moments and for different purposes. When it is invoked in the form of rituals, prayers, beliefs, etiologies, and practices, what kind of work does culture do? How can the work of culture inform the therapeutic process (Obeyesekere 1990) and posit a new kind of politics for clinical work?

Roy Wagner (1981 [1975]) has argued that anthropology as a discipline invented "culture" as a kind of illusion, or "false object," in order for the researcher to arrange and understand his or her experience of alterity. In this view, "culture" is a mediating term that allows the anthropologist to make sense of his or her experience of otherness and commensurate the sense of disorientation that accompanies any encounter with what is radically different from one's self. What the construct of culture shows is its kinship with the anthropologist's worldview and ways of rationalizing experience. In inventing "another culture," the anthropologist not only invents his own; he also reinvents the notion of culture itself (4). As an explanatory concept, culture makes difference translatable and therefore knowable. Along these lines, Wagner warns us that for the purpose of understanding, we must proceed *as if* culture existed as a monolithic "thing," but for the purpose of demonstrating how as anthropologists we attain our comprehension of the other, it is necessary to realize that culture is an invention, a tool—in other words, a prop (8–9).

The relation that the anthropologist builds between two cultures— which, in turn, objectifies and hence "creates" those cultures for him— arises precisely from his act of "invention," his use of meanings known to him in constructing an understandable representation of his subject matter. The result is an analogy, or a set of analogies, that "translates" one group of basic meanings into the other and can be said to participate in both meaning systems at the same time in the same way that their creator does. This is the simplest, most basic, and most important consideration of all; the anthropologist cannot simply "learn" the new culture and place it beside the one he already knows. Rather, he must "take it on" so as to experience a transformation of his own world (Wagner 1981 [1975], 9).

Understood from a linguistic perspective, this kind of translation does not leave any of the languages involved unchanged. Translation is the way in which words travel from one language into another and back; it is a movement into the elsewhere of another language and the coming back transformed into the language of departure. Words are not simply dislocated into another linguistic dwelling, but are called to reshape the space in which they are transported and transformed (Heidegger 1975).

Dr. L seemed to be moving in and out of the different registers outlined by Wagner: at moments she needed to operate as if culture exists as a discrete set of practices (praying in Edo, referring to voodoo rituals, being in contact with family members, visiting the museum) in order to produce a response in Mary and to create a means of understanding of the patient's experience outside of psychiatric diagnostic criteria. In line with a phenomenological approach to mental illness, the ethno-psychiatrists at the Centro agree that to enter the lifeworld of the patient one has to break free from the apparatuses of control of the medical institution, beginning with its classificatory language. They argue that the diagnostic apparatus prevents one from exploring what is behind the patient's symptoms and from listening to the radical difference of what Foucault (1988) called the voices and experience of madness. At other moments, on the other hand, Dr. L implied that over the course of the therapeutic relationship objectified ideas of culture could also be undone, contested, and discarded as not useful for understanding. At the epistemological level, ethno-psychiatrists realize that the evocation of cultural ties is also an invention and a creation. I interpreted it as that intermediate space where translation as a form of relation occurs and produces something new. In this context, translation transfers the subject to an origin from which she has been alienated and which now appears as a completely different reality, a new world. Moreover, when the tightrope walker makes the journey without falling, cultural interpretations allow for other epistemologies and ontologies to be part of the therapeutic encounter.

What the exchange with Dr. L taught me was that the concept of culture at play in this kind of therapy is the result of an encounter, or a series of relations, not only between patients' representations of their experiences and the ethno-psychiatrists' own interpretations of them but also with homes, spirits, and invisible presences in the here and now of the therapeutic consultation. What emerges from these sets of relations is a constantly shifting context where cultural identifications simultaneously allow for understanding, misunderstanding, and the invention of meanings.

The ethno-psychiatrist's imperative is to provide culturally sensitive clinical services by focusing on the different ways in which patients' cultural backgrounds shape their expression of suffering and how forms of identification shift—sometimes dramatically—in the experience of crossing borders, as I suggested in the story of Favor in the introduction. This practice—as with anthropology—tends to recognize difference through the construct of culture, which becomes a shared construct, done and undone within the encounters. In a way, culture works as a signifier onto which difference can be translated and thus signified. When ethno-psychiatrists work *as if* culture is a tool, the underlying idea is that cultural referents can hold a space of difference and suffering that does not stigmatize the patient's experience in the way a psychiatric diagnosis can. Culture—understood in this case as rituals, prayers, magic, possession, spirits, djinn, and other meaningful cultural signifiers—may have the capacity to alter the patient's experience or simply reinscribe it in a world that holds meaning. How different contexts allow for experiences that escape coherence and meaning plays an important role in understanding patients' experiences of what lies at the margins of cultural codes (Corin 2007).

Because of their interdisciplinary training, the ethno-psychiatrists at the Centro bring to their practice a complex understanding of culture and recognize the problems entailed in the therapeutic strategy of reanchoring migrants in their own cultural backgrounds. They know well that the anthropological critique has undone the concept of culture by revealing it as a flexible and conflictual construct, encompassing norms and their transgression, rules and their opposites, and that the self emerges between adherence to existing codes and the constant creation of new ones. In this sense, our approaches to culture were very similar. In my work with them, I was intrigued not only by the ways in which cultural material was evoked and used in the clinical setting and its effectiveness as assessed by clinicians but also by those instances in which patients resisted identification with their mother tongues or etiologies that were too close to them and tainted by unresolved ties. What counts as therapeutic in these moments of identification and dis-identification is a central question. This issue is made even more complex by the fact that what figures as therapeutic in ethno-psychiatry is often in conflict with Western psychiatric practices. The use of culture is thus political in the sense that it creates an interruption, a disturbance, with the dominant discourse of biomedicine. What is important in ethno-psychiatry is how it recuperates the concept of culture after anthropology's deconstruction of it and repoliticizes it by showing its potential to create another discourse on difference.

Within this alternative space, the issue of what counts as human and its relationship to invisible presences and other ontologies is ultimately called upon. The Belgian philosopher Isabelle Stengers—who collaborated with Tobie Nathan on his first experiments in ethno-psychiatry in France—said that every technique needs some kind of invisibles (Stengers 2009). Invisible forces populate our therapeutic traditions, and not just the traditions and techniques of others. Among them, she counted the unconscious, which is irrational, repeats itself, possesses and acts upon us, has a force of its own that is unknown, and appears in the analytic setting before the analyst as a sort of sorcerer. Our Western sense of being human is in part defined by this "invisible," just as Mary and other patients at the Centro defined their experiences as influenced by invisibles. Ethno-psychiatry can thus be understood as a self-reflective practice that constantly reminds us that all therapeutic techniques are culturally and historically situated. In this sense, it functions as a medical anthropology that is attuned to the rituals and invisibles not only of others but of us as well.

JUGGLING WORDS, TRANSLATING WORLDS: THE WORK OF MEDIATION

I met Grace when she entered the rehabilitation program for victims of human trafficking and was referred to Emancipazione Oggi (Emancipation Today), a Catholic NGO that supported women filing criminal charges against their exploiters. She looked very young, although her actual age remained unknown. She had arrived in Italy from Benin City (Nigeria) with a fake passport. On paper she was eighteen. She and I spent a lot of time together over the course of several months. The staff at the NGO asked me whether I was willing to accompany her through the different steps of the program. At first, this meant going with her to the police station to file charges, to the hospital for medical checks, and attending to other needs she may have. When we met, she lived at a shelter for victims run by Catholic nuns in a secret location at the periphery of town. She was in a protected site because she had just entered the program and was in the process of collaborating with the police. Grace's life took some complicated and painful turns over the course of our relationship, some of which led her to attend the Centro Fanon, where she was eventually taken in as a patient.

Following Grace through various institutional settings allows us to look at the ways in which her story is rendered and made intelligible and how different languages and logics translate her into various categories of recognition. I argue that in the ethno-psychiatric setting, what the state hears as a lie or a missed narrative is received as a different kind of truth. In this context, the role of the cultural mediator becomes central; it embodies yet a different kind of translation that enables a relationship of care among all the participants in the therapy. Usually members of migrant communities, cultural mediators translate between migrants and Italians in institutional settings such as hospitals, prisons, schools, shelters, and courtrooms. The mediators' role in ethno-psychiatry helps develop a shared therapeutic frame between patients and doctors.

Let me start from the first time I encountered her story, at the police station on the day she filed a denuncia against her traffickers. I had accompanied her there and sat next to her as she recounted her story to a police officer with the help of a Nigerian cultural mediator who translated from Edo into Italian. Grace spoke broken Italian and needed a translator to understand and answer the officer's questions. The story that resulted from that day of interrogation and that came to constitute the official text of the denuncia runs as follows (this is my paraphrasing of the official document):

Grace is eighteen as she enters the rehabilitation program for victims of human trafficking. She left Nigeria when she was fifteen. In Nigeria she had never had sexual intercourse with a man. Her brother arranged for her to travel to Europe, with the promise that she could pursue her studies there. Grace completed primary school but dropped out of secondary school, as the family had little money. Her parents are divorced. Her father has twenty-five wives and more than fifty children and is completely absent from her life. Her mother has a small seasonal business in the local market in Benin City. She never knew where Grace was taken and what she was doing. She knew only that Grace was in Europe. Her brother's friend traveled with her to Italy and sold her to Edith, the woman who became her madam. Edith told her that her travel from Nigeria to Italy cost them 200 million lire (the equivalent of $100,000) and that in order to pay her debt quickly she had to work as a prostitute. Grace thought that being a prostitute meant wearing heavy makeup and had no idea that she actually had to have sex with men. Her madam told her to put on a miniskirt, a wig, high-heeled boots, and a tight shirt and sent her on the streets with the other young Nigerian women who worked for her. She was told that from that moment on, her name was Juliet, and if someone asked her age, she should say she was twenty years old. After her first sexual intercourse with a client she was taken to the hospital for constant bleeding. Once she was discharged from the hospital, the madam forced her to go back to the streets, even though the bleeding continued. She worked from 8:00 A.M. to 9:00 P.M. every day and gave all the money she made to Edith. She was not able to save any for herself or her family in Nigeria. A month after arriving in Italy, her madam performed a voodoo ritual. As part of it, she made Grace take an oath not to betray her and said, "If you don't pay your debt, you will die. If you tell anyone about what is happening to you, you will become crazy. I bought you with the money I earned from my own prostitution, and now you have to return the money with yours. If you don't respect the pact, you will die in Italy." The police caught Grace several times but never repatriated her. Her madam used to hit her with a belt or punch her in the stomach. She used to slam her face against the wall every time she came home without having earned enough money. One day, she escaped from her madam's house and lived with another Nigerian woman for a few months. During this time, she continued to work as a prostitute, to pay her debt to Edith, but also kept some money for herself. One night, three Italian men raped her. She was taken to the emergency room, and social workers approached her to explain about the possibility of entering the rehabilitation program for victims of human trafficking. In the denuncia, she declared that she had made a conscious decision to join the program.

Right after filing criminal charges, Grace had several crises at the shelter where she lived with the nuns. During these episodes, she would tremble with fear, at times ending up in uncontrollable fits and seizures, being completely unresponsive to the nuns, and becoming physically rigid and stiff. She was afraid to sleep in her bedroom by herself. In more dramatic moments, she would run to the kitchen and grab a knife, saying that she wanted to kill herself. She reported hearing a voice telling her to kill herself. It was the voice of Edith, her madam. For days the nuns did not know what to do, aside from stopping her from harming herself. They described her crisis as follows: "She crawls on the floor as if she was a snake; her body becomes as heavy as a piece of wood that weighed 200 kilos; we can't lift her even if the four of us together try. She says she wants to die." The nuns described her crises as "epileptic convulsions" and justified them as consequences of the subjugation she experienced during what the nuns understood as "voodoo rituals."

Before hospitalizing Grace, they called her pastor from the local Pentecostal church. He performed rituals with water, sprinkling drops of it all over her body, which reduced her to crawling on the floor. He suggested that the nuns contact her madam to tell her to stop performing rituals on Grace. "Otherwise," he told the nuns, "she is going to die in seven days." None of these rituals worked. After another crisis on Christmas night, Grace was hospitalized. Her diagnosis showcased the overlapping languages and criteria that are not usually combined in a single diagnosis: "psychotic syndrome linked to her prolonged exposure to serious psycho-physical traumas." The psychiatrist at the public hospital, Dr. M, explained her "post-traumatic psychotic syndrome" as a consequence of being forced into prostitution at a young age, being raped twice, and being reduced by her madam's voodoo rituals to a state of psychological subjugation. He concluded that she was likely to die or go mad if not treated. The psychiatrist reported her symptoms as "hallucinatory voices of a persecutory type, delirious and persecutory interpretations, anxiety attacks, nightmares, and insomnia." Dr. M was not familiar with ethno-psychiatric practice, but he was trained in *psichiatria democratica*—democratic psychiatry—and had a particular interest in social medicine. He volunteered as a psychiatrist at the local jail and was the only doctor at the hospital who was interested in seeing foreign patients. With Grace, he attempted to translate the symptoms into a language that reinterpreted psychiatric categories. Post-traumatic stress disorder is not a syndrome and does not belong to the spectrum of psychosis. In diagnosing her with "post-traumatic psychotic syndrome," the doctor was rearranging the categories at his disposal to signify a series of symptoms untranslatable to one specific psychiatric category as he knew it.

Apparently, Grace's last crisis started immediately after she found out that the police had not yet arrested her madam. "If she is free, she can do rituals on me," she thought. Moreover, Grace feared that the madam would send someone to threaten her family in Nigeria, thereby disclosing the fact that she was working as a prostitute and had lied to them. As the stories in the following chapters show, the larger networks of prostitution that move between Europe and Africa and the social relations back home have a strong impact on women's experiences, often haunting their imaginary and psychic life.

Meanwhile, the nuns were always with Grace and, at the suggestion of the psychiatrist, tried to collect information about her life before she came to Italy and while in Italy. Nuns, psychiatrists, ethno-psychiatrists, and cultural mediators collaborate at different moments of the rehabilitation program for victims and often share the fragments of a woman's story that each collects in the effort to grasp the larger context of their lives. But Grace's story seemed impenetrable to the nuns; it constantly eluded their attempts to grasp some truth about her past that would explain her current suffering. She often contradicted herself: sometimes she would say that her brother had sent her to Italy; sometimes she denied it. Sometimes she said he was a native doctor, a magician, who tricked her into prostitution, but in other versions of her story he was a craftsman who lived far away from the family and had lost contact with her. She said her mother knew she was a sex worker but then claimed her mother did not know and had not talked to her in a long time.

During one consultation with the hospital psychiatrist, one of the nuns said, "Each time, she tells a different story. It is as if she did not have a center, an identity that could hold, a story to which she could adhere, a culture that could sustain her." Even the Nigerian cultural mediator who worked in the Catholic shelter complained that Grace always lied about her past: "She never gives me the same version of the story." She didn't want to contact her family in Nigeria, especially her mother. "But she is still her mother, after all," lamented one of the nuns. "Why shouldn't she forgive Grace for what had happened to her?" I wondered whether forgiveness was what Grace wanted or if that was just what the nun wanted for her—her language to imagine Grace's project of emancipation and healing. The story she told the nuns did not have the same coherence as the one she told at the police station when she filed criminal charges, although the nuns were looking precisely for that same logic in the account of her life. They wanted to make sense of her difference and what they perceived as her madness.

Dr. M reflected on the nuns' concerns: "The different versions of the story could be a strategy of survival, a defense. If she told the true story she would probably die; she is not able to handle the truth of her own story." He alluded to a dangerous truth that can only be approached through multiple lies, fearful and timid attempts to touch it and own it again (or maybe own it for the first time), with the risk of being annihilated by it. Grace's migration, her exile, can therefore be seen as a possibility to occupy her story differently, in a way that could make healing possible. But this story could not emerge within the hospital through biomedical language, or in her interactions with the nuns.

The hospital psychiatrist's interpretation shows how various actors reacted differently to Grace's numerous narratives. The lack of coherence in each fragment of Grace's account confused attempts to rehabilitate her as a "victim" and free her from subjugation to make her an autonomous subject. Foreign women are recognized and taken on by social services as victims. Without the narrative of the victim, recognizing the other is fraught with the danger of losing one's own center, or, following de Martino (2000 [1948]), of losing one's own presence. For de Martino, the "crisis of presence" refers to the individual's existential fear of being threatened by situations that challenge his or her ability to handle external and internal realities. Foreigners and Italians alike share this danger when their mutual incommensurabilities cause conflict. This is how I interpreted the anxiety and fear I heard in the nuns' concerns about Grace's "psychotic episodes," their discomfort about hearing of the complicity of family members in her choice to migrate, and the impossibility of grasping some coherent narrative that could then be labeled as her story.

As for Grace, she did not have many prefabricated stories at her disposal within the Catholic shelter, other than the story of the "victim" provided by the denuncia, which, as I show in chapters 4 and 5, found its raison d'être in the Catholic rhetoric of confession and redemption. Approached as a victim within the frame of the rehabilitation program, she responded as a victim. Grace's experience also points to something I have observed in other foreign women's lives. They come to inhabit the category of the victim for particular periods of their migration trajectories. While they often have that category ascribed to them, they are never completely subsumed within it, even at critical moments when all other reference points are lost. Hence the confused versions of the past that creep into their narratives are a way of redeeming a story that cannot be told as it attempts to make itself heard. I saw Grace's suffering as an account in and of itself, a way of telling an ineffable story in institutional settings that represent, to her, multiple alterities and that inhibit the production of a single narrative. Her elusive stories could also be interpreted as ensuing from trauma: did they point toward dissociation, a missed narrative—as Western psychological and psychoanalytic theories of trauma would cast it—or were they an account of life in its own right?[7] In the various institutional settings where her stories were heard, the gaps and discrepancies were interpreted as holes in the account, as lacks preventing Grace's narrative from becoming whole. In contrast, in the ethno-psychiatric space, as I show below, discrepancies would be treated as forms of truth, contradictions would hold meaning more than coherence, and silence would convey not the absence of speech or the vacuum of sense but a narrative itself.

When she was discharged from the hospital, she worried about what would happen to her once she had fully recovered: "I don't know how to do anything. What will I do when I get better? I am nothing, I can only go back to the street." Her concern, apart from practical ones such as finding a job, speaks to her fear of being recognized solely as a victim. Being labeled in this way contains the foreigner in a moment of loss, outside of which the risk of experiencing a crisis of presence re-presents itself with full force. The story of victimhood provides a singular fixed narrative—a kind of anchor for some—and also adds another possible version to the other stories women tell in different institutional settings and/or according to various contradictory paths of memory.

After her first hospitalization, I told the nuns and Dr. M at the hospital about the ethno-psychiatric clinic where I was conducting my research. They decided to consult with the ethno-psychiatrists and cultural mediators at the Centro Fanon, and eventually Grace was accepted as a patient. When asked at the Centro about her crises, she responded with frustration and anger at the fact that she had yet to receive her residency permit. She had been in the rehabilitation program for four months, and she had filed criminal charges before that. When she met Dr. A, one of the ethno-psychiatrists at the Center, she refused to talk to him. A Nigerian cultural mediator, Charity, was present during the consultations and spoke Edo with her. They were both from Benin City. Over the years, Dr. A had treated many Nigerian women and had come to be recognized as an expert on issues concerning their treatment; he consulted with the Immigration Office, social services, and mental health practitioners. After a few consultations, he asked Grace whether she was in contact with her mother in Nigeria or with the brother who had sent her to Italy without warning her about prostitution. He was relying on a version of the story that the nuns had reported to him and that mirrored the one she gave when she filed criminal charges. Other questions were more directly about the specific symptoms she experienced. I wondered how she would talk about the voices she heard in her head now that she could speak in her mother tongue. What words would she use to describe her bodily sensations during her crisis?

At first, Grace responded with "yes," "no," or long silences. Eventually, however, Grace started telling a story about the time she had arrived in Italy. It sounded just like the story archived at the police station, with the same coherent rhythm and empty words, caught in the speech accepted by the state. And then she burst into a long list of grievances:

> I am tired of telling the same story over and over again. I gave them my story, and I still don't have a residency permit or a regular job. I am going crazy because my madam knows I reported her to the police. I live with Catholic nuns who pray day and night, and I am still sick and without papers. Why don't their prayers work? If I go mad, it means voodoo works here in Italy as well. This man can't do anything about my papers. What's the point of telling him my story anyway?

Charity not only translated the ethno-psychiatrist's questions for Grace, but, as is common practice at the Centro, was given the space to ask her own questions and collect Grace's story in her own way without specific instructions from the therapist. The idea is to create a space where patients can use their own words and language to express what they are experiencing, and the aim of the cultural mediator is to facilitate this process so that the patients can resort to different etiologies and techniques of cure and borrow from both those of the receiving country and those of their country of origin. In this context, the cultural mediator is asked to be much more than an interpreter, an expert at finding equivalences between languages. Rather, she becomes a juggler of words and a translator of concepts, adept enough at the task to make the words and concepts resonate and reverberate in the language of the other, whether the patient or the therapist.

Even so, for several weeks during the consultations Grace met any question or reference to Nigeria with complaints about not having papers, the denuncia not helping her get legal status, not having money like she did when she worked on the streets, and so on. The ethno-psychiatrist did not make a new diagnosis. In fact, he suspended the previous diagnosis in his attempt to let another story emerge. Dr. A encouraged her to slowly get back in touch with her family in Nigeria and, more generally, with her life there. He suggested that she read African literature—if that was something she used to like to do. But Grace was still very vulnerable, and she resisted all attempts to draw her life and story back to where she came from. She refused to contact either her mother or her brother. Hers was a broken biography, splinters of stories jutting in divergent directions.

When Grace filed criminal charges she was asked to provide a chronological narrative in which the past was recounted with linear transparency. In the therapeutic setting, another kind of memory was invoked: a traumatic one that repeats itself in symptoms and regressions, punctuated by multiple temporalities and interruptions, and that resists direct access. As Dr. A explained, what in part characterizes traumatic memory is that the subject ignores the existence of a past traumatic event in the sense that she does not hold a distinct rational memory of it. Nonetheless, this memory makes itself visible in repetitions, in acting out old patterns of behaviors, and it operates despite the subject's awareness of it. In a way, the patient is possessed by this memory; it has a life of its own and cannot be reduced to a single narrative (Beneduce 2010). There is no coherence. In this clinical space, fragments of memory provide an account that defies categorization. This memory encompasses all the invisibles that the ethno-psychiatric setting can reconvene (Stengers 2009).

Before Grace left the session that day at the Centro, Dr. A told her to write down all the words she heard in her head and urged that if the voices told her to kill herself, she should cry out, "The doctor forbids it!" This imperative seemed to reassure her. Someone was standing up for her against the threatening voices in her head. Through transference, the doctor occupied the position of the healer who speaks directly to the persecutory voices, as a shaman or native doctor would do. Dr. A explained to me that evoking concepts such as witchcraft or the existence of invisible agents as the root causes of the patient's suffering resembles the revelation of a secret. Thus, the therapist needs to position himself as the patient's defense against damaging forces that can bring about illness, madness, and danger. The first step for a therapist is to take the patient's fear seriously and not reduce it to belief. Next the therapist needs to insert himself in the network of power relations that cause the patient's suffering so as to take on the role of the one who can break the spell (Beneduce 2007). In this clinical context, it is not a matter of evoking the magic of the patient's cultural background but rather of making her speak to it in order to free her from its effect. This is how I understood what Dr. A enacted on that day. He occupied the position of the protector—or, rather, he let the logic of the voices in Grace's head assign him this position—who could counteract the malignant forces. But as Dr. L had warned us in the case of Mary, things can slip from your grasp if you do not know how to position yourself in the field of magic, where accusations and counteraccusations become powers that assign positions to those who find themselves in their presence (Favret-Saada 1980).

Eventually, after several consultations, mostly spent talking about the residency permit, a different kind of story seemed to creep into the usual exchange of words. Charity, the cultural mediator, evoked the possibility that Grace belonged to a secret society in Nigeria, which would explain why she resisted revealing the details of her life back home. On that day, Grace had a bad headache that made it more difficult for her to talk. The therapist put his hands on her head and asked her to tell him about her past in Nigeria. "You are safe here, the doctor protects you from the people who want to harm you," he said. She remained silent, with her eyes closed. "Do you have another name, an African name?" "Yes?" "What is your African name?" "Ivié," Grace replied. Slowly she started revealing more. She was worried about going mad because she had not paid her debt to her madam, and she had broken the oath. "My madam will do anything to destroy me, to make me go mad." The ethno-psychiatrist asked Charity what the expression "to go mad" is in Edo. "Iwaré."

"Is it a general term or is it linked to voodoo rituals?" he asked. "It means that the people who do magic to you make you become a cadaver without a body; you become a slave, useless, the living dead, at the threshold of life and death," Charity explained. At that point, Grace started to complain about back pain and her legs being very heavy, as if full of water. She had experienced these symptoms before but had never revealed them to the therapist. He then asked her if she had ever participated in the worship of Mami Wata, the goddess of water, wealth, abundance, and success. After a while, she recounted that her mother had brought her to one of Mami Wata's ceremonies and that for a long time she had worn an anklet as a symbol of her devotion. When she came to Italy she joined a Pentecostal church and ceased worshipping Mami Wata.[8] The interaction was a flurry of words: those spoken by Grace, then translated by the cultural mediator, then taken up by the doctor, and finally bounced back by Grace. Her symptoms seemed to resist any reduction to a clinical record; they pointed instead toward confused relations, opaque memories, and ruptured belongings that exceeded psychiatric diagnosis and could not be made intelligible through biomedical logics.

How could Grace's experience and multiple affiliations be translated in a clinical context that did not use psychiatric categories to find meaning in what exceeded the domain of normality? Could "culture" be used to understand these moments of incommensurability when stories follow different temporalities and categories no longer hold their logic? The ethno-psychiatrist as tightrope walker had to create an encounter with the patient that would produce meaning for both patient and doctor. This meaning, however, could be fleeting and illusory. As one psychologist at the Centro explained, when women speak of voodoo in the clinical space the therapist might assume an understanding of what cultural trait they refer to, but in reality what the patient presents is an element whose contours are very opaque. Voodoo is sometimes called "culture," though it eludes any definition of what culture is. Ethnopsychiatric practice is thus articulated through the making and unmaking, appearing and disappearing of meanings, objects, rituals, and concepts. Moments of commensuration/reification are followed by moments of incommensurability, when "things slip from your grasp." And just like misunderstandings, things that slip through your fingers and accounts that are not linear become important elements of a cure.

Patients often arrive at the Centro after having been diagnosed at the hospital. They are usually referred by other health services or by public and religious institutions. The referral takes place when institutions recognize that the person needs a different kind of treatment and when social workers, mental health practitioners, and volunteers feel powerless and unprepared to manage the patient's request for help. Because ethno-psychiatry is intertwined with practices of cultural and linguistic mediation, at the Centro patients can turn to cultural mediators from the same linguistic group to help. In this context, mediators are asked to explain and clarify symptoms according to the cultural idioms of the country of origin of the patient, and they can also participate in the process of formulating diagnoses and administering a cure (Nathan 2001). Their role is to mediate between the cultural content of the patient's idioms and the explanatory models of the doctors (Kleinman 1988). This allows for a different telling and a different listening.

The stories that resist being told are not necessarily about prostitution or other events that are usually represented and experienced as traumatic; often they concern the time before migrating: stories about homes and family members with whom ties have become more precarious, tense, and persecutory after migration. For example, one of the psychologists at the Centro explained to me that in the ethno-psychiatric setting, a considerable number of women who according to the law qualify as victims of human trafficking do not talk about prostitution as a traumatic experience. They have a more complex relationship to sex work, which at the moment of migration they might see as an entrepreneurial adventure, for lack of better choices. In women's accounts sexuality is mentioned and experienced in multiple ways: in some cases it serves the purpose of migrating, earning money, and supporting family members; in other instances it is thought of as sinful and shameful, especially if perceived through the gaze of the receiving society's institutions; in yet other cases, all these aspects are experienced at once. Women are often caught in these polarized logics, seen as either victims or prostitutes, either traumatized or pathological. In reality, in their experiences these polarities are blurred. They do talk about the crude reality of street violence and sexual abuse that often accompanies prostitution, but this is only one of various ways in which women position themselves and are positioned by others in relation to prostitution.

THE PLAY OF DIAGNOSTIC AND CULTURAL INTERPRETATIONS

One way in which translation works in the ethno-psychiatric setting is through the formulation—or suspension—of diagnosis, a kind of translation itself. Therapists are very cautious about using diagnoses based on the criteria of diagnostic manuals. Yet they are aware of the patients' need to have a name for their suffering. In the consultation, all participants share the process of naming the experience of suffering. Practitioners view the formulation of a diagnosis as an exploratory process during which patients can explain what they experience in their own terms; family members are involved in naming the moments of crisis (often from afar by phone calls made by cultural mediators or patients themselves), and ethno-psychiatrists juggle their own explanatory models and cultural explanations and are conscious of whether or not they resonate with the patient's representation and experiences. In the words of one ethno-psychiatrist, "Coming up with a diagnosis is an open process of exploration, not a process of labeling and fixing. It takes into account multiple voices, and it aims at serving a purpose for the patient, such as being able to name his/her suffering in a way that can be heard and shared by family members and people back home." The assumption is that any diagnosis that claims to have recognized and identified symptoms within an explanatory model is paralyzing. The aim is to have composite diagnoses that draw from plural epistemologies and taxonomies and speak specifically to the patient's situation.

In a context where matters pertaining to gods and spirits are put in dialogue and tension with the language of secular psychiatry and psychoanalysis, clinical practice is fundamentally reshaped and "enchanted" by logics that escape the language of secular time. Diagnosis is thus less a process of direct translation of causes and symptoms into categories and more a form of acknowledgment of a fluid situation where the subject is to be understood not only in psychoanalytic terms but also as defined and constituted by external invisible agents. As in the experience commonly referred to as "possession," these external agents fundamentally position the subject by putting it in relation with forces, spirits, and presences that are constitutive of it—not separate from it, but copresent with it in forms of intersubjectivity that go beyond the Western idea of what counts as human. Just as acknowledging the presence of invisible agents in the clinical encounter decenters the idea of the subject as it is framed in psychological and psychiatric terms, ethno-psychiatric theory and practice decenter psychiatry itself (Beneduce 2006). Ethno-psychiatry produces a rupture within psychiatric practice. On the process of diagnosis, Dr. L explains:

> We often deal with people who don't adhere to a single system of classification; they are suspended in between various possible ways of making sense

of the causes of their suffering. . . . Our practice should facilitate the person's exploration of all the etiologies available to them . . . , in order to make space for their difference to emerge. . . . A diagnosis is . . . a classification, a homologizing labeling that completely misses the patient's difference. . . . Our effort is to look at the migrant's difference and not to put suffering into the box of a diagnostic category.[9]

Naming symptoms and suffering in this setting implies the combination of multiple approaches, languages, categories, and ontologies. Beyond the diagnostic logic of psychiatric and psychological paradigms, the explanation of the patient's symptoms results not from an either/or process (either psychiatric or cultural) but from a process that attempts to blur the boundaries of psychiatric and cultural categories. The suspension of diagnosis represents the attempt to make the space of the clinic receptive to other ways of understanding suffering and open to difference. In ethno-psychiatry, both prognostic and therapeutic efforts aim to allow the patient's difference to express itself and not to reduce it to the homologizing effect of a diagnosis. Approaching diagnosis as a multivocal process resonates with a practice of translation that recognizes a certain degree of incommensurability between languages and ontologies and does not attempt to reduce them to equivalences.

Recognizing the patient's difference is considered a therapeutic act in and of itself. In my fieldwork at the Centro Fanon, I often observed this approach. However, the benefits of demedicalizing suffering had its exceptions. In some cases, evoking cultural material in the therapeutic setting can provoke anxiety in the patient. The attempt to invoke values and cultural material that resonate with the patient's original context can cause distress rather than a sense of holding or a reassuring sense of familiarity. In Mary's case, for instance, Dr. L was aware that the dead husband and his family's magic powers had a persecutory effect on Mary, but she also believed that even if certain aspects of culture are perceived as threatening, working through them can bring healing.

I was caught in another set of questions regarding the failure of culture as a concept that could heal. Or, rather, I understood cultural interpretations as a vehicle of mediation that at times need to be suspended and bracketed, just like psychiatric diagnoses. In one of our conversations, Dr. A told me about the case of Joy, a Nigerian woman who complained about hearing voices and feeling the presence of spirits inside her head. In particular, she had reported a dream in which a spiritual husband sat on her head and ejaculated. Devotees of the possession cult of Mami Wata are married to a spiritual husband (another way to refer to Mami Wata), but their devotion is often discontinued or tainted with ambivalence once they leave Nigeria. Nonetheless, women may experience that the ties with the divinity cannot be completely severed and thus feel haunted by her presence. Joy felt persecuted by the spirit. During one consultation at the Centro, one of the practitioners made a reference to the presence of the spiritual husband in Joy's dream, to which she responded with a high level of anxiety: she stood up and started walking fast in a circle while speaking to the spirits. Dr. A intervened because he realized that the spirits were threatening to Joy, and at that point in the treatment the therapeutic team was not capable of handling such forces. He commented to me that if you invite spirits into the consultation, it is like inviting a ghost: "You must know both how to let them in and how to send them away." In that instance, he reassured Joy that the medications she was taking would help her get rid of the voices and feel better. He therefore resorted to what he defined as an "allopathic-exorcist treatment," not because the presence of the spirits was something to deny (on the contrary, he emphasized), but because he believed that the patient was too vulnerable and the therapeutic team ill equipped to face the spirits.

This further explains how in ethno-psychiatry identifying the patient's positioning with respect to their culture has important implications for the diagnosis and kind of treatment chosen. The patient's suspension between different etiologies can at times mean that he or she may benefit from naming the suffering with a psychiatric diagnosis, precisely the diagnostic domain contested and challenged by ethno-psychiatric practice. Moreover, medications can also figure as part of the treatment if they help the patient cope with unsettling presences and threatening voices. This is what Dr. A described when he discussed Joy's case and the difficulties the therapeutic team encountered dealing with the invisibles that the patient evoked. In this case, the doctor did not use the language of culture to communicate with the patient. Therefore, in the context of migration, as in a postcolonial situation, it becomes impossible to fully inhabit the diagnostic categories or the references that culture provides (Pandolfo 2008).[10] This kind of clinical work suggests and enacts a conversation—an encounter, a translation—between different worlds (and languages) that construct a plurality of meanings, objects, interpretations, and understandings.

Within this setting, not only are there competing and overlapping etiologies at play, but there are also discrepancies between how the ethno-psychiatrists and the cultural mediators approach the question of translation. Leaving room for multiple interpretations of symptoms can coexist with the therapeutic need to name difference through criteria framed in the register of culture rather than that of a psychoanalytic diagnosis. Acknowledging the existence of differences, singularities, and the process through which they constantly reshape each other is not the only practice at play in ethno-psychiatric clinical work. The tendency to explain symptoms through what is recognized as cultural material points to the need—for both ethno-psychiatrists and patients—to name suffering and make it commensurable, understandable, and manageable. This leads me to ask whether cultural explanations can, in this context, become a substitute for psychiatric diagnoses and thus have the same fixing and paralyzing effect of the language of biomedicine.

THE REVERSE OF CULTURE AS THERAPY

What if, from the patient's point of view, exile from one's own world rather than cultural references can provide a therapeutic opportunity? While participating in therapy sessions at the Centro—and later as I started transcultural analysis myself, in the context of my own migration—I often wondered whether departure from one's mother tongue and from what counts as home may allow the subject to rearticulate life in different forms and imagine experience anew in ways that can be considered therapeutic. The ethno-psychiatrists shared this question with me. They often talked about culture as conflictual and violent as well as therapeutic, as a shifting signifier that carries different connotations. They often avoided using the concept of culture but instead referred to "a noncoherent set of cultural and social references that influence patients' ways of experimenting the world," as Dr. P once explained to me. What figures as a reference to patients' background and tradition can also be "poisonous knowledge" (Das 2000), pointing to experiences of suffering that are enmeshed in social relations and not necessarily tied to a specific traumatic event. When Mary referred to her husband's family and the fear of being the victim of their spell, she is referring to social relations that she perceives as dangerous. Frantz Fanon, too, has talked about the practice of tradition as "a disturbed practice" (1965 [1959], 130), and of the impossibility of a return to the past, to a culture that has been tainted and erased by the experience of colonization. For him, the "quest for dis-alienation"—or emancipation—can happen by acknowledging the fracture that violence produces, becoming untangled from the influence of the colonizer's gaze and starting anew (Fanon 1967 [1952]).

For instance, at the Centro, in some cases when the language of sorcery, possession, or witchcraft is evoked to provide a context to a patient who is hearing voices and feeling haunted by other forces, ethno-psychiatrists noticed that patients and family members (who are not necessarily present in the consultation) may react with distrust and disbelief. As Beneduce (2003) explained, people express this kind of distrust in regard to theories and etiologies in order to distance themselves, not because that world has ceased to be meaningful, but precisely because that world is still present and associated with unresolved ties, relations, and debts. In such moments, cultural interpretations appear to be persecutory rather than healing. Here I am referring to the persecutory aspect of cultural references that could lead to a foreclosure of the cure, and not, as Dr. L earlier suggested, a necessary step in the healing process. In this sense, both cultural and psychiatric diagnoses can turn out to be stigmatizing and paralyzing, closing down the possibility of exploring suffering and instead enabling it. Thus, when practitioners describe their practice as a "critical ethno-psychiatry" they refer to the importance of bracketing both cultural and psychiatric diagnoses and allowing interpretations to emerge in the space in between.

In the context of migration to Europe, the psychoanalyst Fethi Benslama (2000) points to the fact that in the sociology of migration, migrants are often portrayed as victims rather than agents. They are passively moved by the need to leave, attracted by the illusion of the wealthy north that alienates them from their cultures. This argument classifies all kinds of migration as banishment (banissement), and it completely effaces the question of desire: the desire to exit, to exile one's self from a context that may have become unbearable. Such is the desire to inhabit another culture and speak the language of the other as an experience of emancipation. Benslama further argues that migration creates a rupture in the course of the life of the subject who has become a foreigner, to himself or herself and to others. This experience puts in question the very sense of being in the world, and the psychoanalytic setting can help the subject inhabit this rupture, tolerate the loss, and thus find a more authentic sense of self.

Benslama's critique of ethno-psychiatry is directed at Nathan's clinical use of culture in the French context. As I explained earlier, while Nathan's model inspired the early phase of the Centro Fanon, practitioners there have also questioned it and developed a critical approach to it. Benslama

(2000) argues that by encouraging foreign patients to address their cultural backgrounds, ethno-psychiatry may risk reducing the specificity of the individual to the anonymity of the group. Thus, contrary to a use of culture as a tool of recognition of difference—which counters the universalizing perspective of biomedical knowledge—this approach might produce precisely the opposite effect. Thinking about Dr. L's explanation of what it means to reify certain aspects of patients' backgrounds in order to create a relationship, I understand reification not as the reduction or translation of experience into fixed meanings but on the contrary as a mean to create a therapeutic relationship. Reification in this clinical context, then, does not fix patients in abstract representations but emerges from the relationship between patients and therapists and enables the circulation of speech and associations. As Dr. L specified, a patient's response to a therapist's use of cultural material reveals what resonates with the patient as a meaningful interpretation. In this sense, reification is a social relation (Strathern 1999) that produces certain effects.

My question about exile—as a way of thinking about the rupture produced by migration and as a potentially healing place—emerges from spending time at the Centro, where cultural representations and identifications are both evoked and suspended and symptoms can interrupt the flow of memory and beg for another listening. In line with a psychoanalytic perspective, this therapeutic choice allows the subject to be in touch with the rupture produced by crossing borders and with the resulting self-inquiry that is peculiar to the individual as such and not as a member of a group. To live in this break means to stutter in one's own language and in the language of the other. Experiencing this uncertainty in a clinical setting—instead of reanchoring the patient in what is represented as his or her culture of origin—can be therapeutic. At the same time, it is essential, in my view, to understand ethno-psychiatry's contribution beyond the Western psychoanalytic conception of the subject as the expression of a singular voice that emerges at the juncture of individual experience, unconscious desires, and the work of memory. Some of the therapeutic choices in ethno-psychiatry position the patient in the frame of external and collective forces that, while being other from the subject and operating beyond his or her will, are constitutive of his or her subjectivity. These invisibles coexist with what in Western terms is understood as the individual, and they blur the distinctions between self and other, knowledge and belief, as we know them. Ethno-psychiatry thus troubles Western assumptions not only about mental health but also about subjectivity and what counts as human.

What is "therapeutic" and what stands for "cultural identification" at different moments in the ethno-psychiatric treatment shift and are in tension. Whenever cultural material is represented as a possible therapeutic tool, or lever, anthropologists raise their guard and denounce its objectification. In the contemporary heated debates about ethno-psychiatry in Europe, psychoanalysts have joined the classic anthropological critique of this practice, which they claim can stigmatize and further the risk of creating cultural ghettos and exotic representations of the other (Benslama 2000; Fassin 2000; Fassin and Rechtman 2005). I believe the anthropological critique of ethno-psychiatry needs to be turned upside down. As the clinical moments I have recounted in this chapter show, clinicians may reify cultural references, but they do so with the awareness of creating a tool in order to produce an effect that in turn produces a therapeutic encounter. The clinical setting becomes a theater of alterity where cultural meanings are produced and shared by the different characters. To apply anthropological theory to the clinical use of culture is misleading and risks missing the point of the political valence of the use of culture in this specific context. The kind of reification I am referring to here is only a temporary tool of recognition, an attempt to translate difference in terms that are intelligible to patients and doctors. It is a means (a technique) that has the potential to go beyond the logic of recognition and blur the distinctions between various classificatory systems and translations. This reminds me of James Clifford's (1997) ways of talking about culture in terms of travel and as a set of circuits to exemplify the complex cultural formations that cannot be contained in the term *culture* and that contemporary anthropology theorizes.

The question about what counts as cultural material that I—as an anthropologist—and ethno-psychiatrists—as both therapists and anthropologists—ask points in directions that are sometimes similar and sometimes different. I am mostly interested in how the play of cultural references takes definite boundaries in the clinical setting (in the form of rituals, languages, prayers, places, voices heard, spirits, invitations to join local Pentecostal churches, to visit exhibitions, to recuperate memories and maintain ties with home) and how those very boundaries are done and undone in the therapeutic encounter. Different intertwined layers of culture and translation are at play. Sometimes aspects of the patient's world constitute the subject; at other times they dissolve it. At some times cultural representations provide containment for the individual; at others they create dangerous identifications. In a way, "culture" resists closure; it works—for both anthropologists and doctors—as a floating signifier. Therapists make and undo reifications in order to create a relationship with the patient. Perhaps, in this relationship, cultural material may also make the subject depart from, rather than fix her in, certain identifications.

As practitioners, ethno-psychiatrists use "culture"—not merely to observe or theorize it (although they do so in their theoretical writings)—*as if* it existed and experiment with what has therapeutic traction. They do not know with certainty what cultural identifications are or what they mean to the patient. They work through intuitions, definitions, constructions, and translations. Moreover, they pay attention to the work that cultural references do, to their effectiveness on the bodies of patients and in their lives (Lévi-Strauss 1968). What is "therapeutic" from the practitioners' point of view also seems in flux: in some cases cultural material is seen as healing because it provides a positive environment, a set of symbols that would re-create meaning in the patient's world. On the other hand, as in Mary's case, being reimmersed in cultural material that the patient perceives as dangerous can be, in Dr. L's words, a way to make her stronger. Ethno-psychiatrists suggest that provoking disruption has the potential to be both healing and ineffective. Continuity with one's cultural background as a healing strategy can go hand in hand with the strategy of distancing from a world that is poisonous and a tradition that has become perverse (Fanon 1965 [1959]). What ethno-psychiatrists view as healing is the patient's ability to hold together different worlds, the one she left behind and the present one in which she is living. In fact, the past should merge into the present and find a place there. Ethno-psychiatrists explain listening as being attentive to the different temporalities of the patient's experience, something that the hegemonic tone of today's psychiatric discourse erases and makes invisible. Therapy is thus the reverse of assimilation; it is a political statement and a way to create experiences of "integration" (through interruptions), a concept that a politics of migration and psychological theories of the subject share in principle while meaning different things in practice.

Gananath Obeyesekere (1985) has reflected on the work of culture as the process whereby painful experiences are transformed, or translated, into sets of meanings and symbols that are publicly accepted in the world of the patient. This kind of work, though, risks failure, just as walking on a tightrope may result in falling, and translating risks betrayal. In other words, culture can fail to provide the materials that are necessary to bring meaning to experience. Obeyesekere argues that success and failure in turn can provide a critique of culture that can connect anthropology and critical theory. I would add that success and failure can also lead to a critique of the play of cultural representations that brings together anthropology and clinical work and that makes them—at moments—untranslatable and incommensurable.[11] This is the conundrum that the ethno-psychiatrists and I shared; from within our own disciplinary perspectives, all of us struggle with concepts and their use.

To conclude, after spending a lot of time thinking about the questions raised by my ethnography, I am left wondering whether something about the ethno-psychiatric use of cultural material presents the possibility that there is a kind of difference that we cannot fully understand. In this specific context, culture works as a site of translation and mediation that has the potential to produce categories of recognition—just as psychiatry does with diagnoses—but it can also create a space for the acknowledgment of difference and provide a language that welcomes the incommensurability of worlds.

I lost track of Mary's stories after her first six months of therapy at the Centro. I returned to the United States and heard that she continued to see Dr. L and the team at the clinic. Grace, on the other hand, remained part of my life even after leaving Italy. We kept in touch through Charity, the cultural mediator who translated for her at the Centro. After several months, she received a residency permit, but it was the wrong one. Instead of the permit for "victims of human trafficking," she received one based on health care. Apparently, her hospitalization history and her crisis at the shelter made her eligible for this kind of permit also. In the bureaucratic labyrinth, her "psychiatric problems" elicited a response faster than her condition as a "victim." This was the reason they gave Grace at the police station, when she asked for an explanation. She was furious. This kind of permit would not allow her to work, and she felt completely disabled. Ultimately, though, she was able to get a new permit, the one granted to "victims of human trafficking." Charity thought that getting a residency permit that enabled her to find a job was somehow "therapeutic" for her. The lack of recognition on the part of the institutions, especially after having signed a sort of pact with them, can be annihilating for those who experience it as a form of social death. Grace was expelled from the shelter.

She was still having crises, but the nuns and the other Nigerian women there believed that she was making them up in order to attract attention and speed up the process of getting the residency permit and finding her a job and a house Her crises were interpreted as manipulative acts rather than a cry that exceeded comprehension. She lived at friends' places for a while, went back to the Pentecostal church that she attended when she worked as a prostitute, and reconnected with people she knew before entering the program. I do not know whether she ever went back to work on the street. With time, she found temporary jobs looking after the elderly. She stopped going to the ethno-psychiatric clinic, and although her crises were not as frequent, they persisted. The rest of her story is still unfolding.

CHAPTER 2

Decolonizing Treatment in Psychiatry

Culture is conflict.

—Psychologist, Centro Frantz Fanon

The Centro Fanon was located at the intersection of two secondary roads in a residential part of the city, in the basement of the local mental health department. The corridors were lit by long rectangular neon lights, and the rooms had small windows high up on the walls. During therapy sessions one could see the feet of the people walking by. The head of the mental health department was a psychiatrist trained in the Italian school of democratic psychiatry, a background he shared with most of the ethno-psychiatrists downstairs. The Centro's therapists, though, had a diverse background that informed their clinical work. Unlike the building, which stood at the intersection of only two streets, the clinical practice inside is located at the crossroads of several clinical and philosophical trajectories.

Ethno-psychiatry's legacy has been traced to the work of colonial doctors such as John Colin Carothers and Octave Mannoni (Mannoni 1990 [1950]; Beneduce 2005; Beneduce and Martelli 2005) and in Italy to community-based psychiatry, Gramsci's political thought, and Ernesto de Martino's anthropological research (Pandolfi and Bibeau 2005). Part of the Centro Fanon's genealogy goes back to, and in part departs from, the work of authors who have addressed the colonial and postcolonial implications of psychiatric interventions both in Europe and in the former colonies (Fanon 1967 [1952]; de Martino 1977; Nathan 1994).

The heated debates over ethno-psychiatry in Europe show that the relationship between culture, suffering, and appropriate therapeutic techniques is a highly controversial topic that risks accusations of racism and new forms of discrimination (Fassin 2000; Nathan 2003; Beneduce 2007). These tensions and controversies are products of ethno-psychiatry's history. Questions of culture, mental health, therapy, and power relationships have reemerged today, despite the fact that ethno-psychiatry and transcultural psychiatry position themselves in opposition to colonial psychiatry.[1] On the one hand, culture is becoming an increasingly politicized domain of public discourse, because it is through the language of cultural difference that the relationship between foreigners and receiving countries is often articulated. On the other hand, ethno-psychiatry, being committed to the treatment of migrants, refugees, and torture victims, finds itself on highly politicized terrain in which questions of citizenship, borders, mental health, and rights intersect in complex ways.[2] In the words of Roberto Beneduce, founder of the Centro, "*Culture* and *cultural difference* can become a useful resource for constructing effective therapeutic strategies, effective dialogues with people, only after we have situated this *and other differences* within recognized relationships of power and meaning" (Beneduce and Martelli 2005, 384; original emphasis). What is at stake in contemporary Italian ethno-psychiatry is the question of difference in relation to healing and suffering and its potential to critique institutions and colonial experiences.[3]

In addition to Nathan and his clinical experience in France, philosophical traditions such as phenomenology and existentialism, as well as the anthropological work of Ernesto de Martino, the experience of democratic psychiatry, and the legacy of Franco Basaglia have influenced the Centro's clinical approach. The specificity of Italian ethno-psychiatry can only be understood against the backdrop of the debates over the deinstitutionalization of the mentally ill and the radical critique of public institutions initiated by Basaglia and the deinstitutionalization movement in the early 1970s (Pandolfi and Bibeau 2005). Crucial to the Italian context is also the work of Antonio Gramsci and his reflections on the complex relationships between hegemony and subaltern cultures, in addition to the role of the organic intellectual in creating a field of political action that could involve subalterns in defining what counts as politics. Moreover, Frantz Fanon's denunciation of colonial power relations and the violence embedded in colonial institutions provides the theoretical ground on which the group of practitioners and cultural mediators base their reflections on history and discrimination, which they incorporate into training for mental health practitioners and social workers in the public sphere (Beneduce 2007). These legacies intersect in the clinical practice of ethno-psychiatrists at the Centro Fanon in ways that are broadly relevant not only for the politics of alterity in clinical settings but also for critiquing multicultural projects of integration and the politics of recognition.

THE CONUNDRUM OF CONTRADICTIONS: BASAGLIA AND PSYCHIATRY WITHOUT THE *MANICOMIO*

Interviewer: . . . Doctor Basaglia, to conclude, are you more
interested in the patient or in his illness?
Basaglia: Definitely in the patient!
—Sergio Zavoli, *I giardini di Abele*, TV7 (1968)

The recent revival of ethno-psychiatry in Italy has its roots in a long-standing Italian intellectual critique of public institutions. Franco Basaglia embodies this critical tradition of politically engaged mental health reform originating in the 1960s and 1970s. Recognized as the leading figure of the democratic psychiatry movement in Europe, Basaglia (1924–81) became the director of the Trieste mental asylum in 1971. There, together with a group of colleagues, nurses, and social workers, he started a systematic critique of mental health institutions and the violence embedded in them.[4]

According to Basaglia, the solution to the closed and violent structure of the mental hospital was not to be found in humanitarian gestures that increased the degree of dependency between reformers and patients in the institutional setting but rather in questioning the power relationships that characterized the practice of institutional psychiatry. This critique established the foundation for an anti-institutional movement engaged in dismantling the mental hospital and turning psychiatry inside out. In 1978, this movement led to the abolition of the mental hospital in Italy. Basaglia interpreted mental illness as a sociopolitical problem and envisioned a public psychiatry able to comprehend suffering and social misery outside hospital walls. Influenced by Foucault's (1988) and Goffman's (1961) work on the asylum, he offered a more complex analysis of the interrelation of mental illness and society's response to the management of suffering. Basaglia was able to identify the intersections of the misery of the asylum and the misery of society.

Franca Ongaro Basaglia, wife and colleague of Franco Basaglia, explained, "Having understood that the asylum did not contain madness, but rather poverty and misery that, not being able to resist harshness and suffering, can be expressed through madness, clearly demonstrated that the asylum, and therefore the psychiatry practiced within it, had an explicitly class character" (quoted in Scheper-Hughes and Lovell 1987, xvi). The *manicomio*—a word whose closest English translations are "mental hospital," "madhouse," or "asylum"—as a microsocial architectural space that reproduced perversions in human relationships created an illness specific to itself: institutional psychosis or institutionalism (11). Because of this doubling of the institution within which two kinds of psychosis—that of the patient and that of the institution itself—mirrored and reproduced each other, no real encounter between doctors and patients can take place. The institutionalized patient is subjected to a pact with the institution that forecloses any possibility of listening to and empathizing with his or her lifeworld. In *L'istituzione negata* (The Institution Denied)—a 1968 collection of essays by Basaglia and his most militant colleagues—Basaglia wrote:

> In order to truly face "illness," we should be able to encounter it *outside* of institutions. By this I mean, not only outside of the psychiatric institution, but *outside* of any other institution whose function is to label, codify, and fix those who belong to them into roles. Is there really an *outside* from which we can take action before institutions destroy us? Can't we, instead, deduce that what we know of the "illness"'s appearance is always, anyway, its institutional appearance? (Basaglia 1968, 374; original emphasis; my translation)

By highlighting the institutional construction of mental illness as a disease, Basaglia radically questioned the psychiatrist's practice and his or her social role and responsibility vis-à-vis patients. Influenced by existentialism and the phenomenological approach to mental illness developed by Ludwig Binswanger, Karl Jaspers, and Eugene Minkowski, Basaglia focused his political and ethical efforts on a reevaluation of the encounter between doctor and patient that the asylum made impossible due to its hierarchical and closed structure. To enter the lifeworld of the mentally ill, one had to break free from the situation of oppression instituted by the asylum and its apparatuses of control. Understanding illness also meant suspending diagnoses and paying attention instead to the suffering hidden behind them. According to Basaglia, "in order to have a relationship with an individual, it is necessary to establish it independently of the label by which the person has been defined" (1968, 31; my translation).

In my conversations with ethno-psychiatrists at the Centro Fanon, Basaglia's legacy emerged as central to their clinical work and their political commitment to question the institutions in control of dispensing diagnoses and cures. Simona Taliani, a psychologist trained in ethno-psychiatry and medical anthropology, with experience in field research in Cameroon and other parts of West Africa, once explained to me that by bracketing the diagnosis the patient was allowed to be a competent historian of his or her own life and memories.

> We provide a clinical space where we put diagnoses and psychodynamic interpretations aside in order to listen to what the other has to say about his/her malaise. . . . Our methodology is meant to accompany the person in exploring all the etiologies that they have in mind. . . . In this way, we are engaged in a political effort to see the other as a political subject that has something to say about his/her story and history.[5]

In the ethno-psychiatric encounter, patients construct their own webs of signification, creating meaning out of present circumstances, perceived pasts, and possible futures. In line with Basaglia's teaching, diagnoses are seen as an expression of the hegemonic power of the institutions that inhibit a real therapeutic encounter. Also, diagnostic categories prevent the production of a narrative that, however tentatively, can link different etiologies and healing practices.

For Basaglia, the phenomenological approach allowed psychiatrists to be exposed directly to the lifeworlds of the patients. Empathy with the patient allows for the creation of "a terrain of encounter . . . from which emotion is not absent, and which allows one to find a path from which to start a therapeutic relationship" (1981, 4; my translation). As Simona explained to me, ethno-psychiatry positions patients as political subjects "not because they are victims of human trafficking or of torture, or asylum seekers, but because they tell us about their suffering in their own terms, by using their mother tongues and local etiologies." This means that in the ethno-psychiatric setting the patient can be in a position where power dynamics are for a moment inverted, "because the most competent one is not the doctor but the patient herself." This is a different therapeutic relationship than the one created by the institution, and it allows for a different listening of the patient's symbolic and psychic life. As she put it, "we use the mother tongue in therapy sessions not because we are anthropologically sensitive to the patient's cultural difference, but because the mother tongue is a political instrument that can be used to say certain things."[6] While the use of patients' mother tongues in psychotherapeutic contexts in Western countries was originally introduced to improve the doctor-patient relationship and to elicit relevant material from patients' cultural backgrounds, it became a way to empower non-Western patients in the receiving society's health care systems (Rechtman 2006). For example, mental health practitioners working with indigenous people in New Zealand and Canada have talked about "cultural safety" as an appropriate therapeutic approach that takes into account power imbalances and institutional discrimination in health care settings (Papps and Ramsden 1996; Kirmayer 2012). According to this model, when patients use their mother tongue they can voice their social, historical, political, and economic backgrounds and more easily position themselves as political subjects.[7]

When phenomenological analysis was no longer sufficient to explain the class nature of illness and the larger social and political contexts that determined its modes of expression, Basaglia turned to Gramsci (1975) and other Italian Marxist thinkers who were engaged in finding a new language to address social change. Phenomenology lacked the potential to generate a political impact and change the lives of confined people. Having an understanding of madness not as a mere social product but rather as a complex nexus of contradictions (institutional, ideological, ethical, medical, political, and social) that manifest in patients' bodies, and questioning the structure of medical knowledge itself, allowed Basaglia to foreground issues within psychiatry and its relation to the law.[8]

The traditional asylums were still governed by the 1904 law that positioned psychiatry within the criminal justice system by assigning it the function of *custodia* (control, custody) rather than of *cura* (care). Basaglia was one of the main advocates of the 1978 Law 180, which ratified the closure of the madhouse and promoted the organization of a community-based psychiatry through the establishment of mental health centers. Law 180, also known as the Basaglia Law, prohibited the construction of new asylums, imposed the gradual vacating of the old ones, and established norms for the creation of community-based sociomedical structures to deal with the problem of mental illness without falling back on institutionalization. By involving the community in changing the cultural attitudes toward deviancy, this law also fractured former relationships between psychiatry and justice and ended the practice of doctors being the exclusive managers of mental illness. It confronted the old contradiction between custody and care—that is, control and treatment—and redefined the institution as a positive space in which a different kind of encounter could take place.[9]

I was drawn to doing fieldwork at the Centro Fanon because of the political sensitivity that animated the work of its members and that was akin to mine. I was particularly intrigued by the ways in which the political dimension of Italian community psychiatry intersected with their ethno-psychiatric approach. Roberto Beneduce once told me the story of how the Centro came into existence and the motivations—clinical and political—behind it:

> In one way or another there was a desire on our part not to lose sight of the legacy of Italian community psychiatry. From our point of view, that legacy was not at odds with the opening up of the cultural sphere; therefore the political and the cultural are brought together, going thus slightly against a tradition that had been very strong in Italy. It wasn't easy to bring together the political and the cultural in the clinical work with immigrant patients because even the most sensitive Italian psychiatry never intentionally developed its medical anthropological intuitions. When Basaglia critiques the mental illness statute he is doing medical anthropological work *avant la letter*. At the beginning of the sixties when he takes up phenomenology, there is a critique of mental illness that is anthropologically rooted, but all these things are dispersed and re-channeled into a single critical analysis of institutions.[10]

According to Beneduce, focusing the critique on institutional settings prevents one from seeing how mental illness is constructed and reproduced not only inside the psychiatric institution but also in the social imaginary. For him, focusing on the social dimension of suffering was "the undelivered promise of the writings of some psychiatrists and psychoanalysts between the sixties and seventies." Having himself migrated from the south to the north of Italy, he drew from both his personal and professional experience to translate Basaglia's legacy into a way to work with foreigners.

The critique of institutional violence and the relationships of domination within institutions that characterizes Basaglia's work echoes Fanon's unveiling of the institutional roots of violence in the colonial context. Mariella Pandolfi and Gilles Bibeau have compared Fanon's "wretched of the earth" to Basaglia's wretched of the "institution denied" to underline how both authors were committed to the same radical denunciation of the perversion of mental institutions that deprive people of their rights.[11] However, Basaglia contrasted Fanon's work in the psychiatric hospital in Algeria with his own. It was in Algiers that Fanon clarified his position as a politicized psychiatrist by realizing that the doctor-patient relationship is always defined by the system. Since the so-called therapeutic act is an "act of silent acceptance of the system" (Basaglia 1968, 378), Fanon saw revolution as the only way to act from and against the institution. Basaglia wrote:

Fanon was able to choose revolution. We, for objective reasons, are prevented from doing it. In our reality, we still need to continue to experience the contradictions of the system that overdetermines us, by managing an institution that we deny, by performing a therapeutic act that we refuse, by preventing the institution—which as a result of our very action has turned into an institution of subtle and disguised violence—from continuing to be *only* functional to the system. We attempt to resist the flattery of new scientific ideologies that tend to hide those contradictions, which it is our duty to make explicit. *We are aware of the absurdity of this wager: we want to keep values alive, while nonrights, inequality, and the quotidian death of man are turned into legislative principles.* (1968, 379–80; emphasis in original; my translation)

Basaglia's idea was to work from within the conundrum of the system in order to address the contradictions of an institution that he fundamentally rejected. The constant process of undoing psychiatry from within differed from Fanon's engagement in the revolution: Basaglia thought that a revolution from within the institution could discard the very assumptions underlying its existence. He called this project *"l'utopia della realtà"* (the utopia of reality). For Fanon, on the other hand, revolution required the radical rupture and negation of the mental institution by stepping outside of it, which he did by resigning from his position as a clinical psychiatrist in the hospital in Algiers.

Italian ethno-psychiatry and the debates that animate it come precisely from the political engagements initiated by Basaglia. The vigilant critique of state institutions coupled with the commitment to rethink public services in the domain of public health index a specific kinship between Italian ethno-psychiatry and the legacy of democratic psychiatry. While this more politicized approach to illness and healing was at first oriented toward the economically and politically marginalized, since the early 1980s ethno-psychiatry has increasingly addressed marginalization and domination through a specific focus on migrant communities. It argues that the health care of foreigners is a political issue rather than a strictly medical one and thus echoes Basaglia's concern with the broad political dimensions of mental health and cure. Similar to the epistemological and methodological break that Basaglia created from within psychiatry, the Centro's ethno-psychiatrists bring into focus, through their work, the epistemological uncertainty that mainstream psychiatry is forced to confront in the treatment of foreigners.[12]

When Michel Foucault wrote about the great reforms of psychiatric power and thought over the twentieth century, he argued that they placed the power relations embedded in psychiatry at the center of the field and fundamentally questioned them. Great reforms are attempts to displace such power, to unmask it, to nullify or eliminate it. He observed, "The whole of modern psychiatry is fundamentally pervaded by anti-psychiatry, if one understands by this everything that calls back into question the role of the psychiatrist formerly charged with producing the truth of illness in the hospital space" (Foucault 1994, 45). Several anti-psychiatries have traversed the history of modern psychiatry. I understand the Italian ethno-psychiatry practiced at the Centro as operating within the field of Basaglia's version of anti-psychiatry.[13]

Beneduce once commented, "I don't want to give up psychiatry," thus evoking for me the importance of a critique from within this practice.[14] This statement resonated with several clinical cases I followed at the Centro. To undo psychiatry from the inside out, ethno-psychiatrists not only put diagnostic categories aside but also maintained relationships—often tense—with all those institutions that used these categories, and they proposed a critique or, we might say, an interruption of the logic of psychiatric knowledge. Take the example of Mary, who was referred to the Centro by social workers who described her as "depressed." Or recall Grace, who was diagnosed at the public hospital with a form of psychosis. In both cases, the Centro's therapists suspended those diagnoses and explored other ways of expressing and explaining symptoms. They sometimes suggested practices such as prayers and rituals as therapeutic, or spoke of magic and spirits, but they also remained aware of the psychiatric diagnoses they were working against. They engaged in conversations with social workers and doctors in charge of patients' cases in other institutions and thus proposed a critique, or, as Rancière (1999) would frame it, a dis-agreement with psychiatry's diagnostic apparatus. Another example is Joy, who was taking psychiatric drugs and was not responsive to the ways in which ethno-psychiatrists were engaging with the language of the spirits she heard. In that instance, the therapeutic team decided to comply with the pharmaceutical prescription and approached her with what Dr. A referred to as an "allopathic-exorcist treatment." Here, too, their practice remained close enough to psychiatric knowledge to be able to dismantle it while not fully rejecting it.

THE END OF THE WORLD: ERNESTO DE MARTINO AND CULTURAL APOCALYPSES

Another central thinker in the genealogy of Italian ethno-psychiatry who contributed to the questioning of Western diagnostic categories and apparatuses is Ernesto de Martino (1961, 1977, 2000 [1948]). Trained as a religious historian and renowned as a philosopher and ethnographer, de Martino engaged in a serious reevaluation of the intersections of history, religion, psychoanalysis, psychiatry, anthropology, and political theory. De Martino's reflections were influenced by phenomenology, Marxism (through the work of Antonio Gramsci), and Benedetto Croce's historicism. His work in the 1940s anticipated many epistemological concerns that lay at the heart of current ethnopsychiatry, including questions of mental health and the conundrum of difference.

Above all, de Martino pointed out the importance of a political engagement on the part of the ethnographer in regard to his or her object of inquiry. Although his initial interest was in colonial societies, he later shifted his ethnographic focus to the marginalized of rural southern Italy, thus continuing a tradition of anthropology "at home" pursued by Italian researchers (Seppilli 2001). According to de Martino, certain magic-religious rituals and therapeutic techniques in Western societies were deeply linked to both hegemonic and subaltern logics of power and domination between different socioeconomic classes. He studied rituals of possession and focused on their meanings for the individual and his or her relationships with society.[15]

His first book, *Naturalismo e storicismo nell'etnologia* (Naturalism and Historicism in Ethnology), begins with a reflection on the crisis of Western civilization and calls for a critical analysis of the history of the West as a fundamental goal of ethnographic work. He later returns to this idea of the undoing of Western categories of analysis through the encounter with the other in *La fine del mondo* (The End of the World), an unfinished manuscript published posthumously in 1977. When we consider our categories of observation, he writes, we encounter a paradox: by employing them in the study of others we will only see projections of ourselves in the alien; on the other hand, by not using them, nothing can be observed. To resolve this paradox, the Western ethnographer must be aware of the historical context that produced his categories of analysis inasmuch as they are not pertinent to other contexts. Through this *epoché*, or suspension of judgment, we question Western categories of observation and contribute to anthropological knowledge (de Martino 1977). This explains why his philosophy was also referred to as *etnocentrismo critico* (critical ethnocentrism).

When ethno-psychiatrists at the Centro Fanon refer to de Martino's contribution to their practice, they acknowledge the importance of inhabiting this epoché that allows for the possibility of listening—within the space of the clinic—to the different etiologies that patients resort to. The experience of crossing borders often creates a condition of being in limbo, in which several explanations of symptoms are possible and appropriate. For instance, in the case of Mercy, a Nigerian woman who was referred to the Centro by the public mental health department, where she had been diagnosed as schizophrenic, the ethno-psychiatric group suspended that diagnosis and asked Mercy how her symptoms would be described in Nigeria, by her family, in her village, and by her healer. Other etiologies used to understand her experience, including the language of possession and spirits, of devotion to Mami Wata, and different forms of ties associated with voodoo rituals, were discussed in the therapeutic process. I began to understand this reference to cultural interpretations as a way to situate the patient and her experiences in a context loaded with political and symbolic meanings that the psychiatric diagnosis of schizophrenia had leveled out. In this sense, the ethno-psychiatric turn to culture repoliticizes those experiences that psychiatry translates into diagnostic codes. Another example of how migration can create a limbo where explanations of symptoms become more complex is Favor's story (see introduction). Favor was no longer sure whether the effects of voodoo rituals performed in Nigeria were still effective in Italy. She seemed to question the truth of her crisis because she was in a different context, or in between worlds, where meanings once in place no longer held.

As Piero Coppo has pointed out, ethno-psychiatry is first of all a method that allows for different etiologies to be evoked and used in the clinical encounter. It is radically different from transcultural psychiatry, which, despite its cultural sensitivity, continues to use psychiatric categories. One could argue that by functioning from within the psychiatric paradigm, transcultural psychiatry as a clinical practice does not take fully into account the radical change that some experience in crossing borders. Ethno-psychiatry, on the other hand, takes other cultures' forms of knowledge about health and therapeutic practices seriously and thus deconstructs certainty within Western psychiatric knowledge. Ethno-psychiatry then is not a subfield of psychiatry but a way of reconceiving the clinical response to the patient. The encounter with alterity—be it ethnographic or psychopathological—asks for a radical revision of the disciplines that history has produced. Ethno-psychiatry looks at psychiatry as a historical product, a culturally shaped technique and episteme among others (Coppo 2005).[16] This kind of revision resonates with de Martino's invitation to critique Western consciousness.

Throughout his work, de Martino was concerned with what he terms the *"crisi della presenza"* (crisis of presence) of modern civilization, which involves the place of the individual within society. As I briefly mentioned in chapter 1, the "crisis of presence" refers to the fear we may experience of losing control of external and internal realities when faced with frightening situations. Influenced by Heidegger, Sartre, and Hegel's master-slave dialectic, de Martino developed his own understanding of what it means to be in the world (see Saunders 1993). In *Il mondo magico* (The Magic World, 1948), de Martino first introduced the "crisis of presence" concept in a discussion of the Malaysian context. He described the experience of *latah,* the dissociative state in which a person becomes vulnerable to external influences, imitating and echoing others, and generally losing the boundaries of his or her own personality and sense of self. In this crisis, "the distinction between presence [as consciousness] and the world that makes itself present crumbles" (de Martino 2000 [1948], 93). He refers to the subject's risk of no longer being in the world, of "not being-there" *(il rischio di non esser-ci).*

Although de Martino seems to be interested in the crisis of presence more from existential and historical perspectives than from a strictly psychoanalytic one, in an article titled "Crisi della presenza e reintegrazione religiosa" (Crisis of Presence and Religious Reintegration) published in the philosophical review *Aut Aut* in 1956, he establishes a parallel between certain instances of loss of presence and mental illness. The person suffering from a mental illness may lose the ability to engage dialectically with the world and to relate to the object as outside of one's self. The subject loses the ability to relate to the world symbolically and instead identifies with it. At the core of this crisis is the anxiety that "underlines the threat of losing the distinction between subject and object, between thoughts and action, between representation and judgment, between vitality and morality: it is the cry of one who is wobbling on the edge of the abyss" (de Martino 1956, 25; my translation).

De Martino (1956) suggests that religious rituals could resolve the crisis of presence by reestablishing ties between the individual and the social and reanchoring the subject within the symbolic order through what he calls "cultural redemption" *(il riscatto culturale).* Religious and magical rituals help people overcome the sense of loss and alienation they experience with the crisis of presence by providing them with a structure that allows the reestablishment of boundaries between themselves and the world. Traditional and religious therapies aim to reintegrate the individual into the community. In this sense, de Martino's reflections are a prelude to contemporary ethno-psychiatric practices that figure religious rituals and the vocabulary of magic as an important part of the therapeutic process. As in Mary's and Grace's cases, encouraging patients to perform rituals that are meaningful to them, evoking the language of possession and spirits, and listening to the cultural signifiers that patients bring to the clinical space are among the therapeutic modalities that ethno-psychiatrists apply in their work. Allowing for the patient's modalities of healing and suffering to be expressed and experienced in this setting creates an alternative space to public health care institutions where rituals can be performed as part of the clinical encounter and relationship. In chapter 1, I interpreted Dr. L's and Dr. A's references to the language of voodoo and magic in their clinical encounters with Mary and Grace as a way to let them talk about practices that were familiar to them. The doctors thus hinted at their competence and familiarity with African contexts, and this opened up a different account and therapeutic experience. Whether this strategy is effective and curative depends on each individual case, but acknowledging the validity and power of rituals is a way to acknowledge the existence of other worlds and their truths.

At the same time, however, inherent in this approach is the risk of reifying these magic-religious experiences by framing them in the domain of "culture." As I argued in the previous chapter, in clinical work taking this risk seems to be a necessity that can lead to productive outcomes: grasping the patient's reference to cultural material and/or suggesting it as part of therapy may seem like a moment of inevitable essentialization. One could look at this process as a form of condensation of meanings, temporal and uncertain, a provisional translation aimed at producing understanding or, more simply, at creating the space for speech to occur. Ethno-psychiatrists have referred to this process in different terms: "partial coherence" or "epistemological temporariness" (Taliani and Vacchiano 2006). In a conversation with Francesco Vacchiano, an anthropologist and one of the therapists at the Centro Fanon, he described this dilemma as follows: "It is true that cultures can be incommensurable and untranslatable, but in psychotherapy we need to be able to do some translations, even when they seem to be a stretch. As therapists, we need to use a strategic essentialism without becoming relativist."[17] Vacchiano's mention of "strategic essentialism" reminded me of Gayatri Spivak's use of this idea. In her earlier work, it refers to a strategy that, if applied judiciously, can be effective in dismantling hegemonic structures or alleviating suffering (Spivak 1993). As Spivak explained, "A strategy suits a situation; a strategy is not a theory" (4).[18] As such, it takes up categories or identifications at critical moments and reifies them in order to do something political and/or clinical with them. It anchors things so that there can be something to push against. In the clinical context, the references to patients' cultural backgrounds can thus have an unpredictable epistemological value: they may provide a terrain on which to build a (therapeutic) relationship or something to leave behind. This process implies that practitioners have some knowledge of the patient's cultural references, but they simultaneously let the patient find hidden paths within and outside the constraints imposed by culture, or even by trauma itself. Mary's therapist explained that culture can be used strategically to create a reaction and allow patients to position themselves vis-à-vis their own backgrounds. When Mary responded to the invitation to go to an art exhibit, we learned something about her imaginary of statues and her fear of being exposed to other Nigerians who may find out about her health issues. Or, as in Grace's clinical experience, the cultural mediator's questions about the possibility that Grace belonged to a secret society in Nigeria allowed the therapist to ask other questions about devotional rituals; in this way, they were able to evoke her relationship to the goddess Mami Wata, and she could express her fears about voodoo and the possibility of madness.

De Martino was in conversation with several Italian psychiatrists and psychoanalysts on the question of the crisis of presence and its pertinence to psychopathology and clinical work, among them Giovanni Jervis (1994), Bruno Callieri (2001), and Michele Risso.[19] Considered one of the pioneers of Italian ethno-psychiatry for his clinical work with southern Italian migrants in Switzerland, Risso was profoundly influenced by the work of de Martino on magic, evil eye, and bewitchment and contributed in fundamental ways to the psychopathology of migration and to contemporary ethno-psychiatry's attempt to situate symptoms in larger historical, cultural, and political contexts (Risso and Böker 1992).

In de Martino's work, the crisis of presence is not only an existential category that produces anthropological understanding; it also addresses the broader question of the historicity of man. The crisis is linked to the question of "cultural apocalypses" that he develops in *La fine del mondo* (de Martino 1977). Here de Martino reflects on the uncertain boundaries between the pathological (and individual) and cultural dimensions, between the psychological register and the historical-anthropological temporality of being. De Martino's project is the first attempt in anthropological theory to reflect on these issues from multiple and complex angles. On the one hand, he considers the macro dimension of cultural apocalypses and, on the other, he is attentive to the micro dimensions of the catastrophic event, or the risk of self loss and pathology (Pandolfi and Bibeau 2005). An exterior catastrophic event can put the sense of self in danger, but it can also be translated into a return to the world in ways that were previously unimaginable. Nonetheless, subjectivity is inherently at risk of losing itself. For de Martino, it is precisely this dimension of risk, both ontological and historical, that constitutes subjectivity.

In *La fine del mondo,* de Martino sketches the first critical analysis of psychological and psychiatric categories, thus anticipating the most recent medical-anthropological critique of diagnostic criteria and its application in the context of Italian ethno-psychiatry. He points out that cultural psychiatry can illuminate the links between psychological disorders and the failure of culture's task of holding the individual's inner and outer worlds and assigning meaning to events for him. According to de Martino, a transcultural approach to psychiatry serves a double purpose. Not only does it allow for a study of the sociocultural dimensions of mental disorders and the recognition of the effectiveness of culture-sensitive therapies, but it also has important epistemological implications inasmuch as it contributes to critical approaches to the diagnostic categories of psychiatry as a whole.

When ethno-psychiatrists at the Centro Fanon describe their process of assessing the patient's psychological condition, they refer, as one of them put it, to their "prudent use of psychiatric diagnoses." The aim is to let Western psychiatric diagnoses be undone and questioned by the patient's own metaphors, interpretations, and worldview. In this way, multiple models are at play and provide different angles on symptoms and experiences, without reproducing a hegemonic discourse on mental health. As I discuss in chapter 1, practitioners at the Centro view diagnosis as an exploratory process to learn the patient's interpretations rather than to label symptoms. They also approach diagnosis instrumentally (Beneduce 2010). If they are asked to write medical certifications for asylum seekers, for example, and know that a certain diagnosis would make the seeker's appeal more believable and therefore more likely to be approved, they may decide to use the language of psychiatry to describe the patient's symptoms. In this sense, diagnosis becomes a political tool and is used as a form of social currency. It begets forms of recognition that are in line with the receiving country's standards of truth and authenticity in judging the validity of foreigners' life narratives. It is often the case in the stories of asylum seekers and victims of human trafficking—stories punctuated by violence and abuse, betrayal and destruction—that verbal accounts do not have the same type of persuasive power as medical certifications (Fassin and D'Halluin 2005).

COLONIZING DISORDERS

Categories of psychiatry and medicine have a history of their own that shows that they played a decisive role in the confrontation between dominant and dominated cultures, even with the aim of fostering cultural sensitivity. In the name of respect of and sensitivity to difference, old power dynamics can reemerge under different guises. For example, the Centro's ethno-psychiatrists are aware of the striking continuities between the viewpoints and diagnostic categories of psychiatry in the colonies and of contemporary health practitioners working with foreign patients in the public system in Italy. The debates that most animate ethno-psychiatry today remain inextricable from colonial and postcolonial situations where relationships of power between colonizers and colonized have produced certain interpretations of mental illness and cultural difference.

During the colonial and decolonization periods, psychiatry and psychology contributed to the culturalization of racial representations and the essentialization of cultural difference. Several studies of indigenous populations conducted by psychologists and psychiatrists from the 1940s to the 1960s marked the birth of ethno-psychiatry and gave it a specific ideological tone.[20] In the early 1950s, John Carothers (1954) interpreted the Mau Mau's opposition to colonial governance as an expression of local "customs," or, in other instances, as a psychological reaction to the conflicts produced by the encounter with European powers and their "modernity." His analysis of the Mau Mau anticolonial movement in Kenya as cultural behavior was one example of psychiatry's collaboration with the colonial power structure to study indigenous mentalities and behaviors to better govern them (Carothers 1953).[21] In this way, the political dimension of these acts of resistance and the historical subjectivity of the people involved in them were completely reduced to cultural difference or psychopathology. The construction of an African racial and cultural stereotype served to legitimize and justify colonial power, as well as to reduce local movements of resistance to psychopathology (Vaughan 1991; McCulloch 1995; Collignon 2002). In the colonial context, psychiatry doubled its function of control by reducing historical dynamics and political revolts to "symptoms" varying in nature: a complex of dependency on the colonizer (Mannoni 1990 [1950]), conflicts deriving from the exposure to the colonizer's culture, and the speed of the transformation of traditional models into European ways of being "modern."

Other studies conducted on the mental health of colonized populations had very different political implications. During the decolonization movements, some psychiatrists and psychologists defended the colonized. Octave Mannoni in Madagascar and Frantz Fanon in Algeria, for example, were actively engaged in a radical critique of colonial power and the relationships of domination and racism established by it. Mannoni, although sympathetic to the Malagasy rebellion against the colonizers, interpreted the suffering and rage that followed the imposition of forced labor and the Malagasy revolt as "the congruence of two personality crises" (Bloch, introduction to Mannoni 1990 [1950]).[22] He identified the dialectic between the "inferiority complex" of the colonizer and the "dependency complex" of the colonized as the defining dynamic underlying their relationship. According to this dialectical relation, Europeans projected onto the local populations their fears, while the Malagasy projected onto the whites a dependency transfer that mirrored their relationship to their ancestors and the hierarchical religious structure according to which the dead represented a moral authority—the superego, which dictated the conduct of the living.[23] While the Malagasy equated the "colonial fathers" with their ancestors who protected and dominated them, the colonizers interpreted this form of dependency as the expression of the blacks' inferiority and subordination to their rule. According to Mannoni, the colonizer translated the Malagasy sense of dependency into an inferiority complex in order to legitimize the relationship of domination and the abuse of the colonial power.[24]

The nature of the misunderstanding at the root of Mannoni's interpretation brings us back to a crucial question in ethno-psychiatry: How is culture used and manipulated to make sense of difference, even in situations in which this very appeal to culture conceals rather than explains the dynamics of power and domination at the heart of conflicts? Maurice Bloch argued that the reason for this misunderstanding was Mannoni's arrogance. As a psychoanalyst and anthropologist, Bloch wrote, Mannoni "disguises his ignorance of Malagasy motives only by substituting other motives deduced from theories originating in the highly specific intellectual tradition of his own culture" (in Mannoni 1990 [1950], xix).

This is precisely the critique that, a few years after the publication of *Prospero and Caliban*, Fanon developed in *Black Skin, White Masks* in order to respond to Mannoni's interpretation of the colonial encounter. Fanon argued that Mannoni psychologized the colonial situation and reduced the conflicts between the colonizer and the colonized to a sophisticated dynamic that kept the colonized in a position of dependency. While Fanon recognized the honesty of Mannoni's study of "the extreme ambivalence inherent in the colonial situation," he denounced the tendency, characteristic of psychological research in general, to achieve a certain exhaustiveness that lost sight of the real (Fanon 1967 [1952], 83). Fanon did subscribe to the aspect of Mannoni's analysis that broached the problem of colonialism as the "interrelations of objective historical conditions" and also as the "human attitudes towards these conditions" (84).

Fanon contested the assumption that certain complexes of the colonized—such as the inferiority complex of the Malagasy—were latent from childhood and manifested from encounters with the white man. He argued that this attempt to make the inferiority complex something that predated colonization echoed psychiatry's mechanism of explanation, according to which "there are latent forms of psychosis that become overt as the result of a traumatic experience" (85). Instead, Fanon looked at the colonial situation both as the emergence of a particular encounter between "the white" and "the negro" that "only a psychological analysis [could] place and define" and, most important, as the expression of racism that needed to be confronted from a militant position of denunciation rather than from a purely intellectual analytical position (85). Fanon argued that the colonial encounter needed to be analyzed not only from its pathological roots but also for its political, economic, and cultural implications. This more nuanced approach was lacking in Mannoni's work.

The problem that emerges from these debates is that colonial psychology and psychiatry seemed to erase the political meaning of struggles, movements of resistance, and rituals. Cultural difference was invoked in place of the political. In this context, the meanings of culture, of its paradoxes and dynamics, are often distorted. The risk of using culture as a way to flatten the political dimension of suffering has its roots in the colonial context and in the controversial ways in which culture came to figure as a static criterion with which to interpret behaviors and emotions. Nevertheless, the colonial context also gave rise to the work of militant psychiatrists like Fanon, who argued that suffering and domination are enmeshed in both the political and the cultural. Said otherwise, the political and cultural cannot be understood independently. A certain use of "culture" can actually recuperate the political dimension that medicine has erased and thus function in a very different way from its colonial use. The Centro Fanon's clinical work is inscribed in this line of therapeutic and political intervention that has repoliticized the field of culture and used it as a way to address difference and interrupt the universalizing language of psychiatry.

CULTURAL THERAPEUTICS AND IMPOSSIBLE RETURNS

In *Black Skin, White Masks,* Fanon denounces the trauma that the gaze of the white man imposes on the black man. Colonization happens at the deeper level of the soul, and it creates a form of alienation that the black man experiences as an interior disintegration. The gaze of the white person turns the body of the black person into a speechless body, fixed in its silence: "I am being dissected under white eyes, the only real eyes. I am *fixed*" (Fanon 1967 [1952], 116). Overnight, Fanon writes, the black person's customs and their sources are wiped out "because they [are] in conflict with a civilization that he [does] not know and that impose[s] itself on him" (110). In *Towards the African Revolution* (1967 [1964]), Fanon explains that the consequences of this dialectic are the sense of guilt and inferiority experienced by the black man. In order to avoid feeling guilty and inferior, the oppressed gets caught in two possible patterns: he either proclaims his unconditional adoption of the new cultural models, or he irreversibly condemns his own culture. Influenced by Sartre's existentialism, Marx's theories of alienation, and Hegel's master-slave dialectic, Fanon argues that the gaze of the other shapes the colonized identity. We always perceive ourselves as something other than ourselves; identity is always alienated in the other.[25]

Colonization produced a fracture, which Fanon considers irreversible. This fracture echoes de Martino's "cultural apocalypses" and the experience of the "crisis of presence." As a disruptive event, colonization brought about the erasure of the natives' systems of reference, cultural patterns, and ties to the past. This process—which de Martino would interpret as a radical loss of oneself and of one's presence in the world—alienates the colonized, who is thus reduced to the "inferior race," which denies itself by absorbing the convictions, doctrines, and attitudes of the "superior race" (Fanon 1967 [1964]). In the colonizer's language, this alienation appears under the name of assimilation. In the dialectic of nonrecognition, which is inscribed in the colonial encounter, the black self is a construction of the white man, and he is fixed in the image of himself that the white mirrors back to him.[26] This delusional world, this process of mystification intrinsic to the colonial situation, produces simulacra of the past. The disappeared culture of the colonized thus becomes inaccessible precisely because it is reduced to a copy of itself. Fanon writes:

> Not with impunity, however, does one undergo domination. The culture of the enslaved people is sclerosed, dying. No life any longer circulates in it. Or more precisely, the only existing life is dissimulated. The population that normally assumes here and there a few fragments of life, which continues to attach dynamic meanings to institutions, is an anonymous population. (Fanon 1967 [1964], 42)

What does it mean, for Fanon, to get disentangled from the web of alienation the white man's gaze produces in the black's image of himself? According to Fanon, disalienation or emancipation from the perverse relationship established by colonialism cannot happen through a return to origins because the presence of the colonizers has transformed the culture that once existed. There is no culture, custom, or tradition to go back to; the white man has obliterated them. To become emancipated by the colonial situation one has to take responsibility for this fracture and get uncaught from the web of images and copies of one's self that the other projected: "I am not a prisoner of history. I should not seek there for the meaning of my destiny. I should constantly remind myself that the real *leap* consists in introducing invention into existence" (Fanon 1967 [1952], 229; original emphasis).

Fanon interprets all ties to the past or attempts to recuperate a relationship to the origins as moments of further alienation that repeat the process of becoming a stranger to one's self. Emancipation takes place by cutting ties with the past and the culture that the encounter with the colonizer has contaminated. By rejecting the system of domination, one can attain freedom, which implies another rupture, almost a second act of self-effacement. The search for emancipation in the past is a "retroactive operation" that encases a person in a dead culture, in "the culture put into capsules" (Fanon 1967 [1964], 42). This process is not a creative act of reappropriating one's own origins but a further act of self-destruction because the domination of the white man has destroyed and erased the culture. To go back to it is to revisit the event of alienation and to reinhabit it but with no possibility of revitalizing it. In order for the revolution to happen, African people must not be guided by the past but by the present and the future.[27]

When I asked Beneduce why he named the ethno-psychiatric center after Fanon, he explained that the similarities between the increasing numbers of documented and undocumented foreigners in Italy in the early 1990s and the colonial situation described by Fanon were so striking that his name imposed itself on the clinic, whose goal was to bring together political engagement and clinical intervention for postcolonial populations facing different forms of institutional racism. He continued:

> The figure of Fanon seemed central to me, not as a metaphor or as a rhetorical image, but because he had succeeded in bringing together the contributions of psychoanalysts with the historic problems of language. . . . That is, the psychoanalytic subject in its relationship to history, and therefore the limits of a traditional approach with the battles of history and with the problems brought about by the relationships of force between colonized nations and colonizing nations.

Fanon's work was very appealing to the group of ethno-psychiatrists and cultural mediators who in the mid-1990s started the Centro. First of all, Fanon's reflections on the colonial situation allowed them to frame foreigners' mental health issues in the context of postcoloniality and psychiatry's colonial legacy. Moreover, Fanon provided a method to think about the relationships between psychoanalysis, history, and subjectivity and to address both the sociohistorical and psychic dimensions of experience as contingencies that have an impact on people's being in the world.

Though Fanon foregrounds the violent and alienating aspects of a tradition tainted by domination, that same tradition can still provide cultural signifiers that people resort to in an attempt to restore meaning to experience. In a thought-provoking piece, Simona Taliani speaks about the blind spots in Fanon's reading of culture and the past. She argues that by denouncing the world of spirits, invisible presences, and the symbolic dimension of tradition as belonging to a past that has been erased forever, Fanon crystallizes "traditional" culture and conceives of it as fixed in a past that cannot be reclaimed

(Taliani and Vacchiano 2006). But rituals and beliefs have lives of their own that undergo a process of resignification. In this regard, Fanon seems to deny the possibility of resorting to a world that still holds meaning and is populated by ancestors and divinities that form a community with the living and share a history with the humans that belong to it. From her position as a practitioner, Simona asks, "What kind of humanity can emerge from this further alienation from one's own imaginary and symbolic world?" (114; my translation). Still further, I ask, after Fanon, how can we think of the role of spirits and demons, ancestors, and rituals in shaping people's imaginary without losing sight of the transformative and disruptive impact of history and its violence?

At the Centre George Devereux just outside Paris, Tobie Nathan and his team designed a form of therapy for foreigners and their families that took into account and used their own systems of classification and expression of mental illness. Nathan was influenced by Devereux's (1978) approach to the relationship between culture and psychiatry, according to which bare facts always belong to at least two different discourses that complement each other but can never be understood simultaneously. Nathan's ethno-psychiatry is positioned at the intersections of psyche and culture and explores the boundaries between the two without trying to explain one level of discourse in terms of the other. Ellen Corin (1997, 347) has pointed out that for Devereux and Nathan, "culture and psyche are doublets or homological structures containing the same basic elements governed by analogous mechanisms."

Nathan has shown how clinical work with foreigners raises the problem of what therapeutic techniques and theories are appropriate to apply. Since patients and therapists do not typically share the same therapeutic and epistemological frame, it becomes crucial to find a space of mediation in which to negotiate a common therapeutic frame. Nathan (2003) introduced the idea of organizing therapeutic groups composed of multiple professionals: Western mental health practitioners trained in psychoanalysis, practitioners from other parts of the world who speak the patients' language and are familiar with therapeutic practices of their countries of origins, and cultural mediators.[28] The composition of the therapeutic group is aimed at facilitating the move from one etiological theory to another without interrupting the flow of speech in the therapeutic setting. The presence of a mental health practitioner from the patient's country (who often also serves as a cultural mediator) is meant to re-create a familiar cultural environment in order to ease the expression of the symptoms. Magic-religious practices such as prayers, healing through protective amulets, exorcism, and chanting of devotional songs are an integral part of the treatment.

As I noted previously, one of the central themes in Nathan's work is the metaphor of culture as a womb; while it contains and protects, eventually it expels and forces us into a relationship with alterity, with a world other than the mother. In this sense, the womb is a space that articulates ambivalences having to do with confronting the other. Corin (1997, 350) explains the metaphor of the womb in this way: "Just as the psyche is protected by a 'membrane' regulating exchanges with the environment, identity is enveloped by a second structuring membrane framed by culture from the outside." Displacement and migration can create a rupture in this "membrane" that facilitates the assignment of meaning to different experiences. In Nathan's work the purpose of therapy is to reconstitute this structure by reanchoring the patient in her cultural background.

In his later work, Nathan continues to think about the containing and structuring functions of culture and how it can be applied as a therapeutic lever, but he departs from the metaphor of the womb and turns to that of traumatism. The latter becomes the interpretive frame through which symptoms are interpreted and treated. His approach to clinical work is generally oriented more toward the effectiveness of certain healing praxis than toward interpretation. The performance of rituals, the fabrication of objects and amulets, and the recitation of sacred texts are more central than the interpretive process of unveiling meaning starting from the patient's words, silences, dreams, and *actes manqués*. The attempt to reanchor the patient in her own cultural universe serves the purpose of reinscribing symptoms within a frame that assigns them meaning and of reorienting the patient within what ethno-psychiatry figures as "tradition." "Symptoms are like text without context," Corin (1997, 352) writes, and therapy attempts to reconstruct the context in which symptoms appear coherent. In Nathan's work, this context is often referred to as the patient's "culture." Reinserting the person within a cultural frame by eliciting traditional etiologies is thus a therapeutic technique.

Nathan's conception of culture as a frame that can give coherence to experience differs considerably from Fanon's view that any attempt to return to an original culture is destined to reproduce alienation. I asked practitioners at the Centro Fanon how much Nathan's model influenced and shaped their clinical practice and how they reconciled—if they

did—Nathan's and Fanon's different approaches to culture in the therapeutic encounter with patients. Beneduce explained:

> Nathan's model influenced the birth of the Centro Fanon and my approach
> toward patients a great deal, because the meaning of therapeutic trigger by
> way of cultural materials seemed extremely rich to me. When I say "thera-
> peutic trigger of cultural material"—Devereux's expression—I am referring
> to the waterfall of psychic and relational events that I saw emerging in the
> moment when I could evoke with my patients situations, say, in Africa,
> which I had been able to personally explore in my work there. And they were
> events that multiplied every time I would evoke metaphors, places that they
> knew, that they had heard of, political figures from their national histories,
> references to people that were familiar to them. This produced a kind of
> radical shift in the therapeutic scene.

Nathan thus provided a technique that can have the radical effect of
unlocking chains of memories and associations in therapy. This is radical because it contrasts with the clinical encounters foreigners have in
public hospitals, where the language of biomedicine forecloses the circulation of other epistemologies. While Nathan's psychoanalytic background informs his approach to the ethno-psychiatric setting, he also
believes that the hegemonic discourse of psychoanalysis cannot always
address the complexities of patients' cultural backgrounds. In his book
Médecins et sorciers (1996), he contrasts psychoanalysis with the thinking of traditional healers, which he considers more open to difference
and able to reorient the patient within a signifying frame.

Overall, Nathan is interested in the effectiveness of what takes place
in therapy, in the processes of influence and suggestion activated in the
therapeutic setting. In *L'Influence qui guérit,* he argues that "the psychoanalytic apparatus, by its very organization, triggers processes governed by analogy," even when the participants are not aware of it
(Nathan 1994, 120). The material setting itself—the objects used, the
words pronounced, the rituals performed, the languages used—can produce more transformations in the patient than psychoanalytic theories
of the unconscious and transference. The power of performativity inherent in rituals and words is at the core of the healing process. For Nathan,
healing takes place when the therapist is able to inhabit different systems of thought and draw from different traditions of healing and the
patient is reinscribed in his own belief system.

The paradox of Nathan's project lies in several aspects of his work.
While on the one hand he describes the ethno-psychiatric setting as a
"space of mediation" that allows migrant patients to negotiate their

multiple belongings to different cultures and to rearticulate their relationship vis-à-vis "home," on the other hand, he also engages in a project of reanchoring patients in their past cultural traditions, regardless of the experiences of migration and rupture with that specific past. Therefore, the ethno-psychiatric setting seems to mirror the polysemic and fragmentary nature of patients' experiences; in this sense, Nathan assumes a dynamic concept of culture as a domain in constant transformation. Nonetheless, the therapeutic strategy of referring patients back to their "culture" also implies a static idea of culture as a homogeneous placeholder of meanings, behaviors, beliefs, and conceptions of health and illness. Nathan's clinical application of "culture" could overshadow a more dynamic understanding of the simultaneous processes of identification at play in the therapeutic context where cultural signifiers are created, contested, reaffirmed, and validated. Ethno-psychiatrists at the Centro add to Nathan's approach an understanding of cultural interpretations that is rooted in ethnographic work and that allows for the emergence of new notions of the individual, one who is embedded in tradition while at the same time deeply rupturing and transforming it. The experience of displacement often intensifies the tensions between continuity and transformation and exposes individuals to an often challenging negotiation between what is perceived as "tradition" and what is encountered as "new."

One of the ethno-psychiatrists explained to me that in her clinical work the concept of culture was extremely complex to utilize and that the impasse lay in the impossibility of analyzing the clinical encounter according to a perspective that was simultaneously anthropological and clinical. She believed that when therapists used culture as a clinical tool, they could get caught in a series of complex processes of manipulation and rearticulation of the concept. This comment reminded me of Dr. L's suggestion that Mary attend the art exhibit. She elaborated that in some consultations it is necessary to essentialize culture so that patients can respond to certain reified ideas of their cultural background and thus create—or re-create—points of reference. Nonetheless, she added, in other cases it is crucial to deconstruct that very idea and free the patients from culturally shaped forms of identifications. Since several of the ethno-psychiatrists at the Centro are also trained as anthropologists, they are faced with the dilemma of how to reconcile or keep separate the anthropological critique of culture and its clinical application. Do these orders of reflection belong to radically different epistemologies, or can they coexist? In the ethno-psychiatrist's words, such friction cannot find an ultimate resolution, and functions as a reminder for practitioners of the need to go back and forth, from the anthropological to the clinical and vice versa. As I show in the previous chapter, in the clinic what may appear as a reification of symbols is soon after followed by a deconstruction. These are different phases of the ethno-psychiatric work. Dr. P, for example, talked of his therapeutic process in ethno-psychiatry as divided into two main steps. The first one involves reanchoring the patient in cultural referents that are familiar and not necessarily benign and in helping the patient make peace with a cultural and historical context that manifests itself in cultural signifiers, relationships, and ties. The second step involves freeing the patient from those cultural identifications that are persecutory and facilitating a process of reinvention of one's own signifiers and representations.[29]

By focusing on cultural otherness and on the importance of traditional etiologies, Nathan's model tends to neglect the socioeconomic causes and consequences of migration. Although his approach includes a critique of the public health system, which refuses the foreigner access, and is also an attack on psychiatric knowledge's inability to account for cultural difference, it can be read as a way to inevitably naturalize cultural otherness. Didier Fassin (2000) has strongly criticized French ethno-psychiatry as the legacy of colonial psychiatry inasmuch as it fosters the creation of ghettos in line with the republican idea of citizenship. He sees the practice of Nathan's ethno-psychiatry as a way to create a model of government that mirrors the colonial endeavor to control and marginalize the colonized in the name of scientific knowledge and clinical intervention. I believe that ethno-psychiatry as practiced at the Centro Fanon opens up spaces of therapeutic intervention that are more complex than what Fassin portrays in the French context. It is not about creating ghettos, even though this may be one possible drift of ethno-psychiatry. In my observation, practitioners are aware of the political and social dimensions of migration, which, according to Fassin, is lacking in Nathan's work. Beneduce once explained to me that in his clinical work it was crucial to foreground the suffering of the migrant as a political experience embedded in colonial and postcolonial experiences:

> Patients remind me of the fact that they don't have a passport, or a job, or that they feel looked upon with disdain by the authorities, or by the social workers, or by the [Italian] population, that they weren't able to feel comfortable when they were in France or in England because they remembered

what their grandparents had told them about the colonial experience. That history and their current precarious position represent variables that are just as important as the cultural ones on which Nathan had constructed his fascinating work.

Working from within the tensions and contradictions of Fanon's reflections on culture, and Nathan's use of the same concept, creates a space for thinking critically about relationships of domination and their consequences for mental health and therapy. The combination of these approaches minimizes the tendency to reify culture, on the one hand, and, on the other, to reduce it to a ruin of the past that is unattainable in the present. At the Centro, practitioners are inspired by Nathan's model of therapy because they take seriously the effectiveness of symbols and etiologies from the patient's cultural background, and they consider culture to be therapeutic inasmuch as it provides a context wherein symptoms acquire meaning for the patient. Their critical ethnopsychiatry, though, proposes an approach that places interpretation in between psychiatric and cultural references. In other words, clinical work is not about choosing either a psychiatric or a cultural interpretation but offering a different kind of listening. In this way, clinical practice reinterprets and translates Basaglia's and Nathan's legacies.

While Nathan mainly focuses on the deconstruction of diagnostic criteria without looking at the larger political implications of migration in the lives of the patients, Fanon's lesson forces us to face the concrete ways in which foreigners are marginalized and suspended in a constant threat of not being recognized or legitimized in the receiving country. Following Fanon's approach to clinical practice allows the group at the Centro to always position their practice in the field of the political, in the sense that it incorporates a political critique of not only psychiatry as a hegemonic discourse but other ideological fields that influence foreigners' precarious conditions. Not having a passport, a residency permit, or a job is an important variable in the clinical work, just as Nathan's analysis of cultural variables is effective in curing patients. The challenge the Centro Fanon's group faces is to keep these two approaches together, in tension with each other, while being vigilant to the risks inherent in the political context in which the encounter with the other takes place. Their use of culture, I argue, functions as a way to repoliticize the discourse about difference. While in the colonial context psychiatrists mostly used culture to explain colonized behaviors and psychic life, and thus depoliticized the weight of symptoms or of political resistance, in the context I am analyzing the use of culture has the opposite effect. It repoliticizes the field of culture and provides a language to talk about difference that other institutional settings and biomedicine itself are lacking. The Centro's clinical approach can be portrayed as a form of "politico-therapy" (Beneduce 2007).

OUTSIDE THE CLINIC

The ethno-psychiatric project does constitute a political effort to question universalistic conceptions of mental health and healing by opening up a new field of practice in which cultural difference becomes central; but it can posit "culture" as the exclusive domain of the other and as a fixed container of meanings that does not allow for a radical questioning of institutional discourses on mental health and difference. This latter point is what Rosalba Terranova-Cecchini,[30] a leading figure in Italian transcultural psychiatry, has argued about contemporary ethno-psychiatry. She claims that reflecting on the difference of foreigners alone does not challenge official psychiatry enough to rupture its models and practices, which are, in fact, influenced by transcultural processes (technological, scientific, ideological) in contemporary society (Terranova-Cecchini 2002). It is only by extending the same reflections on difference to Italian patients that psychiatric criteria can be questioned at their roots. She bases her claims on her own transcultural therapeutic work with Italian patients, in which she takes into account their cultural and symbolic background as central to clinical work. Terranova-Cecchini points to what may be a limit in ethno-psychiatry: the fact that it does not necessarily allow us to face the hidden "truths" about ourselves, the issue of difference within Italian society, and our own archives on the colonial past and Italian migrations.

At the time of my research, though, one of the Centro's main activities was to work with Italian social workers, mental health practitioners, state officials, school teachers, and volunteers who served the foreign population, and to address the issues of difference and discrimination that implicate foreigners and Italians alike. I followed the ethno-psychiatrists outside of the clinical space for long meetings with elementary school teachers in neighborhoods where foreign children went to school and at local and national conferences where they shared their clinical expertise with doctors, practitioners, and social workers. At that time, ethno-psychiatrists also consulted with the local Immigration Office on state-funded programs for asylum seekers and victims of human trafficking and were involved in various programs for foreigners in the juvenile penitentiary system in Turin and other northern Italian towns. The Centro was an important point of reference for the state and all those NGOs working on issues of migration and social integration. In these meetings, I often heard them tackle issues of discrimination and prejudice as they emerged in the consultations with the state or in supervisions with other Italian actors. In many ways, the work of this group of practitioners ventured outside the walls of the Centro into other institutional contexts, thus extending their critique to fields well beyond psychiatry.

PART TWO

Entering the Scene

The Immigration Office

It was one of those foggy and humid autumn days typical of the Padana Flat. On my way to a meeting at the Immigration Office, I ventured into a neighborhood of the city that I didn't know well but later became important for my field research. The office was not far from Piazza della Repubblica, the large rectangular plaza that hosts the market of Porta Palazzo. Once a meeting point for southern Italians who had migrated north to work in the Fiat factories, the market is now home to the African, Middle Eastern, and Chinese stands that cover the entire area with fruits and vegetables of various sorts. I spent a lot of time there buying food and talking about new recipes with vendors. The Porta Palazzo neighborhood has seen the coming and going of many different communities over the past fifty years, which means it, more than any other part of the city, bears witness to how layers of migrations have been woven into the urban fabric of Turin. Today Chinese supermarkets are the most popular purveyors of body lotions, yams, and palm tree oil for Nigerian customers; African hair dressers are favored throughout the neighborhood among both Africans and Italians looking for an alternative or "exotic" look; and a vast variety of calling centers offer competitive rates for calls home, wherever that is.

The Immigration Office was located in the heart of this neighborhood, in one of the gloomy, narrow streets characteristic of the historic city center, flanked by buildings that time and pollution have covered with a grea patina that on that day blended with the gray of the overcast November sky.

Unlike most of the streets in Turin, the winding Via del Cottolengo does not meet perpendicular to its intersecting fellow streets. Maybe it is because it was designed to border the enormous complex of the Cottolengo—a city within the city, with its churches, convents, hospitals, orphanages, and hospices enclosed in walls—that the street itself had to acquire not only the name but also the irregular sinuousness of the complex.

The Cottolengo, also known as Piccola Casa della Divina Provvidenza (Small House of Divine Providence), was established thanks to the imagination of a village priest, Giovanni Cottolengo, who, amid many difficulties, between 1832 and 1842 founded, organized, and managed this vast monument to charity. The Cottolengo was meant to provide asylum and refuge to the marginalized, the handicapped, the mentally ill, and the deformed. It was what I imagined as the last *girone* (circle) of Dante's Hell, where the disfigured creatures that no one was allowed to see, because they evoked too explicitly the resemblance between man and beast, were kept.[1]

This vast complex once aroused a mixture of respect and fear even among those who were not so faithful to the Catholic Church. Somehow a secret fortress, where the rejected found a home and where the tragedy and paradoxes of certain lives found meaning in the grammar of divine providence, the Cottolengo soon became a world-famous institution. In popular parlance, the name "Cottolengo" was added to the list of synonyms for "idiot" or "imbecile"; in Turin's dialect, the force of this newly acquired adjective was condensed into just two syllables, *cutu*. A tourist guide describes the Cottolengo as "a permanent miracle that is renewed daily in the neighborhood of the Valdocco, . . . with more than four thousand inmates, with the most indescribable deformities, the most disparate forms of poverty, and the most devastating diseases" (Antonetto 1999, 192). The same guide reminds the traveler that there is another Turin beyond the facade of the nineteenth-century baroque city of the House of Savoy—which ruled the Kingdom of Italy from 1861 to 1945, when the republic was proclaimed—and the more contemporary one of the automobile industry and the working class. It is the city of faith, made up of a fervent movement engaged in serving the unserved and underserved. It consists of powerful charitable and religious organizations that run hospitals, hospices, and shelters and that derive their strength from serving the abject. The word *Cottolengo*, therefore, evokes among the faithful an image of both tragedy and benevolent grace. Among the less faithful, it is an ambivalent image of power and wealth.

At the time of my research, the Immigration Office was located in one of the buildings of the Cottolengo, one of many that had fallen into disuse. Abandoned by the previous tenants, the building now hosted social workers, bureaucrats, cultural mediators, and the hundreds of foreigners who came daily to request documents, employment, housing, and other forms of assistance. The uncanny returns in the ways in which urban space accommodates different categories of marginal citizens at different times. The imbeciles of the Cottolengo and the foreigners of today often share life stories whose paradoxes and misfortunes are somewhere between tragedy and surreal comedy.

CHAPTER 3

Ambivalent Inclusion

*Psychiatrists, Nuns, and Bureaucrats
in Conversation*

One day in early November 2002, I accompanied Dr. R to a meeting at the City Hall Immigration Office. Dr. R was an ethno-psychiatrist at the Centro Fanon where I had done fieldwork for a few months. He had invited me to come along to his meeting to learn about the work that the group of ethno-psychiatrists did with the state on the matter of victims of human trafficking. He had explained to me that the collaboration with the Immigration Office was important—though at times very challenging given the divergent positions he and state officials had in regard to the matter at hand—because many of the foreign women in the state-funded rehabilitation program for victims were also referred to the Centro Fanon as patients.

For the past two years, Dr. R had been working as a consultant for an aid program for victims sponsored by the Ministry of Equal Opportunities and by the municipality of Turin. Outside of the strictly clinical space, the Centro Fanon's practitioners were involved in supervising the work of bureaucrats, social workers, Catholic nuns, and lay volunteers who were involved in various ways in the implementation of the rehabilitation program for victims of human trafficking. To better understand the cultural dimensions of both the women's suffering and their difficulties in adjusting to the expectations that the Italian institutions had of them, this group of professionals and volunteers turned to the advice of ethno-psychiatrists, anthropologists, and cultural mediators.

"Progetto Freedom" was the name of the program instituted by Article 18 of the Immigration Law for the protection of victims of human trafficking. In Turin, it started in 2000 and lasted until 2007. It was managed and monitored by the local government (not by state-subsidized nonprofits, as is the case in other Italian cities), and it gathered a network of NGOs, social services, hospitals, and Catholic associations that assisted women who had decided to leave prostitution and were, according to the law, victims of human trafficking. The program is organized into several phases. The first step is to file criminal charges against one's own traffickers. In addition, women can leave their previous residence and live in a shelter for six months or up to a year. In Italy, Catholic nuns usually run this kind of shelter; that is, the task of orienting foreigners is often delegated to religious institutions. In Turin, the project also aimed at supporting and training women in various professional skills. In seven years, approximately six hundred women were able to use the program.

The Centro Fanon was one of the associations that participated in Progetto Freedom's network. Dr R's role in the project was twofold: as a therapist at the Centro, he treated women patients who were in the program and who had been referred to the Centro for psychological support; as a consultant for the state, twice a month he supervised the work of government officials, bureaucrats, social workers, volunteers, and Catholic nuns who implemented the program and helped the women through it. From the perspective of bureaucrats and volunteers working for the state, ethno-psychiatrists were "cultural experts," as one social worker once put it, and could understand and explain the women's "cultural difference."

Outside the Immigration Office there was a long line of people waiting in the cold to get inside: men and women from different parts of the world wearing worried expressions, waiting for something that could change their lives but rarely does. I imagined this "something" could be recognition by the institutions; papers to prove their legal status and their right to access services; or who knows what other hopes, dreams, fears, and disillusions they carried with them as they approached the office. The building itself had the same color as all the others on Via del Cottolengo: once a bright gray, it had turned into a gray so dark it could be black. Looking at it, one could see the effect of long decades of the local authorities' scarce interest in cleaning and restoring old buildings in this section of the city.

Dr. R and I entered the building, at 26 Via del Cottolengo, and walked down what seemed like an endless hallway—reminiscent of an abandoned hospital or elementary school from the turn of the twentieth century—before reaching the room where the meeting was to take place. The room resembled one of the classrooms at my parents' parish where I attended Catechism as a child. It reminded me of how much I disliked the stories about sins and penance that I had to listen to every week. All these memories came back as I entered the meeting room. Soon, though, my attention was drawn to the present, and to the fact that I was not there to listen to preaching or moral instruction but for a very different purpose. After greeting the participants, Dr. R introduced me as a trainee and anthropology student doing research on immigration issues at the Centro.

This was the first of many meetings of Progetto Freedom that I attended with Dr R. We often met on the bus on the way to the immigration office and exchanged comments and ideas about the meetings. I rarely talked at these meetings and could easily go unnoticed. I was always intrigued by how they provided rich and sometimes disturbing examples of the different practices and languages used to make sense of the foreign other. The women were in the background, present in the forms of lives turned into "cases" to be discussed. In this way, the fragmented and distant past was translated into the coherence of a story—a life story—that unfolds in linear time. The opacity of experience and memory was thus crystallized in an account that could be looked at, analyzed, and sometimes solved, like a riddle.

On this day, all the participants were already there when we arrived, waiting for the ethno-psychiatrist to begin the supervision. The meetings' moderator, Silvia, a social worker in her fifties, was also the coordinator of Progetto Freedom. Her role consisted of receiving and orienting the women who decided to enter the program as well as coordinating and monitoring the various associations involved in the program's implementation. More specifically, Silvia oversaw social workers and Catholic nuns who ran the *comunità d'accoglienza* (roughly translated as "host communities" or "shelters") intended as temporary residences for women in the program. The people who usually participated in the meetings with the ethno-psychiatrist were the ones who both ran and lived in the host communities and were in close contact with the residents. The questions at the heart of these meetings revolved around the application of the law—before which we are all equal—when dealing with foreigners and their cultural difference. Participants sometimes sought expert opinions from ethno-psychiatrists for what they perceived as "difficult cases."

On that day, the social worker in charge of the project, two state officials, two educators from an NGO, three Catholic nuns in charge of different shelters, three lay volunteers, the ethno-psychiatrist, and I were present. The pressing problems for the day were the cases of a Nigerian woman and an Albanian woman who lived in different shelters for victims.

Sister Minerva introduced the story of Prudence, a Nigerian woman and former prostitute who had recently moved into her shelter, by saying that hers was "a confused story, full of holes." After giving birth to her son, Prudence was hospitalized because she refused to talk or eat for several days. To the nun, she appeared emotionless. The few words that she did speak expressed that she did not want to keep her baby, whom the doctors had told her was going to be a girl. But the baby was a boy, and she did not want him because he might harm her, and he looked too black. Sister Minerva suggested that "Prudence might be under the effect of the evil spirit of the voodoo rituals." A Nigerian cultural mediator who worked for the Immigration Office was able to contact Prudence's family in Nigeria, who told her to pray for Prudence in order to counteract the effects of the spell. Silvia had reassured Prudence that she and Sister Minerva were praying for her, and Prudence's pastor in Nigeria was also sending her his blessings. Prudence was moved and began to cry. Sister Minerva continued by explaining that Prudence refused to breast-feed the child because she did not want to hurt him, but at the same time she wanted to keep producing milk. Silvia filled the group in on other details of Prudence's story. For example, she claimed that the child's father was an elderly Italian man, a former client of hers, who offered her a large sum of money to have an abortion. Sister Minerva added that at times Prudence's body became temporarily paralyzed; during these episodes she would not speak. Instead, she used one of her trembling hands to communicate. At other times, her emotions seemed uncontrollable; she cried a lot. Neither the Sister nor the social worker knew what to make of Prudence's state, and they each turned to the ethno-psychiatrist for advice: "Does Prudence have a psychiatric problem? Or are there any cultural reasons for the ways in which she expresses and experiences her suffering? How should we proceed in order to help her and the child?"

Dr. R explained to the group that Prudence's was a "complex and didactic case that could teach us important things about the methodology we apply in our work with migrant women." "At these meetings," he added, "we deal with the suffering of these women, and we try to understand the cultural idioms, the different representations of the body, of sexuality, of illness in their cultures." He stressed the importance of working on the cases as a way to call "our practices" into question. He admitted that being confronted with issues such as sexuality, prostitution, death, and illness was not an easy task. Therefore, these supervisions were also meant to train the group to work as a team and to establish a common language with which to discuss similar cases. He then commented, "Only ten years ago, it would have been unimaginable to bring together religious people, psychiatrists, bureaucrats, and anthropologists in an institutional setting to come up with common strategies to deal with a given social issue. Today, the dimension of migration introduces an additional variable in our practices, which forces us to constantly cross thresholds."

It is precisely this idea of being pushed to cross thresholds when working with foreigners that triggered my interest. I noted an interesting parallel between the crossing of boundaries inherent in migration and the crossing of disciplinary, vocational, and professional fields that occurred in work with foreign populations. This crossing also entailed a critique of the boundaries between different domains of knowledge and practice. Later, as I reconsidered Dr. R's words, I realized that for the group of people involved in the implementation of Progetto Freedom, working with foreign women provoked a renewed and interdisciplinary approach to their work, and it raised questions about cultural difference and its implications for the state's pedagogical techniques of securing order and producing citizens. It also questioned the state's project of integration and multiculturalism. I was reminded of Pia Covre, an Italian sex worker and advocate, who described the immigrant prostitute as a paradigmatic figure of singularity that is indigestible for the state and institutions. How can the migrant prostitute fit into the grammar of the law when her difference seems unruly and constantly exceeds the boundaries of the state's discourse? For me, these meetings were made even richer by the fact that it was not only bureaucrats and social workers questioning their own practices by acknowledging cultural difference as an important variable in implementing the law but also members of the church who were questioning their own methods of assistance, all the while aiming to conform to Catholic teachings that we are all God's children and are therefore equal before the Father. This new scenario of collaboration was made possible, even necessary, by increasing waves of illegal and legal migration that had arrived in Italy over the previous fifteen years, which the media and social services had portrayed as an emergency. It was a scenario that lasted for several years, from approximately 2000 to 2008, when the Centro Fanon's practitioners started distancing themselves from the Immigration Office's approach on issues of immigration and stopped consulting for the state. The passing of the Maroni Decree in 2008, which strengthened the already restrictive and punitive approach to migration, created and legitimized a new institutional language of discrimination that made the work at the threshold of different fields undoable.

At the time of my research, however, the collaboration between ethno-psychiatrists and state officials allowed for a space of reflection on difference. In this context, the migrant prostitute embodies the conundrum of difference that does not have a language of its own and therefore creates a rupture in the dominant discourse of the law. In this chapter, I trace the ways in which state and religious institutions attempt to resolve this dilemma by turning to ethno-psychiatry, a discipline that is, as we have seen, itself at the threshold of different epistemologies and fields such as psychiatry, psychoanalysis, and anthropology, among others. In this way, through the language of therapeutics and cultural difference, ethno-psychiatry provides a radical critique of psychiatric, legal, and moral categories of inclusion and challenges current politics of recognition. Its political impact derives precisely from the ability to cross thresholds and question established categories. Here I want to focus on how the state translates the ethno-psychiatric approach into its own categories of difference. What dynamics are at play when the various actors involved in Progetto Freedom transpose ethno-psychiatry's discourse on difference onto their own practices and ways of knowing in order to improve projects of integration, rehabilitation, and recognition of the foreign other? In attempting to rehabilitate the foreign prostitute through a culturally sensitive approach, the therapeutic state rearticulates her marginality but does not succeed in undoing it. She remains at the margins.

ADVOCATES, CRITICS, AND SUBJECTS

Dr. R explained that the ambivalence Prudence expressed toward her son could be explained as a psychiatric disorder and, at the same time, by taking into account local etiologies. But this could only happen with the help of the Nigerian cultural mediator, who could clarify what was typically "Nigerian" about Prudence's reactions to her son. First, Prudence perceived the child as threatening because he was too black. Silvia added, "Other Nigerian women have had the same reaction in relation to other women of color; they don't want to be identified with them." Whether it was true or false that the father of the child was white was not very important, Dr. R commented. Nonetheless, his presumed whiteness evoked a complex history of colonial and postcolonial encounters, a theme that Fanon powerfully addressed as a psychiatrist and as an activist.[1] Dr. R introduced Fanon's ideas about power relationships and discrimination, creating a parallel between the colonial situation and the contemporary context of migration in Europe. Fanon was often evoked at these meetings, an invisible and yet tangible presence, a reminder of a past still alive in the stereotypes, prejudices, and practices of institutions and the people who represented them.

On that day, the analysis of Prudence's story did not go any further. All agreed that a psychologist from the Centro Fanon would visit her at the hospital to evaluate her. We moved on to the other case, which one of the nuns brought before the group, of the Albanian woman, Elma. In her early twenties, Elma had been in the program for victims for several months and had completed most of its phases. The main goals of the rehabilitation process are to provide training, support, and professional orientation for the women. Women must attend Italian classes; sessions aimed at professional development such as taking care of the elderly, cooking Italian dishes, learning how to housekeep "Italian-style"; and doing internships sponsored by the local government in factories, restaurants, and other workplaces that offered the possibility of long-term employment. Elma had a job as a maid at a hotel and had been waiting for her residency permit for months. At the time of the meeting, she lived in one of the Catholic shelters. Sister Anna told the group that when Elma realized that her residency permit was constantly being deferred, she started losing weight and crying a lot, and "she had fallen in love with a foolish man." Elma fainted easily and did not want to take the bus to work by herself. Sister Anna explained that, in her opinion, "she was regressing." Elma had reached "a certain degree of autonomy and independence," and now she seemed to be losing it. In this context, autonomy and independence stand for women's shift away from the prostitution networks. In the language of the state, women who have been able to move away from their previous exploiters and are on track in the program are on their way to becoming "autonomous." In order to do so, they are required to spend a period of time during which they depend on the assistance of social workers, mental health practitioners, religious people, and volunteers who are in charge of accompanying them through the phases of the program and who act as the gatekeepers of rules and norms. Therefore, the rhetoric of rehabilitation and emancipation at the heart of these programs goes hand in hand with practices that infantilize women (Agustin 2007). They end up being recognized as either a victim in need of protection and support or as a prostitute that society must redeem and reconstitute as a self-sufficient human being.

"When social recognition is lacking," remarked Dr. R, "the person faces the experience of social death, and she can show serious psychosomatic symptoms." Women who have entered the social protection program have to abandon their hope of using sex work to gain economic independence and help their families back home. If the institutions do not grant the documents of recognition that they promise, the person can experience a sense of social annihilation.

"Yes, I agree," answered Silvia, the social worker in charge of the project, "but the ways in which they respond to the long delays on the part of the institutions also depends on the maturity and fragility of each woman." She gave the example of Nigerian women who, "thanks to their stubbornness," are able to handle the frustration of waiting for the documents to be issued without experiencing psychological distress. The women from Albania, on the other hand, had proved to be more "immature and impulsive," more easily discouraged and emotional.

"We should devote more time to mapping, for each woman in the program, their personal resources, the kind of social networks they can count on (family members who have migrated with them to Italy, the churches that they attend, their friends), so that we can also map their fragility/vulnerability," suggested Dr. R. He stressed the importance of knowing whether a woman who attends a Pentecostal church, for example, reacts better to the difficulties of adapting to the time line of the program than one who has no religious ties. "We have to remember that for each and every one of these women, the experience of the program brings out their most regressive and hysterical behaviors," he commented. They compare one another's progress in the program, become jealous if one has received her papers and the other is still waiting for them, and if one has found a job or has a boyfriend.

While I was listening to the discussion, I kept an eye on the clock that was hanging on the wall, both as a reflex to keep track of time passing and because I had planned to go back to the Centro Fanon for an evening consultation once the meeting was over. I automatically performed the gesture of checking the time only to discover a good hour into the meeting that the hands of the clock were either moving imperceptibly or not changing position at all. I thought it was ironic that even the clock at the Immigration Office was caught in an impasse, incapable of measuring time any longer, proof that time was frozen. I also remembered Fanon's (1963) "petrified world of colonization," where the colonized are deprived of their freedom and dynamism by the colonizers and thus turned into stones, ontologically nonbeing.[2] This frozen quality of colonial time—a sociocultural stasis—that denied agency to the colonized by turning them into zombies suspended between an impossible past and an indefinitely deferred future seemed to be crystallized in the broken clock on the wall. Its inertia became a metaphor for the inertia of institutions and their practices and the effect it produced on people. During the period I attended these meetings, it never occurred to anyone to remove it from the wall or to replace the battery.

Sister Anna brought my attention back to the case of Elma. Lately she had started explaining her long wait for the residency permit as "God's will." "I told her to leave God alone," remarked the nun harshly, while commenting on the fact that Elma was Muslim, as if this latter detail would make the statement about God's will less authentic.

"I would be cautious with the statement about God," Dr. R noted. "Being able to appeal to the order of the religious to make sense of an intolerable experience can be a way to manage the frustration that goes with it; it can be a strategy to answer to the disappointment one experiences in his or her current situation." He added that secular society offered fewer resources to cope with the challenges of life.

"To me, this is blasphemy!" Sister Anna responded immediately.

"And maybe it is," reasoned the doctor, "but it allows the woman to name her frustration and what she perceives as her misfortune. This response may lead to other responses, to other explanations; the lack of alternative answers often leads to totalizing visions of life and the world."

The ethno-psychiatrist ended the meeting by reminding the group of the paradoxical nature of their role in the context of Progetto Freedom. He explained that given their responsibilities with regard to the implementation of the law, they acted and were perceived by the women as the gatekeepers of rules. But because they also shared the everyday frustrations of the women and witnessed the quotidian difficulties of being foreign in a society that had its own timing and norms, it was crucial, he suggested, that they also act as advocates for the women and as critics of the law itself. "In this way we can approach them in a therapeutic way. We listen to their sense of uncertainty, to their vulnerability, and, when possible, we leave aside the mandate we have in regard to the law and become their allies, even if only powerless allies. In this way we implement the law and simultaneously critique it."

This meeting offers an opportunity to hold open the space between the law and its application long enough to glimpse the structures and forces at work in this margin and to listen to different voices and interpretations of the law. This is what Dr. R referred to when he mentioned that the law should be simultaneously implemented and critiqued. The content of the law creates the possibilities for practices to be enacted and positions taken. As an ethnographic problem, the law is experienced as distant and simultaneously as penetrating people's everyday lives, and it provides a lens through which one can reflect on the state's pervasive yet elusive practices. Veena Das and Deborah Poole explain how in modern European political philosophy the state has been defined by a clear-cut division between the external sphere of the law and the internal sphere of ethics, between the state as repository of universalistic reason and the family as repository of primordial relations: "In this vision of political life, the state is imagined as an always incomplete project that must constantly be spoken of—and imagined—through an invocation of wilderness, lawlessness, and savagery that not only lies outside its jurisdiction but also threatens it from within" (2004, 7). Furthermore, the bureaucratic state establishes itself as rational by creating, at its margins, segments of the population that are represented as being ruled by passions, credulity, and passivity and that therefore need to be studied, integrated, and managed. Das and Poole write, "Margins are peripheries seen to form natural containers for people considered insufficiently socialized into the law" (9). Margins, then, are both peripheral and central to the functions of the state.

The meetings at the Immigration Office provoked several questions that resonate with this articulation of the state and its margins. First, they bring up the issue of the state being a distant presence in people's lives that itself becomes visible through its affiliation with particular institutions and laws that address specific sections of the population. In this case, it is "victims of human trafficking" and how to take into account difference while applying the rationality of the law. Moreover, the foreign women's stories told during these meetings, together with private conversations that I have had with many women involved in the rehabilitation program, made me aware of what I would call an "intimacy with the law" that some women end up creating by both adopting the label of "the victim" that the law makes available for them, and by using it consciously in order to get access to rights and services. The law, therefore, penetrates women's lives and they, in turn, translate what the law offers them into their own terms.

WHO DOES THE LAW WANT ME TO BE?

In 1998 the law on immigration (Law 39), also known as the Martelli Law, was revised and became what is commonly referred to as the Turco-Napolitano Law (Law 40), named after its sponsors, Livia Turco and Giorgio Napolitano, deputies in the Democratici di Sinistra (Democrats of the Left) party at the time. In the spirit of improving previous legislation on matters related to immigration, Law 40 was conceptualized to better regulate flows of migration to Italy, to facilitate the regrouping of migrants' families, and to strengthen the programs aimed at integrating foreigners into Italian society. One of the new aspects of the revised legislation concerned the "provisions of a humanitarian nature," within which Article 18 declared that victims of human trafficking had a right to a temporary (six-month), renewable residence permit. This permit is granted to allow non-nationals to escape from situations of violence and abuse. According to the law, people who qualify as victims, by proving they have been forced into prostitution or have been victims of violence, can participate in a rehabilitation and social integration program. The residency permit is granted based on "the severity and imminence of the danger and the importance of the contribution made by the foreign national in combating the criminal organization or identifying and aiding in the arrest of those responsible for the aforesaid crimes" (Signorelli and Treppete 2001, 41).

Although informal and less structured rehabilitation programs for victims of violence had been in place since the early 1990s, when foreign prostitution became a concern of immigration policies both nationally and internationally, Article 18 legalized these processes in an attempt to change the arbitrary treatment of victims of human trafficking.[3] With this legalization came official funding for the implementation of the rehabilitation programs by the Ministry of Equal Opportunities, regional governments, and municipalities. What had once been informal and often improvised became a formalized field of intervention with rules, funds, stricter criteria for who could benefit from the programs, and a more formalized language in which to publicly talk about a certain segment of the migrant population—the prostitute.[4]

The Regulation for the Implementation of the Unified Text on Immigration (Law no. 40) was issued in 1999, one year after the Italian government had passed the revised law on immigration. Article 27 of the Regulation outlines two different procedures for obtaining a residency permit: one is known as *percorso sociale* (social itinerary) and the other as *percorso giuridico* (juridical/legal itinerary). Both procedures have the prerequisite that the person involved is in physical danger. As explained in the *Manual for Interventions in the World of Migrant Prostitution*—published to guide those involved in the implementation of programs for victims—the social itinerary is "made available when the danger originates with the woman's (or man's) efforts to escape from the control of a criminal organization" (Signorelli and Treppete 2001, 42). In such cases, "the risk of retaliation results from the simple fact that the woman has left her exploiters and has contacted an association to ask for protection and help" (42). She is not required to pursue criminal action against her traffickers, and it is the role of the association or legal agency to present a request to the chief constable, who may then issue a residency permit entirely at his own discretion. The legal itinerary, on the other hand, requires that the person collaborate with the police or legal authorities by filing criminal charges, or a denuncia, against traffickers. The distinction between the two procedures is somewhat slippery insofar as when filing criminal charges a woman is presumably always in a position of danger and vulnerability.[5] It is unclear when this kind of danger is considered serious enough to exempt the woman from denouncing her exploiters. Therefore, the ambivalence of Article 18 lies in the fact that while it is meant to protect and integrate foreigners into Italian society, it functions as a mere instrument to fight criminality.[6]

I interviewed several administrators and lay volunteers who worked either for the Immigration Office or for associations involved in the implementation of Article 18. They mostly complained about the fact that legal authorities rarely used the social itinerary and instead favored the legal itinerary. Therefore, in order to enter the program, women who are classified as victims must pursue criminal action against those they identify as their exploiters. Generally, either government social services or other organizations involved in aid programs for victims of trafficking ask women who enter the program to sign an agreement in which they commit to following all the steps leading to the issuing of a residency permit. In many cases, women can draft the denuncia with the help of organizations whose mission is precisely to support them in filing criminal charges against their traffickers and in drafting the formal document for the authorities. After the document has been produced and handed over to the police, they receive what some Nigerian women call in English "the slip," referring to the small piece of paper that documents their enrollment in the program. The slip also serves as a temporary residency permit and as a confirmation of the authorities' receipt of the denuncia. With this in hand, women gain access to social and educational services, and can register with the Employment Office. The overall purpose of the social protection program, as a lawyer-activist in Turin who is an expert on Article 18 told me, "is to cut the unnatural link between the victim and her persecutor, and to allow her to undertake a process of lasting and definite social integration." Moreover, he explained that the idea that foreign women who come out of prostitution need to be "accompanied and supported in order to become autonomous and independent" is at the core of public discourses that identify migrant prostitution as one of the "most insidious forms of modern slavery."

Without questioning the overall importance of the program in achieving what is publicly portrayed as the "freedom and independence" of foreign women, two leading figures in the national debate about human trafficking and the implementation of Article 18, Luigi Ciotti and Lorenzo Trucco—a priest and a lawyer, respectively—have summarized the core meaning of the program as follows: "Among all these other goals, the most fundamental element of the program is the residency permit; without it, it is neither possible to 'raise your head again' nor to pursue the paths that lead to autonomy and legality."[7]

In talking to women in the rehabilitation program, I often noticed how the residency permit represented different things for them simultaneously. For some, it became the repository of dreams, expectations, and hopes for a better life. While waiting for it to be issued, the permit was often endowed with an almost magical virtue of social integration (Fassin and Morice 2001) and with the power to mirror an image that reconstitutes women as legal subjects, as subjects that can be accommodated in the commensurable logic and language of the state. In other words, by receiving the recognition of what, following Fanon (1967 [1952]), I would call "white approval"—the approval of the receiving country—foreigners can be resurrected from the state of nothingness that being labeled "illegal" and the lack of access to services had produced in their lives (Ong 2003).

Often, though, receiving the permit is very deceiving. Amen, a Nigerian cultural mediator who worked for an NGO that helped women file criminal charges against their exploiters, was very clear when she explained to me that at first the permit may provide women with a certain sense of security, but in the long run it does not change anything. "Once they receive it, they look at it and wonder what that piece of paper can do to their lives," she said fiercely. She added:

> It is more important for the Italian associations that women are granted the permit than for the women themselves. They want work; they want to make money. Receiving the residency permit is disappointing. It doesn't necessarily lead to a better life. Those who are happy with it are those who are already employed and making money. The others, 99 percent, go back to the street and instead of giving money to the madams, keep it for themselves.[8]

As a tangible sign of state recognition, the residency permit paradoxically functions as a surreal object: instead of providing real job alternatives and access, it legalizes those who continue to work in prostitution with the benefit that they can often do it independently from their previous exploiters. Women discover that although they could not do much without papers, they can hardly do more once they obtain them. Not only does this "new birth" sometimes lead to a falling back into nothingness; it also leads to the erasure of a difference that exceeds the category of the victim and eludes legal control. This is the indigestible otherness that Pia Covre evoked in her speech: "For the State, which confers rights, the migrant prostitute is an emblematic figure of singularity; she embodies something extra which is indigestible, an immeasurable difference that no prostitution policy wants to remove or mitigate" (see introduction). What is at stake in this erasure is that the kind of subjectivity foreign women are allowed to perform before the Italian state is dichotomized: she must be either a victim or a prostitute, either with agency or without it. As victims they are recognized as legal subjects, but they do not have access to better jobs; as prostitutes they are not included, but they work—although illegally—and make money. Herein lies the residency permit's perverse function: it grants recognition without guaranteeing employment. Ultimately, in financial terms, women were better off when they worked as prostitutes.

As the story of Elma demonstrates, the experience of waiting for the state's recognition can be disruptive and destabilizing to the point of being comparable to a social death, as Dr. R, the ethno-psychiatrist, pointed out. In most Italian legislation on immigration, Article 18 is often referred to as an ambivalent instrument of protection and integration. The ambivalence, according to these debates, lies in what some have called its "prize nature." In fact, both state agencies and the people in the program easily interpreted it as a reward for women or men who cooperate with state authorities to fight international criminality. According to this position, the residency permit becomes the reward for those who file criminal charges against their traffickers by giving a personal account of exploitation and corruption.

The reward quality of this piece of legislation also disguises a form of betrayal. In fact, exposing oneself as a victim before the state entails the risk of receiving no real reward in exchange. An activist who works for one of the most important nonprofits in Turin involved in the implementation of programs for victims once explained to me that "the limits of Article 18 are that it makes promises of integration into Italian society—a job, a house, a residency permit, access to services and education—that the institutions are not capable of keeping." Nonetheless, especially in the aftermath of the August 2002 revisions of the immigration law—sponsored by the deputy Umberto Bossi, leader of the Lega Nord (Northern League) and Gianfranco Fini, leader of Alleanza Nazionale (National Alliance)[9]—Article 18 is also referred to as a "normative oasis,"[10] or as an anchor of hope for those seeking legality under increasingly punitive and exclusionary rules. In fact, the Bossi-Fini Law was the culmination of more than a decade of anti-immigrant discourse supported and nourished by extreme right-wing political parties with racist tendencies often disguised under a discourse of nationalism.[11] Furthermore, while it also introduced new restrictive rules on issues of labor contracts, regrouping of migrants' family members, citizenship, health care, and political exile, it did not challenge the rights for victims of human trafficking. Article 18 remains the only regulation that allows illegal foreigners who are already present in the country—and who are not eligible for refugee status or medical reasons—to apply for a residency permit. In other words, a foreigner cannot be recognized as an "economic migrant" if she or he works in prostitution. In these cases, full legal recognition can be granted only by appealing to the law for the protection of victims.

In many conversations I had with women about the act of filing criminal charges, I heard the same comments repeated time and again: "Now that we have told our stories to the police, how is it that we still have neither the permit, nor a job, nor a house of our own?" It was obvious to me that the residency permit, along with the right to access services, was the long-awaited reward that made filing criminal charges a more bearable experience. The denuncia was a means of obtaining those benefits that illegality and working in the street did not grant them. I remember very vividly the frustration on Grace's face; she was just fifteen years old when she left Nigeria and started working as a prostitute in Italy. She had been hospitalized several times with a variety of psychiatric diagnoses. A year into the program, she complained to me about the number of times she had had to tell her story to doctors, police officers, lawyers, and psychiatrists to convince them to give her a residency permit—with no success. I also remember her disappointment when, later, she found out that the authorities had issued her a residency permit for medical reasons—based on the records of her hospitalizations—rather than for being a "victim," which meant she would not be able to work. Different kinds of documents interpellate women through different specific categories. This explains why foreigners make the law work for them by choosing the victim role that allows them to access some of the rights and entitlements of economic migrants. Different hierarchies of suffering are formed through the complex economy of permits (Ticktin 2011). Outside of the legal and juridical debates, women often do see the residency permit as a reward or a prize for having entered into a pact with the state and having met its conditions. This is often an ambivalent reward, a promise partially kept, a betrayal disguised as legality, an outcome that reveals the limits and risks of the desired object—state recognition.

CROSSING BORDERS: THE EMERGENCE OF TRAFFICKING

What are the legal and juridical debates—at the national and international levels—surrounding the institution of Article 18 and the emergence of an industry of public assistance designed to address the question of victims of human trafficking? And how do these debates produce specific discursive constructions that delimit the position of the migrant prostitute? Here I want to examine how the intersection of law, jurisprudence, borders, and practices of inclusion and therapeutics articulate the kinds of subject positions that women occupy.

In Europe and North America over the past two decades, the discourses on migration, prostitution, and crime have largely overlapped, often using the terms interchangeably or as synonyms. Most important, in the new Europe—characterized simultaneously by the abolition of internal borders between the European Union's member-states and, thus, by the free circulation of goods, services, capital, and people, and by stricter external border control—trafficking as a legal and social

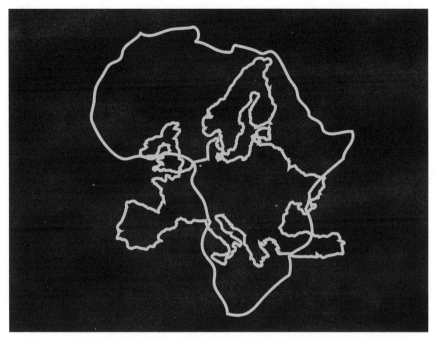

FIGURE 4. *A Map Is Not a Territory*, No. 1. Courtesy of Fiamma Montezemolo.

issue has been intrinsically linked to the tightening of immigration laws and the enforcement of border regimes (Andrijasevic 2003; Berman 2003). In the specific case of Italy, trafficking and the laws aimed at fighting it also need to be understood in the context of current Italian legislation on prostitution and the international laws against human trafficking.

First of all, trafficking is often equated with slavery, thus combining a contemporary phenomenon with an older category. The Italian Penal Code (1930) deals with the question of slavery in the section regarding the protection of the individual, understood as the expression of personal freedom. Articles 600–604 of the code deal with "slavery or slavery-like conditions, slave trade or commerce and buying and selling of slaves." This law was originally conceived to repress any legally established form of slavery and to sanction it when committed abroad against an Italian citizen in those countries where the legal status of slavery was recognized. The law also addressed the question of the "white slave trade" at the beginning of the twentieth century, the phenomenon of deporting white women to the colonies to work as prostitutes. These old norms had been in disuse for many years. At the beginning of the 1980s, there was a shift in the discourses on trafficking and immigration due to the increasing number of illegal foreigners entering Italy, and the Penal Code norms were reactivated in the context of so-called modern slavery.

The term *modern slavery* had already been at the center of international debates on trafficking in human beings, leaving its definition open to various interpretations. It refers to buying and selling things and people but also to sexual exploitation, forced labor, and debt bondage, all categories in and of themselves that are anything but unequivocal. In everyday speech, the term seems to still refer to the slave trade, thus evoking strong similarities between narratives of "white slavery" and "trafficking" (Bernstein 2007a, 2007b; Doezema 2010). What is clear in these debates is the fact that migrant prostitution, trafficking, and exploitation get lumped together as if referring to the same experience. Understood from this semantic field, prostitution is always a slavelike condition and therefore the literal antithesis of freedom (Bernstein 2007; Ramberg 2014).

The jurisprudence indicates that laws based on the concept of modern slavery are inadequate to deal with the contemporary issue of sexual abuse of migrant women who work in the sex industry. The case of the Article 18 program of rehabilitation is complex because it demonstrates that foreign prostitutes are not merely passive or exclusively victims of networks of exploitation. The reality, as always, is more nuanced. Although the majority of them are in one way or another induced into prostitution—in forms that generally occur in the street and involve great risk and exposure to violence—their experiences rarely coincide with the precise profile of the victim outlined by the law. Women's discrepant narratives force us to deal with the fundamental issue of the relationship between freedom and prostitution, trafficking and migration, and to push beyond these dichotomies. The legislation sets the terms of the debates, and individual stories are made to fit those terms. In this way, women's choices and desires, their decisions and free will, are distorted and translated into pieces of a victim story.

The other Italian law that to this day provides a point of reference on the issue of prostitution is the Merlin Law, named after the socialist senator Angela Merlin. The law was passed in 1958 with the title, "Abolition of the regulation of prostitution, fight against the exploitation of the prostitution of others, and norms for the protection of public health." The traditional approaches that characterize policies on prostitution are the prohibition, regulation, and abolition models. None of these is ever adopted in its entirety. Every legislative choice contains within it traces of the other models. The first function of the Merlin Law was to put an end to the institution of *case chiuse* (brothels). It is a radical policy aimed at abolishing regulation and eliminating the criminalization and/or regulation of something considered a purely private matter. For the first time, it questioned the assumption about the irrepressible male sexual urge that brothels were supposedly necessary to satisfy.

Prior to this law, Italian legislation prohibited prostitution by declaring it illegal. The first examples of this approach are to be found in the fifteenth century. In many Italian cities, even before the unification of Italy (1861), prostitution was a sin or an immoral act to be condemned. Although all parties involved could be prosecuted—clients, prostitutes, and exploiters—in practice, only prostitutes were sentenced by the law (Signorelli 2000). In 1860, however, a different model was adopted. The Cavour Regulation established that prostitution was no longer a crime but a necessary social practice. Though it was still considered immoral, its containment was justified on both moral and health grounds. Based on the French regulation passed by Napoleon in 1802, the Cavour model aimed to control the spread of venereal diseases while permitting sex for payment. Public health, order, morality, and decency were at the core of this law. Brothels were legalized, and prostitutes were listed in special registers and deprived of their identity cards. Women were kept under surveillance by the police and required to undergo medical exams.

In this context, passage of the Merlin Law in 1958 marked a radical shift inasmuch as it both shattered the belief that prostitution was needed as an outlet for the male sexual urge and emphasized the concept of individual rights and responsibilities. Based on the principle of egalitarianism and decriminalization, this law was inspired by the idea that prostitution should not be permitted in a society all of whose members are considered equal. Sexual exploitation, brothels, and trafficking for the purpose of sex work are to this day condemned, but prostitution in and of itself is not considered a crime. The Merlin Law remains in force.

In Europe, the early 1990s were characterized by a general atmosphere of moral panic involving migration, sexual slavery, and child abuse. During this time, "trafficking for sexual exploitation" was denounced as a violation of human rights in many parts of the world. In 2000, the United Nations signed the first "Protocol to Prevent, Suppress, and Punish Trafficking in Persons,"[12] which established an international standard by which to define trafficking. Despite the differing views on prostitution as either a legitimate form of labor or as a violation of human rights, the protocol defines trafficking as "the recruitment, transportation, transfer, harboring or receipt of persons, by means of the threat or use of force or other forms of coercion, of abduction, of fraud, of deception, of abuse of power or of a position of vulnerability or of the giving or receiving of payments or benefits to achieve the consent of a person having control over another person, for the purpose of exploitation."[13]

This heightened attention to "trafficking"—conveyed through the media, legal discourses on illegal migration and criminality, and the moralizing rhetoric on modern-day slavery and coerced prostitution—fundamentally obscures the degree of personal agency required to migrate, as well as all the experiences of migrants who are not involved in sex work. The discourse on trafficking both functions and is articulated by fixed dichotomies such as victim/agent, slave/sex worker. It sustains itself by drawing from the most extreme cases of abuse and violence that foreign women face as illegal migrants and coerced prostitutes because these cases are "easy" to think about (Agustín 2003). The legislation, too, relies heavily on narratives of female powerlessness and childlike sexual vulnerability and thus constructs women as either "innocent victims" or "guilty migrants" (Miller and Vance 2004; Gozdziak and Collett 2005; Kempadoo 2005). As I show, what challenges this binary mode of representing migration, prostitution, and trafficking are those cases that do not fit any of these dichotomies.

For example, Ife told me that she came to Italy because there was no future for her in Nigeria. In Italy she worked as a prostitute for several months, which she saw as an opportunity to make money and escape from a place that had nothing to offer her. She later decided to file criminal charges against her madam, not on moral grounds, but on practical ones. She needed a residency permit in order to stay in Italy and have access to health care. She was also tired of giving her madam most of her income. She wanted to send more money home and keep the rest for herself. In her case, entering the rehabilitation program did not mean leaving prostitution but breaking the ties and debts with her madams. Another woman, Peace, wanted to become a nurse but could only enter Europe with fake documents and through the prostitution networks between Nigeria and Italy. After working on the streets for a year, she decided to appeal to Article 18 and gain legal status. After receiving the papers, she was able to enroll in a nursing program. For

Ani, who came from Romania, prostitution was a solution that both she and her mother opted for to solve the family's financial problems and lack of employment. Ani was the eldest of six, and she was responsible for supporting the younger siblings.

The complexity of women's trajectories and stories—often punctuated by the participation, consent, hesitation, and support of family members, friends, and partners in the planning of migration—is often completely erased or misrecognized by the state. By instituting practices such as filing criminal charges against traffickers in order to receive a residency permit, laws against human trafficking induce women to constitute and re-present themselves as innocent victims who have been abused by criminal groups. As a consequence, these laws fail to address the structural and social conditions that may lead women to choose prostitution as a way to leave countries that offer no future prospects. Even more alarming is that these laws also fail to address the receiving country's lack of job opportunities for those who decide to leave prostitution. It is not uncommon to hear about former prostitutes who have become madams after going through the rehabilitation program. Or, as Amen, the NGO worker, pointed out, some women leave their exploiters, file criminal charges against them, receive the legal papers, find nothing better, and turn to prostitution again, maybe in nightclubs rather than in the streets and independent from any network. Therefore, the line drawn between the innocent victim and the willful illegal migrant—categories that determine whether a person will be protected or punished—is dangerous and inconsistent. Most victims are also economic migrants whose victimization involves debts and abusive working conditions, not just straightforward kidnapping and exploitation (Chapkis 2003).

The protagonists of the debate on human trafficking and prostitution in Europe are mostly first world activists who take one of the two main positions. On either side, migrant women are the object of debate but rarely active participants in it. On one side of the debate, some advocates, by focusing on and emphasizing the violence and risks to which prostitutes are exposed, refuse the idea that sex work can ever be a "job" and categorically deny that foreign women may sometimes independently choose, among different possibilities, to sell sex for economic ends. They portray women as passive, backward, and, often, in need of education and domestication. Echoing Covre, they need to be made digestible. These antitrafficking positions, while denouncing the brutal circumstance of migration and prostitution, can also fuel the arguments at the core of anti-immigrant politics. When migrant prostitutes are portrayed as "slaves" who have been brought to Europe against their will, states are justified in taking on the role of the arbiter. By identifying and excluding those who represent a threat to the European Fortress, states can decide to repatriate or deport those illegal migrants that they consider threatening.

On the other side of the debate, the activists who recognize women's active participation in making decisions about their migration advocate normalizing sex work in order to make it less dangerous and more socially acceptable. They propose that sexual labor be recognized as legitimate employment, thus guaranteeing labor rights to those who decide to work in the sex industry. The great majority of advocates for this position are nonmigrant women who identify themselves as sex workers. As I noted above, in most cases foreign women involved in prostitution view their sexual activities as a temporary means to an income, and they resist explicit identification with their work. Several women I encountered talked about sex work as a way to make a lot of money in a short time, after which they imagined looking for other jobs. This means that they typically did not participate in labor activism and political associations fighting for the rights of sex workers. Pro–sex work advocacy elides the marginal status of migrant sex workers vis-à-vis the law and the dimension of illegality that characterizes most experiences of migration, or how foreign sex workers may not see it as a vocation.

It is at the intersection of these different discursive fields on trafficking, prostitution, and migration that Article 18 has emerged as a legal space, an "oasis of legality," and as a good practice aimed at dealing with the question of integration and difference in Italian society. The complexity of these discourses was never explicitly talked about at the meetings at the City Hall Immigration Office in Turin, but it certainly contributed to the challenges that the participants experienced implementing a law that, though claiming to promote integration and inclusion, may also serve to justify anti-immigrant positions.[14]

The "trafficking" discourse is one context of the meeting at the Immigration Office where I found myself on that autumn day. This discourse portrays women as ignorant, naive, and vulnerable to deceit rather than able to plan and make decisions about their lives. By relying on the idea that women are forced into prostitution and cannot disentangle themselves from a situation of subjugation ("slavery"), this discourse constructs the foreign prostitute as an object in need of intervention and assistance, a subject who needs to be freed and redeemed. Within these debates their stories are framed through either the paradigm of the victim or that of the free subject, leaving no room for experiences that exceed them, intertwine them, or completely elude them. There are discursive gaps and silences through which women who sell sex slip. Even those who position themselves as helpers, and condemn trafficking and prostitution, often end up reproducing the marginalization they denounce (Agustin 2007; Peano 2010). Ethno-psychiatry attempts to open up these discourses and reflect on the gaps they produce.

It is not my intention to argue that women are never exposed to serious risks, nor to suggest that they do not experience violence and abuse while involved in prostitution.[15] On the contrary, many women I met endured harsh conditions and dangerous situations while working on the streets. Some had been raped, abused—sexually and verbally—and exploited by their madams. At the same time, I also want to stress that the discourse on trafficking reproduces the marginalization of women by constructing them as victims. The state relegates them to a position of emblematic singularity because the foreign prostitute has no representation. She occupies the position of the "nonperson" (Dal Lago 1999) until the state produces her visibility by labeling her as clandestine, illegal, and finally victim. Unlike Italian prostitutes who have established themselves as workers who enjoy rights, the foreign prostitute exists neither as a "worker" nor as a "sex worker." Naming her as victim is a strategy to confine her disturbing presence within the security of the language of the law.

In the Italian context, the impetus to think differently about foreign prostitution comes from Pia Covre and the members of the Italian Committee for the Civil Rights of Prostitutes (Corso and Landi 2003; Corso and Trifirò 2003). Drawing from Agamben's (1998) rethinking of the question of sovereignty and exception, they refer to the idea of "bare life," of "the life unworthy of being lived," in order to talk about the conditions of foreign women who have arrived in Europe and work as prostitutes (see also Beneduce and Roudinesco 2005). Deprived of any kind of rights, the prostitute is turned into a victim. In this way, the state, the church, and other institutions recuperate some sort of relationship with the rejected, and she is made into the object of their practices of recognition. Her difference thus becomes visible and digestible.

On the one hand, the Italian sex workers' viewpoint is extremely valuable for thinking about the conditions of illegal foreigners in contemporary configurations of Western nation-states and receiving countries. On the other hand, it is assumed that the majority of foreign prostitutes take on the identity of sex workers as their main persona. The Committee challenges and critiques the rhetoric of victimization in order to claim access to civil rights for those among them who make a conscious decision to be sex workers. What this argument risks obscuring, though, are the dreams and hopes of many women for whom irregular (indeed illegal or "unrecognized") status and money, not sex, may be the heart of the matter.

What I want to argue is that while the Italian Committee's position opens up the possibility to ponder the space of nonrights and of intractable difference/marginality that the migrant prostitute occupies, the voices of the foreign women still seem to remain at the margins of even this discourse. Some of them hope for inclusion and recognition and are driven by dreams of fitting into the society that has shaped their imaginaries of emancipation, success, wealth, stability, and, as a young woman from Romania once shared with me, their dreams of "just becoming like anyone else in Italy: with a regular job, a place to live, a husband, and eventually children."

THE THERAPEUTIC STATE

After that first meeting at City Hall, I was intrigued by the questions that were emerging. I also thought it was important to consider the concerns the participants had about the women in the rehabilitation program. They seemed to struggle with how to relate to difference and how to translate the knowledge provided by ethno-psychiatry into more culturally sensitive practices. Twice a month for over a year and a half, I attended the meetings of Progetto Freedom with Dr. R. We always met in that room with the clock that had stopped measuring time. The two other characteristics of the room that stood out were the very bright fluorescent light that was on even during the sunny summer days of June and the incessant ringing of participants' cell phones. The phones remained on and active during the supervisions with the ethno-psychiatrist in case of an emergency call from the host communities or from one of the women in the program asking for advice or help with some everyday matter. Overall, the level of attention was high, and people seemed very responsive to Dr. R's explanations and analyses of the different "cases." However, he often mentioned to me the difficulty of working with this group. Certain dynamics and ways of approaching foreign women on the part of the participants were very hard to reorient. He expressed his frustration that even after years of group supervisions on these issues, prejudice would somehow imperceptibly—or not so imperceptibly—reemerge in their practices or ways of talking about the women. He observed that there were unexpected continuities between the discriminatory categories that colonial psychiatry used to describe the mentally ill and the deviant and contemporary attitudes adopted by social workers and health practitioners working with immigrant patients (Beneduce and Martelli 2005). I often thought he must have felt a bit like the clock on the wall: struggling to move forward, yet somehow caught in an impasse that prevented his supervisions from having a radical impact on the group.

In the months that followed that first meeting, other supervisions would usually start with the social worker in charge of the project presenting an overview of recurrent issues and challenges posed by the women. One day it was the fact that many of the women in the program went to the office to find out how to have an abortion because they could not afford to have a baby; another day it was the fact that the Romanians outnumbered the Nigerians in the program, and they confronted the institutions with a very different set of issues, mostly referred to as "cultural problems." At other times, it was the concern that the shelters could not host more than two Nigerian women at a time. In fact, past experience had proved that a larger group of Nigerian women created conflicts. Jealousy and power struggles among them—all explained through the logic of voodoo rituals happening outside the shelters but influencing the relationships between the women inside it—did not make Nigerian women the easiest guests to have. Another day it was the difficulties some Catholic nuns had dealing with the sexuality of the women who, regardless of the rules of the program, still secretly saw clients while referring to them as "boyfriends." How to deal with all these different situations in a culturally sensitive way was at the heart of the meetings, and the municipality often sought out ethno-psychiatrists to provide advice and expert opinions on these matters.

These meetings offer an example of the postures of the state vis-à-vis the foreign other in general and the foreign prostitute more specifically. They raise a question about how, by turning to ethno-psychiatry, the state attempts to apply a therapeutic ethics to the law in order to manage the "stranger" and include her within its boundaries. By this I mean that the actors engaged in Progetto Freedom recognized a lack in the language of the law that made their work with foreigners ineffective. Hence the need to resort to the vocabulary of emotions and their place in making sense of the social world and to accord more importance to individual cases—strategies that, in part, the ethno-psychiatric approach could provide. As Foucault's (1991) work on biopower shows, notions of sovereignty have changed in the shifting emphasis from territorial jurisdiction to practices aimed at the management of life. This has had important implications for the ways state power has been reconceptualized. Most recently, burgeoning literature on the state has characterized it with different adjectives, each emphasizing one predominant modality in managing life: the therapeutic state, the pedagogic state, the hygienic state, the immunizing state (e.g., Das and Poole 2004).

The meetings at the Immigration Office suggest that institutions dealing with migrant populations have a growing interest in the ethno-psychiatric approach to cultural difference. This new tendency is in part justified by the fact that working with people from other cultures triggers, among Italians, certain "cultural anxieties" that do not find explication in the language of the state alone. Turning to the language of anthropology and psychology seems to provide the institutions with tools that are better suited to broach the issues raised by the foreign other.

By pushing institutions to adopt a therapeutic and culturally sensitive approach to the legal implementation of social and cultural integration into society, the other performs a paradoxical function. On the one hand, it destabilizes universalistic and rationalist discourses of the state by introducing the vocabulary of emotions and cultural difference. On the other hand, this language risks reinforcing the idea that the other never quite fits into the logic of the state because her cultural difference is framed as incommensurable with it. That other is therefore bound to remain at the margins of the state.[16] As Das (2004, 249) has explained, "It is part of the logic of the state that it constructs itself as an incomplete project, because there are always margins in which people have to be educated to become proper subjects of the state."

I see the appeal to ethno-psychiatry on the part of the Italian state as an attempt to incorporate cultural difference in evaluating the behaviors of foreigners while engaging in a therapeutic discourse that emphasizes the role of emotions in the construction of the social world and introducing other ways of understanding the body and suffering. Through ethno-psychiatry, the state tends to simultaneously reconstruct women's identities as inherent in their own cultural background and as individuals rather than as anonymous victims or stereotyped members of a given national group. This is in line with an ethno-psychiatric approach that locates the individual within a collective memory, within history and its intricacies.

When the participants in the meetings at the Immigration Office ask questions about the behaviors of Nigerian or Romanian women who are in the program, the expectation—and often the outcome—is to establish recurrent patterns of cultural conduct to which they can refer when dealing with the women's emotions. The tendency to look for patterns or codes to decipher alien ways of reacting, responding, and adjusting to the program of social protection reflects an anxiety about confronting often-unfamiliar ways of inhabiting the world. In this context, the purpose of ethno-psychiatry is partly to depathologize women and offer a counterdiscourse to psychiatry by introducing cultural variables. The aim of this approach is not to reconstitute codified ways of referring to certain behaviors but rather to destabilize any monolithic and static understanding of illness, culture, and what it means to be a human. Its purpose is not to medicalize culture but rather to show the individual dimensions of suffering, to reclaim experience from the homogenizing effects of diagnoses and state categories of recognition.

For example, in the case of women like Prudence, who was hospitalized because she was diagnosed with a psychiatric disorder, the ethno-psychiatric approach suspended diagnostic interpretations and provided a different reading, attentive to the individual as such and to multiple and alternative etiologies. In Prudence's case, the ethno-psychiatrist suggested seeking the advice of the Nigerian cultural mediator in order to consider other interpretations of her suffering. Despite the effort to problematize suffering and not treat each individual case in the language of Western diagnostic parameters but rather through a multiplicity of angles that included etiologies closer to the backgrounds of the women, the group at City Hall tended to translate this knowledge into typologies of "cultural suffering": the Nigerian women's distress usually fell under the explanatory models of possession and witchcraft, both experiences linked to their devotion to Mami Wata; and the Romanian women's suffering often found explanations in the hardships under communism. In other words, the ethno-psychiatrist's efforts to counter a universalizing tendency to interpret these cases were often translated into other codes and models that effaced the women's individuality/difference.

Ethno-psychiatry's intent to critique the state's approach to the integration and rehabilitation of foreigners gets caught in a paradox. On the one hand, it functions as knowledge that challenges the rationality and universality of the law and that disrupts the binary modes of representing foreign women (e.g., as victim/agent). On the other hand, its use of cultural difference is rearticulated by the state in normative and objectifying ways. The production of typologies translates into a familiar language that is radically unfamiliar and destabilizing. The violence of this logic lies in the need to incorporate the question of radical difference within the boundaries of the state, be it represented by madness or by culture, in order to manage its disruptive force. Prudence is either mad or Nigerian, equipping the state, in either case, with a language to digest her difference. Even in the event that she is a "crazy Nigerian," the state can now address the new configurations of difference through ethno-psychiatric discourse.

Despite the potential of ethno-psychiatry to challenge the universality of dominant discourses, the therapeutic ethos of the state conceals practices that include the other by fundamentally domesticating her difference. When ethno-psychiatrists interact with state officials, they act as tightrope walkers. In order to understand difference, ethno-psychiatrists foreground the women's emotions as symptoms that need to be taken into account, or they make claims on the women's cultural backgrounds to disentangle them from the label of the "victim" and to show them as individuals with their own characteristics and modalities. Their alterity is gradually made more acceptable to Italian institutions because it is translated into individual idiosyncrasies, everyday gestures and reactions, mental states, and emotions. And yet, like Prudence's story, individual stories are used as didactic cases by ethno-psychiatrists themselves in order to establish general modalities of intervention with foreign women. Therefore, stories continue to be formulated through the language of culture, law, psychiatry, or a general therapeutic approach to citizens in need of assistance and care.

As I mentioned earlier, the "victim" label allows the state and the church to recuperate some sort of relationship with the rejected who otherwise would be destined to remain outside the realm of the law. In this way, the incommensurability of the foreign prostitute's position is erased, and she is incorporated as a victim, a category that pertains to the margins. Ethno-psychiatry, by attempting to shift the gaze of the state from the anonymous victim to the individual women and their particular stories, problematizes the margins but without making them necessarily less marginal. Herein lies the project's power and its limits in the ways it allows for discrepancies to emerge in the discourse of the state and in the space of the margins. The ways in which ethno-psychiatry's contribution to the understanding of suffering in the context of migration is received and translated by the institutions does not guarantee that the margins cease to remain marginal. This argument could be extended to the politics of multiculturalism in general, in which ethno-psychiatry can get caught. Despite claims of inclusion and of under-standing difference, the state's translation of the foreign prostitute into a victim gestures toward a translation that removes her difference, whether digestible or not.

The therapeutic state asserts itself through the language of emotions and by helping others. It constitutes its own authority (indeed, its centrality) and integrity by reconstituting the other at the margin, from which the foreigner must appeal for inclusion and rights. From migrant to victim to patient subject to the therapeutic state, the marginality of the foreign woman is resignified but not undone. The very path she must travel through the therapeutic state makes her continued marginality a necessary condition for her inclusion.

PART THREE

Entering the Scene

The Police Station

Inspector Preda's office is located at the end of a long and busy corridor on the second floor of the Turin Police Department. The first time I went there I realized that there was something very familiar about it, even though I had never been in the police station of a big city. There was a frenetic coming and going of people in the corridor. Police officers in uniform transferred piles of documents from one office to another, while officers in civilian dress disguised as drug addicts escorted all sorts of "criminals" who could be distinguished only by their handcuffs. A few foreign women were sitting on a bench outside of one office with bored and annoyed expressions on their faces. Their sunken eyes, made more evident by the faded makeup from the previous night, the sleepy expression, and their tight and colorful clothes told an obvious story. "They must be the outcome of the early morning roundup," I thought to myself.

Inspector Preda shared the office with two other colleagues from the patrol squad. The room was big enough to fit three desks—each facing the center of the room—and to make you feel uncomfortable walking between them for lack of space. The leaning piles of folders, scattered papers, framed photos of family members, computers, and maps of the city that cluttered the desks were the same you would find in any office in any police station. What caught my attention were the walls: each portrayed the officer occupying the desk in front of it.

On the wall behind Inspector Preda was a large, detailed, and colorful map of Nigeria. This was obviously a crucial tool for his job, for people's stories drew migration trajectories that originated in small villages and crossed remote areas of the country. Inspector Preda was known as "the inspector of Nigerians," a title he earned thanks to the hundreds of denuncias he had collected from Nigerian women over the years and because he had a personal interest in the country, which he had visited a few times. He always worked with a Nigerian cultural mediator, Promise, who was in charge of translating the women's stories into Italian. Next to the map there were several photos, all occupying a big glass frame: Nigerian landscapes, the inspector posing with Nigerian colleagues at the Lagos police station, and Nigerian naira banknotes. They were displayed like trophies, not because they represented some sort of award, but because, I imagined, he must have placed them there with the same pride and honor as if they were. They were testimonies of his travels to Nigeria and an assurance of his knowledge and cultural competency, which made him the resident authority. Next to the map was a photo, just as big, of the football team Juventus, a Turin symbol for which I felt generations of alliance and devotion.[1]

Next to his desk and his section of the wall, his colleague sat in front of a very different background. Two outdated calendars with photos of naked—or almost naked—women were in the center of the wall. That the year and month had already passed could be interpreted in two ways: either he was so uninterested in the calendar that he didn't realize it hadn't been updated for a very long time, or, more likely, it was the photo that was of interest to him. Either way, there was something disturbing about the whole situation: not only did these calendars picture naked women in an office that mostly received women who used to work or still worked as prostitutes, but they also gave the sense that time had hit the same impasse that foreigners confront when they apply to receive a residency permit. Next to the calendars, I noticed some recent photos of a woman with two children, the officer's family members, I guessed.

The third inhabitant of the office had a whole different set of decorations on his wall. He also displayed the cover of an old calendar, dated 2000, which portrayed the photo of a triumphant Mussolini under the title, "Long Live the Duce 2000 Times Over" (2000 volte viva il Duce). I shivered. I was not sure which sight—Mussolini or the naked women—made me more uncomfortable. And then I spotted yet another old calendar of naked women with a postcard attached to it portraying Berlusconi, prime minister at the time, with the caption, "A concrete promise: bread and pussy for all" (Un impegno concreto: pane e figa per tutti).

CHAPTER 4

Denuncia

The Subject Verbalized

It was May 2003, and I had recently met the people who work for Emancipazione Oggi, a Catholic NGO founded in 2000 whose main mission is to fight foreign prostitution as a form of modern slavery. In their work to get foreign prostitutes off the streets and into a state-sponsored rehabilitation program, this group mostly helps women draft their denuncias, the first step of the program.[1] The denuncia is the victim's written testimony, drafted in the style and format required by the police. Early one morning I went to the organization's office to meet with Mara, the social worker in charge of taking women to file their denunciations. She invited me to go with her and Joy, a young Nigerian woman, to the Police Department, where Joy was supposed to meet with the inspector and a cultural mediator.

When I got to Emancipazione Oggi's office, Joy was already there in the waiting room. The warm spring sun coming in from the open window illuminated her face. She looked very young and tired, or maybe bored, and she did not seem to notice my presence. Joy had contacted the organization at the suggestion of another Nigerian woman who had gone through its rehabilitation program. Joy explained, "I was afraid of my madam and didn't want to work on the streets, and my friend helped me escape." Mara was busy gathering all the documents that the police required: Joy's passport, medical records, and a photo. The appointment was in half an hour. We were almost ready to go when the phone rang. Mara answered and had a brief conversation with the police inspector. She came into the waiting room and, with an expression somewhere between frustration and amusement, announced that the appointment had been canceled. The inspector had said to her, "I am unable to verbalize the Nigerian woman today, please come tomorrow" (Oggi sono impossibilitato a verbalizzare la Nigeriana; venite domani). I gathered that he meant he could not collect Joy's deposition, but I had never heard the expression "verbalizzare la Nigeriana." I myself was amused and somewhat disturbed by it. To verbalize something means to put it into words, to put it on record. In Italian, a *verbale* (the noun derived from the verb *verbalizzare*) is an official document that contains the transcription of a damaging admission to the police. A denuncia is also called a verbale. In this sense, it involves translating the spoken into the written. From the state's perspective, this step in the victim rehabilitation program constitutes women as legal subjects by means of "being verbalized" through the mediation of a police officer and a cultural mediator. The practice of filing criminal charges takes place by means of translation and represents the act through which women enter into a pact with the state. They are thus translated and transcribed into a document. They are voiced into being as subjects of the law—something that vaguely resonated with the biblical power of God's verb calling man into existence, thus making language and existence coincide.

Mara asked me if I would be willing to accompany Joy to the police station by myself the next day because she had other appointments she could not cancel. I agreed. Joy was disappointed and annoyed that her wait would be longer than expected. We agreed to meet the next day at the same time. As I left that morning, Mara jokingly said, "Bring Joy back to us verbalized!"

The next day I went with Joy to the police station. Before being admitted into Inspector Preda's office, Joy and I sat for a long time on a bench with other women who had been detained in the previous night's roundup. They did not seem interested in talking to us. Some of them looked disoriented and scared; you could guess from their expressions that it was their first time there. Others had the expression of someone who was going through a formality yet again, like a routine that would not change the course of her everyday existence.

Since 2002, when Italian immigration laws became more restrictive, newspapers have been reporting almost daily on Operation Clean Streets and Operation Field Drainage/Land Reclamation (*operazioni di bonifica del territorio*), police operations designed to eliminate networks of prostitution (Palidda 2000). *Bonifica,* or reclamation, was central to many discourses of fascist modernity. It started as a conversion of swampland into arable soil but soon turned into the fascists' desire to purify the nation of all social and cultural ills. *Bonificare* saw human society as an organism that can be manipulated by means of a vast surgical operation (Ben-Ghiat 2001). Today, these police operations—conceived of through the language of a contaminated territory that needs to be drained[2]—involve physically removing foreigners from certain neighborhoods. The idea is that their presence pollutes the land on which they walk. Some policemen refer to these interventions as "negro hunting" or "ethnic cleansing." According to these policing strategies, foreign prostitutes are taken to the police station, where they are usually kept for the night; their names (mostly fake), pictures, and fingerprints are taken for the record; and the next morning they are released with expulsion papers and an injunction to leave the country within a week. Some of them are taken to one of the Temporary Detention Centers, where they wait indefinitely to be repatriated to their respective countries.[3] The majority, though, leave the Police Department with expulsion papers, trash them as soon as they are out of sight, and go back to the life they had before, either by choice or for lack of a better one. When women rely on the help of NGOs or Catholic associations to mediate between them and the police,[4] they are usually accompanied through the different steps of the rehabilitation. This way, they have a better chance of sticking to the program and receiving the residency permit that grants them the right to work.

As we were waiting in the corridor, I suddenly remembered what made the whole atmosphere of the police station so familiar. It reminded me of the numerous TV series I had seen about the police and the Carabinieri (the national military police) that state television (RAI) had produced over the past twenty years. During my undergraduate years and then later during field research, I watched many of them, mostly because there weren't better detective stories on TV and I was intrigued by the emphasis that state television put on rehabilitating the Italian forces of law and order. The Italian state was attempting to restore national unity in a country that right-wing, anti-immigrant and separatist discourses were constantly portraying as at risk of being divided in two—North and South—and of being "invaded" and "infected" by growing numbers of illegal migrants. These series create a social imaginary in which the police are engaged in an express mission to heal and cure the country and thus to expel the causes of contagion.

In Italy the rhetoric of illness and treatment has shaped much of the national discourse on difference and identity over the past two centuries. In 1861, the newborn nation was portrayed as "young and ill"; it needed to reinforce and heal itself of its internal divisions. The health metaphor still characterizes political discourse today. The social body is portrayed as sick, and the prescriptions for curing it are varied: rehabilitate the finances; eradicate or uproot the cancer represented by the mafia; and "heal" undocumented migrants. Medical language is applied to discourses about the legalization of migrants as well: *sanatoria* (literally, "healing") refers to the process of granting legal status to undocumented foreigners who can prove they have regular employment. Expressions such as "contamination," "immunity," "expel the clandestines," and "eradicate the plague of trade in women" are used to address issues of national security and order (Diasio 2001; Esposito 2002).

When it was finally our turn, Joy and I sat down in front of the inspector. The Nigerian cultural mediator was late. Inspector Preda asked me to explain to Joy that she was there "to tell her true story of how she was brought to Italy," and he stressed "true" by gazing into her eyes with a piercing look. Later she would have to go to court to testify against her traffickers. He insisted that she had to tell him her real name, the date and place of her birth, and all the exact events—in the precise order in which they had occurred—concerning her travel to Italy and her involvement in prostitution. Providing false information would be punishable as a crime. He was not there to put her in jail, but she had to tell him nothing but the truth.

Before beginning the actual interrogation, he sent her into another office where staff took her fingerprints and a photo. This was the normal procedure to apply for a residency permit. He asked her to fill out a form with her personal information, current address in Italy, religion, mother tongue, names of siblings, father, and mother, and their addresses in Nigeria. The name of the village where she was born was not marked on Inspector Preda's map, so it took him some time to locate it. After several questions, he guessed she was from Ondo State, that her mother tongue, unlike most Nigerian women in Italy, was Yoruba and not Edo, and that she was born in a village close to the city of Akura. An expression of relief and pride spread across Inspector Preda's face for being able to locate places with very little help from Joy. Soon afterward, when he realized that the Nigerian cultural mediator did not speak Joy's language, he became concerned. I wondered how they were going to communicate and expressed my concern, trusting that he felt the same and would look for another translator. On the contrary, he quickly settled the problem by saying that English would be good enough for Joy, the cultural mediator, and him to communicate in. The layers of translation were becoming intricate. As it stood, everybody was going to communicate by translation: Joy and the cultural mediator would move between English (sometimes pidgin) and Italian, the cultural mediator and the police officer in Italian and English, and Joy's mother tongue would only remotely echo in the answers she gave in broken English.

Based on the form that Joy and I filled out together, the police officer wrote the first paragraph of the denuncia as follows:

> My name is Joy Aimiose, and I was born on September 7, 1985, in (at) Akura, in Ondo State. Before I left for Italy, I lived in a village near Akura with my mother. My father's name is Benjamin and my mother's is Jenny. My parents are separated. I am one of two children: myself and my older brother who makes a living as a "magician" (who cheats people) and who never got along with my mother. My mother is a housewife and my father a peasant. My father married another woman, with whom he had no children. I have no identification: no passport, no national citizenship certificate. For the purpose of this testimony, I declare my residence as the "La Rosa" cooperative, where I live at the moment and which assists me with the program of protection and social integration in which I willingly accepted to participate in order to remove myself from the conditions imposed on me by the person that forced me into prostitution.

While waiting for the cultural mediator, Inspector Preda asked other questions in order to trace where Joy used to live when she worked as a prostitute. I translated for him.

Cristiana: Where did you live?

Joy: Via S. Secondo.

C: Did your madam live with you?

J: Yes.

C: Were there other girls in the same apartment?

J: Yes.

C: How many of them?

J: Three.

C: Does your madam have children?

J: Yes, two.

The inspector wanted to identify Joy's managers. He took out a "catalog of madams" that he had meticulously put together during his career as "the police inspector of Nigerian women," opened it, and pointed to a photo of a Nigerian woman. Joy did not recognize her. He tried another photo, which she did not recognize either. He looked at me and commented, "They often don't recognize their madams because they always wear different wigs. They are so skillful at disguising themselves! You would not believe it!" Looking somewhat defeated in his effort to solve the riddle of Joy's "story" efficiently, he put the binder away and resigned himself to proceed with the denuncia in the usual way.

The Nigerian cultural mediator, Promise, finally arrived. She looked very much at ease in the police station environment: everyone knew her and greeted her warmly. She was dressed in a dark blue suit that looked very professional. Without introducing herself, she sat right next to Joy, asking me to move to a seat behind them. Promise, as she later explained to me, came from an area of Nigeria that borders Cameroon, and she did not speak Yoruba, Joy's mother tongue, nor could Joy speak her language. While the inspector was dealing with computer problems that prevented him from typing the document, he urged the cultural mediator to start the interrogation. She then proceeded quickly and efficiently to ask Joy questions in English. Joy, on the other hand, was hesitant—sometimes not sure of the exact answer, other times not sure of her English. She struggled to look for words that she did not know so she could tell her story in a linear way. Chronology, with its coherence, was precisely what was expected of Joy on that day at the police station. Five long hours of interrogation followed.

The cultural mediator was completely in charge. She asked a series of questions in English almost without interruption: very precise details about people, journeys, addresses, dates, encounters, place descriptions, relationships between people, debts, and money (borrowed, earned, returned, lost, and lent). In the space of a few seconds, she translated Joy's stammered words into Italian and transformed them into a polished and ordered text: the denuncia. Meanwhile, the inspector had become an anonymous clerk following the orders of a superior who dictated to him.

> *Promise:* How were you brought to Italy? Did your madam come to get you in Nigeria?
>
> *Joy:* No.
>
> *P:* How did it work?
>
> *J:* Through a friend of brother Daniel who live in London.

P: Did you know why you were coming to Italy?

J: No.

P: Why didn't you ask before leaving Nigeria?

J: Didn't know.

P: How did it work with passports?

J: With fake name, a Muslim name.

P: When did you leave Lagos? What day, month, and year?

J: Don't remember; maybe October 6th of 2000.

The document that Promised dictated to Inspector Preda based on this first part of the interrogation read as follows:

> It was my brother Daniel who, unbeknownst to my mother, invited me to his house in Lagos and then put me in contact with a Nigerian guy named John who immediately promised that he would be able to help me get to Amsterdam so that I could finish school, and who then organized my departure for Italy. I state that in Nigeria I had never heard anything about girls being brought to Europe for work or school and then forced into prostitution. I left from Lagos on October 6, 2000, around 11:00 P.M. I traveled with a passport that had my photo but not my personal information. I don't remember the name that was on the passport, but it was definitely a Muslim name. In fact, they had made me dress as a Muslim woman in order to render the personal information on the passport more believable.

It became clear from the very first moments of the denunciation that Joy's hesitance and stuttering did not come through in the document. By being inscribed in the orderly written text, her trembling voice, broken sentences, and confusion were completely erased. Yet she was performing the very act that granted her access to services and rights and that would eventually allow her to become a legal subject in Italy.[5]

This ethnographic moment showed me the intricacies of translation at play in this context and how in the process of drafting the denuncia, Joy's story was simultaneously revealed and disguised. That is, the revelation of certain details of her story masked other parts of her experience. The law's goal is to save foreign prostitutes from "victimization," to give them back their agency, and to restore their sense of dignity. But while the language of the state aims to recognize the other, it also dispossesses the subject of her stammering voice, fragmented memory, and opaque story. By ordering all the details and anecdotes in a chronological account, the denuncia inscribes the women's experiences in a linguistic form that is not theirs, and it deprives them of the possibility of telling their stories according to the different trajectories of memory that correspond to various experiences. On the one hand, the law and Catholic groups involved in aid programs for victims portray the moment when women file charges as one of freedom and redemption from slavery and as a way for the women to regain agency in their lives. In this frame, prostitution is the negation of free will and independence. On the other hand, for the women, filing criminal charges is not necessarily freeing; they sometimes see it as yet another form of subjugation that suppresses their own projects of emancipation.[6] While most of these women do not necessarily identify with the state's categories of inclusion, they use them in pragmatic ways to access rights and services.

What concerns me in the case of "victims of human trafficking" who appeal under Article 18 is the fact that the subject, as a subject of the law, can only be instituted through various layers of translation. I argue that the testimony produced in the denuncia cannot be understood through the victim/agent trope of the bureaucratic state. These are categories that the state uses to make the other digestible through a process of what I call "confessional recognition." The state grants legal documents on the condition that women go through a program of reeducation that mirrors the religious logic of confession, penance, and redemption.

At stake in the practice of filing criminal charges are the various ways in which cultural mediators and women who file denuncias maneuver the bureaucratic language of the state to access services and rights. In other words, while the state provides a monolithic idea of the victim, the processes that I am describing show how multiple voices, subject positions, and untranslatable experiences come to influence the production of the final account filed at the police station.

THE MAGIC OF TRANSLATION

The interrogation continued, punctuated by the same rhythm of detailed questions and fragmented answers, followed by the precise rendition of both into the text of the denuncia.

> P: And then what happened? You have to tell me nothing but the truth, step by step. How many people were traveling with you?
>
> J: No people.
>
> P: Do you remember their names?
>
> J: No.
>
> P: Where did you go after Lagos?

J: Kano.

P: How many days did it take you to get to Kano? Where did you sleep while you were there?

J: One night; stayed in hotel.

P: How long did you stay there?

J: One week.

P: Did you travel by plane or by bus?

J: Bus.

P: Where did you go after Kano?

J: Amsterdam.

P: Who arranged the trip to Amsterdam?

J: A woman, Edith, work in airport.

P: How did it work with the documents?

J: Fake document. Edith say I put it in toilet on the plane and say I am from Freetown.

In Lagos, I found accommodation in a hotel for a few days while I waited for the person who was supposed to move me from Lagos to Kano. And that is what happened. The trip from Lagos to Kano lasted an entire night and for a few hours the following morning. On the bus, there were many other people, but my guide gave me the impression that I was the only person he was in charge of. Once I arrived at Kano, my custodian, after showing me a hotel where I would wait for a few days, left, without even saying good-bye to me. I stayed in Kano for approximately one week; evidently some other person took care of the cost of the hotel, because I paid nothing. In the lobby of the hotel, I encountered two Nigerian men who were waiting for me. The following day, they brought me to a woman named Edith, who worked at the airport. Before leaving, Edith told me that once I was settled aboard the airplane I should rip up my passport and throw it in the toilet, which I did a few hours into the flight. If, upon my arrival in Amsterdam, anyone asked me where I was from, I was simply to say that I was from Sierra Leone and that I was born in Freetown.

P: Where did you stay when you reached Amsterdam?

J: A man's house.

P: What was the name of the Nigerian man who brought you to Italy from there?

J: Matthew.

According to the instructions I received in Nigeria, once I arrived in Amsterdam, I was to head toward the exit (of the airport), take a taxi, distance myself from the area, and then call a phone number that I had been given; someone would come and pick me up. When I arrived in

Amsterdam, however, I was very confused. As such, I decided to check in at the Immigration Office in the airport; I told the officers that I had no documents and no money and that I was from Sierra Leone. Then, the agents, without asking me any more questions, accompanied me to a shelter in the outskirts of Amsterdam, where there were people (men, women, and children) of varying nationalities. I stayed in this shelter for a month. After a month, I called the phone number that had been given to me in Nigeria. A man's voice responded and informed me that he would come to pick me up. After about two hours, a young man, roughly thirty years old, named Matthew arrived near the front door of the shelter.

P: What did you do with him? Were you still a virgin?

J: Yes.

P: Did he rape you?

J: Yes.

P: In what Italian city did you arrive?

J: Turin.

P: What day and month?

J: Maybe November 15th.

P: How did you get in touch with your madam?

J: Matthew sold me to her.

Matthew brought me to his house and made me follow him into a room and, that night, regardless of the fact that I begged him to leave me alone, abused me by raping me. This made me suffer a lot and it contributed to confirming my conviction that I had fallen into the hands of bad and unscrupulous people. We arrived in Turin the following day. It was November 15, 2000, a date that I will never forget. That day he sold me to Grace, my madam.

P: At what address did you live? What floor? What was the layout of the apartment? How many rooms were there?

J: Via San Secondo, first floor. Don't remember . . . one bedroom, bathroom, kitchen . . .

P: Did other women live with you and the madam? How many of them? Do you remember their names?

J: Three girls. Don't know the names.

P: Did they tell you how much money you were going to pay for the journey?

J: 75 millions lira, not the money they told in Nigeria.

The madam then brought me to the dwelling in which I was to stay with her and some other girls. I specify that the house was on Via S. Secondo, in the vicinity of the Porta Nuova train station. I don't remember the house number, but if I were to go there in person, I would no doubt be able to recognize the location. The apartment, on the first floor, is comprised of one bedroom, one large living room, a bathroom, and a kitchen. In this apartment, I found another three girls and my madam's boyfriend. I don't remember their names. When we arrived at the apartment, the madam told me that I had to give her 75 million lire, a sum that only later I was able to quantify as more than three times the fee agreed upon before leaving Nigeria.

P: Did your madam do voodoo to you?

J: Yes.

P: Did she force you to work as a prostitute?

J: Yes, but I don't want to for three months.

P: When did you start to work on the street?

J: January.

P: Did she ever beat you? How? With shoes or with a belt?

J: Yes, she don't give me food.

P: Did it happen before you left Nigeria or in Italy?

J: Italy.

P: How much money did you give your madam a day, a week, or a month? How much money did you give her in total since you have been in Italy?

J: 900,000 lire for post; 500,000 rent every month; 80,000 food every week.[7]

The day after my arrival in Italy, Grace cut pieces of the nails on my left hand and a lock of hair from my head. She then made me give her some pubic hairs and my underwear, which she stained with blood after having made an incision in one of my fingers. In making me give her these "things," which she organized in a cardboard box after having wrapped them in a piece of fabric, she demanded that I always do everything she ordered me to; otherwise, something awful would happen to me—sickness or insanity. She then made about twenty incisions above my breasts with a razor blade. She then forced me to start prostituting myself immediately. Despite the fact that she mistreated me and beat me almost every day, I resisted her for three months. She denied me food and forbade me to leave the house. In the end, not knowing what to do or who to ask for help, I had to give in: halfway through the month of February, I began to prostitute myself. Grace explained exactly what I had to do with the clients, how much time to spend on the encounters, how much money to ask. I had to pay Grace 900,000 lire per month for my post, which would be added to the 500,000 lire per month in rent and the 80,000 lire per week for food.

"You don't have to worry, but you must tell me nothing but the truth. I don't ask these questions to put you in jail, but to catch your pimps and put *them* in jail," said Promise, in an attempt to reassure Joy and encourage her to say more. But Joy's account did not become any clearer. Meanwhile, I sat behind them and frantically took notes throughout the entire interrogation because I was not allowed to tape record it. The inspector seemed too absorbed in writing at the computer and the cultural mediator too focused on asking questions and dictating the text to be bothered by my presence. I felt that I had become invisible to them. I wondered if Joy felt invisible, too, but for different reasons. She was, in a way, dispossessed by her own stuttering, by her lack of words. The moments of silence and emptiness in her account were suffocated by the pressing rhythm of the bureaucratic language, so masterfully conveyed by the cultural mediator's voice and translation.

The story continued to unfold as Joy provided more details about her shifts on the street, the services that clients requested, the amount of money she was able to send to her family in Nigeria, and how she eventually escaped from her madam thanks to a client. Her declaration, on that day, ended as follows:

> Since the day I contacted the people of an association that helps women that endured adversities like mine, I have been living safely in a house run by that same association. I was informed about everything that the Italian legal system provides for people in situations like mine. Even if it has cost me quite a bit, I agreed to reconstruct my entire story. I am prepared to do all that is requested of me in order to bring the person who treated me like an animal for three long years to justice. I hope to be able to receive a residency permit, find an honest job, and calmly live a normal life. My dream: to become a nurse. In regard to all that I have declared in this long deposition of mine, I confirm that I am fully willing and able to answer any additional question that is asked of me.

This first visit to the police station was just one of many that I made during a year of research with women who were in the social protection program for victims. I examined over one hundred denuncias filed through the Catholic association between 2000 and 2004, as they were being drafted, proofread, and later filed at the police station. Of these, around seventy were approved in approximately ten months to one year. The number of denuncias and the number of victims who apply for documents through this program, and their fate once they enter the bureaucratic pact, serve as a barometer of Italy's shifting moral practices of recognition (Povinelli 2002).[8]

The form of the document is standardized. It starts with "My name is . . . " and is written in the first person. It unfolds with the descriptions of the woman's background in the home country (family structure, class milieu, level of education, date and place of birth), the various phases of her journey to Italy, the story of "betrayal" through which she became a victim, the violence of being exploited as a prostitute, and finally the declaration of consciously choosing to file criminal charges and to enter the rehabilitation program.

The drafting of the text—either in the police station or at the Catholic organization—always takes place in the presence of a cultural mediator who is fluent in Italian and one of the languages spoken by the woman who testifies. A police officer then has to certify it with an official stamp and signature. In general, both the mediator and the denouncer speak the same mother tongue. For example, in the case of women from Romania, Albania, Moldavia, and Ukraine that I met during my research, the cultural mediator was always a native speaker from their home countries. Nonetheless, as in Joy's case, the mediator and the denouncer sometimes need to resort to yet another language, usually tied to the legacies of colonialism (English, French, or Spanish).[9]

In the process of translation, some women experience ambivalence and unease denouncing people whom they perceive as "benefactors" as well as "exploiters," insofar as they made it possible for the women to migrate, make money, help their families, and make new lives for themselves. Diana, a young woman from Romania, told me that she denounced her exploiters only because the police caught her. "But I felt horrible," she said. "They were not so terrible with me, and while I worked for them I made enough money to support my family back home for the rest of their lives." Edith, a cultural mediator from Nigeria who helps women file criminal charges, once told me, "There are many things from the women's stories that I don't translate; otherwise they would never get the papers. I can't translate that their mothers or sisters helped them make the decision to migrate and that they knew about the prostitution." Thus, cultural mediators often decide to hide this type of family involvement from the state because it could jeopardize the woman's status as a "victim," and the state's entire rehabilitation effort would cease to have meaning. Edith also made it clear that she, as a cultural mediator, had the power to mold the story so that women could qualify as state-recognized victims. She added that women decide to make a denuncia not necessarily to abandon prostitution but often to disentangle themselves from their madams and the monetary obligations they demand. Some women want emancipation from their exploiters but still consider prostitution a quick and easy way to make money and therefore continue to do sex work even after filing criminal charges. This allows them to continue sending money back home and keep the rest for themselves.

When I later talked with Promise about her role as a cultural mediator at the police station, she revealed that in her extensive experience translating for Nigerian women, she had witnessed many shifts and changes in the kind of stories they would tell her. In the mid-1990s and early 2000s, she commented, women were unaware of the kind of work they would be involved in once they arrived in Italy. She thought they were "real victims" back then and that Article 18 was an effective legislative tool that helped women free themselves from prostitution networks. "Nowadays," she claimed, "women know very well that prostitution is in the picture; I consider them 'victims' because I know they have no future in Nigeria. But I know they know, and their parents know as well, that they will work as prostitutes in Italy; but it is fine for their families as long as they send money back home."

The state cannot account for the fear and sense of guilt provoked by the action of denouncing family members who were involved in the women's migration. Also, the police station is not a space where the fear of going mad, which paralyzes some women, can be heard. When a woman denounces her exploiters she often sees it as breaking an oath, which will result in the curse of madness. In Joy's case, one of her brothers organized her travel to Europe. When I spoke to her after the meeting at the police station, she admitted that she feared the consequences of what she had just done: "My family will be threatened with death in Nigeria! And what if my madam curses me and I go mad? I still have to pay my debt to her; otherwise, bad things can happen to me and my family." The state cannot recognize this fear of descending into madness; it exceeds its categories and simultaneously reveals the state's lacuna.

Through the act of denuncia, women are expected to provide details of their story that can be used to prove their victimhood. The state, for its part, provides a frame within which such stories can be told in what appears to be a culturally sensitive manner. Especially when it comes to Nigerian women, the word *voodoo* typically appears in the document and is often a topic of discussion among police officers, care providers, and psychologists. This attempt to make the law culturally appropriate by introducing a term to describe Nigerian women's experience of "swearing oaths" at shrines, either before their departure from Nigeria or upon their arrival in Europe, serves a double purpose. On the one hand, it points to the breaches within the bureaucratic language that allow for the acceptance of concepts, such as voodoo, that gesture toward cultural sensitivity but also reify the women's alterity. On the other hand, in drafting a denuncia, the concept of voodoo is manipulated to prove the women's degree of victimhood: they were coerced to obey their exploiters by means of exotic cults and occult threats. This is the magic of bureaucracy. References to voodoo stand in for a complete loss of the expression of personal desires and choices, something the women know too well when they file criminal charges and decide to subscribe to the category of the victim, whether it truly applies to their story or not. They know how to talk about voodoo in the way that police officers use it, and they know how to do things with it. In a sense, the very act of talking about it is effective, almost as if the power of voodoo continues to produce consequences by simply invoking it, whether in the space of a ritual or in that of the police station. In fact, the denuncia itself is a form of initiation, a rite of passage that marks the pact women make with the state. In this sense, denuncia continues the magical effect of bureaucracy. In certain institutional settings, referring to voodoo is crucial because it meets one of the criteria that measure the degree of subjugation women experienced. Words make things happen. Women know that being a "victim of voodoo" makes them more eligible for the rehabilitation program.[10] The label of the victim, therefore, has a double function: although it erases the ambivalence and complexities of women's experiences by reducing them to a category defined by the state, it opens up opportunities that are directly tied to gaining legal status.

The nuances of what it means to be a victim, and how that is woven together with the conscious choices of women, who often see prostitution as a necessary step in their migration experience before they can land on the shores of Europe, do not emerge in the denuncia. This can be read as a contradiction of the therapeutic state that, as I discussed in chapter 3, pays attention to emotions and feelings in order to approach women in a culturally appropriate way. In fact, the state recognizes only the range of emotions that can be ascribed to a victim: fear of her exploiters, lack of awareness that she was getting involved in prostitution, and betrayal. The possibility of "choice" and the idea of self-realization through sex work and exploitation remain unthinkable (van Dijk 2001) and untranslatable. "I kind of knew that I was going to work as a prostitute for a while, and then I would find a normal job," shared a woman from Benin City, "but I never thought it meant working in the streets at night. I needed money to support my siblings in Nigeria after my parents died." A young woman from Romania pointed to a similar experience when she told me:

> I left my country because there was no job, and I didn't want to depend on my parents. The people who brought me to Italy told me that I would work as a baby-sitter, but I knew I would work as a prostitute. I thought I could do it for two or three months of my life, make a lot of money, and then go back to Romania, but then the months passed and I stayed. I have sent my family enough money for them to live well for several years.

Promise, like other cultural mediators working in similar institutional contexts, is caught in the conundrum of translating this kind of testimony, which cannot be understood through the simple victim/agent dichotomy that the state applies. She explained that today parents and family members in Nigeria also have to take part in voodoo rituals by swearing before a magician (native doctor) that their daughters and sisters will pay back their debts. Sometimes, as part of the ritual itself, denuncia is mentioned among the things women (and families) swear they will never do. Along these lines, Promise told me about a young Nigerian woman and her family who had to swear inside a cemetery in Lagos that once in Italy she would never escape from her madam. If she did, her parents would have to bring her back to Nigeria as a cadaver and bury her. Just as the language of voodoo has made it into official documents produced by the Italian state, denuncia is now becoming an element that could determine whether the voodoo rituals performed upon women's departure from home will work for or against them. In a way, filing criminal charges itself can be read as a form of voodoo, a ritual that creates a pact between the participants and then initiates a series of consequences in their lives. It creates a tie with the state, and the state, in turn, takes on the power of the un-witcher who, through the act of denuncia, unties the woman from the bondage of voodoo. The state thus simultaneously invokes magic and exorcises its power by fully embodying it.

Promise struggled with these stories but knew they could not be verbalized in the official document because they would create a different kind of victim. As I mentioned earlier, the woman who migrates in full awareness that she will work as a prostitute is a figure of untranslatability that neither the state nor the church, as I will show in the next chapter, can comprehend as such. I called it an "indigestible" presence. In this sense, Promise lamented that while the first denuncias she drafted in the early years of her work as a mediator were true stories—or at least truer—now "it had become fiction" and the whole rehabilitation program was a "market of lies."

Moreover, Promise struggled with her own role vis-à-vis the state and the women. Having gone through the rehabilitation program for victims eight years before she began working for the state, she knew women were in danger when they filed criminal charges, but that it was only by entering the program that they could gain legal status in Italy. Furthermore, though the kind of victims the state wanted to redeem were not the victims she encountered in her work, she had to translate one type of victim into another in order to make women fit the category that the state could recognize and accept. In a sense, she, like other cultural mediators who played a similar role in courtrooms and police stations, had become a ventriloquist of the state, someone who voiced a story in the language dictated by bureaucracy while making it seem as if it was spoken by someone else, the "I" of the account. As a ventriloquist, however, she did not passively master the state's language but could purposefully use it to help women obtain legal status.

THE STATE'S VENTRILOQUIST

There are two main phases in the crafting of the denuncia. The first one is articulated through the cultural mediator's questions and the woman's responses. This is a dialogic moment. The second phase consists in the moment of inscription, when the spoken is turned into the written text, the testifier's mother tongue into formalized Italian, and the dialogue becomes a monologue that is dictated to the police officer (himself turned into a scribe).[11] The dialogic process produces a monologue in the first person—the "I" of the foreign woman—that is voiced by the cultural mediator. Following Roman Jakobson (1966), I call this type of translation a transmutation. The woman's words are rearticulated, transformed, partly erased, partly produced, transmuted, and rendered by the cultural mediator, who makes the final choice of the terms that will fix the woman's story in the official document. The cultural mediator often also translates bodily gestures and expressions (of sadness, concern, relief) into words, thus adding—and creating often de novo—details that are included in the document but that the woman herself never verbalized. Thus, different layers of verbalization intersect in this process: the women's experiences, the mediator's translation of words and affects, the fragmented story that becomes an official testimony, and its effectiveness in assigning a certain subject position to the testifier who, once "verbalized," can be accepted as "legal." Here I argue that the first-person testimony is not actually a monologue; it is in fact the result of various voices and languages that, through translation, are conveyed and condensed in the text. I call this process a "dialogized" monologue.

On that day at the police station, in the process of filing criminal charges, Joy occupied the position of an "I" (the first person of the denuncia), crafted for her by the bureaucratic language of the police document and internalized by Promise. In reading other denuncias, I realized that most of the statements sound alike, and the women are often aware of the questions they will be asked to qualify for the rehabilitation program. Therefore, although Joy's voice was transformed and lost in the cultural mediator's translation, her position as a legal subject was constituted in the very process of drafting her story. In this context, foreign women achieve social intelligibility and existence at the price of new forms of subjection. More precisely, they achieve a monolithic intelligibility through the standardization of their story. As Judith Butler (1997, 20) writes, "Bound to seek recognition of its own existence in categories, terms, and names that are not of its own making, the subject seeks the sign of its own existence outside itself in a discourse that is at once dominant and indifferent. Social categories signify subordination and existence at once."

The act of denuncia becomes emblematic of this fundamental tension and ambiguity embedded in the constitution of the subject. But what is the status of the "I" that is recorded in this document? What kind of subject is it? In what ways does the formal legal process of filing criminal charges produce the subject while simultaneously alienating her? The "I" of the denuncia is partially abstracted from the experiences of the women, who often tell stories that are not translated (or translatable) into the document or give details that are then transformed to fit the genre that the state requires. The subject is reduced to anonymity. The kind of recognition granted through the denuncia comes at a price: the woman is partly dispossessed of her voice and narratives, both of which are rearticulated and distorted in the act of granting her legal status.[12] At the same time, this kind of dispossession—which is a form of state recognition—allows her a degree of access to services and rights she was previously denied.

I use the figure of the ventriloquist as a metaphor for the role of the cultural mediator in this context. The ventriloquist's craft is to manipulate his or her voice so that it appears as someone else's. Etymologically, *ventriloquism* means the ability "to speak from the stomach" (from the Latin words *venter*—belly, stomach—and *loqui*—to speak). In ancient Greece, it was originally a religious practice aimed at interpreting the spirits' messages to the humans. A famous example is the priestess Pythia, who used this technique at the Temple of Apollo in Delphi. It was believed that the spirits of the dead resided in the stomach of priests and priestesses, through whom the spirits delivered their prophecies; the sound emerged from the interior of the diviner while his or her facial expression and lips remained fixed. The Greeks called this art gastromancy, which was a form of necromancy, a mode of divination of the dead. It also resembled possession rituals and the ability of the diviner to channel the spirits' messages. In the Middle Ages, ventriloquism was associated with witchcraft and magic, thus reinforcing its function as a link between the supernatural and the human. In its contemporary form, it has lost the religious and magical connotations and has become a form of stagecraft in which the ventriloquist has the ability to manipulate his or her voice and make it appear as if it came from a dummy or puppet.

Because ventriloquism can be understood as the art of seeming to speak when one is not—the art of deception, of simultaneously voicing and silencing—I draw from it to understand the ways in which the subject is produced through processes of erasure and creation, verbalization and obliteration. In ventriloquism the voice is dissociated and split from the subject of enunciation. The puppet appears to be moving its lips but is not the actual speaker. The ventriloquist, who appears to be silent, is the real master and manipulator of sounds, words, sentences, and gestures. The voice that we hear is disembodied and has undergone a process of aberration (the voices of ventriloquists often have a metallic sound). In ventriloquism as we know it today, there are traces of its old kinship with witchcraft and possession, a resemblance that makes the spectator wonder where the distorted voice comes from.

Although my aim here is not to create an exact parallel between the practice of denuncia and the ventriloquist's technique, I use it to note some interesting and productive similarities. Cultural mediators who translate for "victims of human trafficking" are often masterfully reproducing the bureaucratic language to make confused accounts intelligible for the state. The different voices, registers, and versions of stories (complex and contradictory) that the woman produces during the interrogation need to be distilled into a clear voice and narrative. It is as if the task of the translator is to absorb the woman's fragmented answers and reorganize them in a form that fits both the document and the categories the institutions require. In a way, she "digests" them to later deliver or "regurgitate" them. In this sense, ventriloquism—and the ways in which foreign prostitutes are integrated into the state—is almost a symbolic form of cannibalism. Cultural mediators take on this task—which I figuratively refer to here as digestion and regurgitation—and ventriloquize a language that belongs neither to them nor to the women who testify. They ventriloquize the language of the cannibal state. Through this language, not only do they provide a coherent and transparent story, but they also condense—out of the cacophonic and composite stories behind the constitution of the self—the "I" of the account into a stable self. These mechanisms of translation and manipulation resemble a form of state magic that turns the denouncer into what may appear to be a partial puppet of the state. What I claim is that in the practice of denuncia certain fixed roles are inscribed in the text and thus assigned to the participants, who can decide whether or not to take them on but not to play them in a different way. In other words, once women step into the rehabilitation program for victims, they turn themselves into the victims that the state can comprehend and integrate and thus digest. At the same time, the denouncer can consciously use the ventriloquist to make sure her story is inscribed in a way that the state recognizes. In this role, she makes statements—through the voice of the cultural mediator—that confirm and sustain a certain identity of the victim.

Cultural mediators, in ventriloquizing the bureaucratic language, seem to be possessed by a voice that comes from somewhere else. I see an interesting doubling here in the cases of Nigerian women's denuncias in which voodoo rituals are often invoked to prove victimhood. Women are represented as possessed and threatened by the spirits that are mobilized by voodoo. In a way, the state objectifies voodoo and turns it into a cipher of the women's culture that supports their case as subjects who lack free will (and thus the state functions as a mediator of some sort). In being positioned in the "I" of the denuncia, women are also "possessed" by the state's voice, which comes from somewhere else and operates by assigning them an identity. The state conceives of the embodiment of this voice as a way to be freed from victimhood and from voodoo's ties. A Nigerian cultural mediator once told me that she treated denuncias as a form of counter-magic, as a strategy to undo the influence of voodoo rituals in the lives of women who feared filing criminal charges.[13]

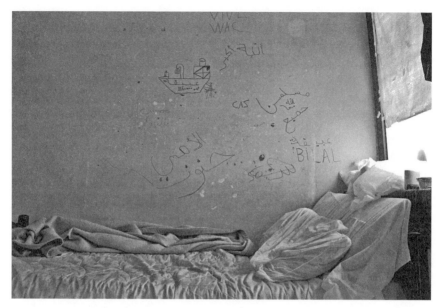

FIGURE 5. Turin, Italy, 2012. Photo by Elena Perlino.

Viewed from this perspective—and not from the state's point of view—the self of the denuncia is fundamentally split; it is produced through deferral and alienation, and it appears at the cost of a disappearance. I turn once more to what Fanon (1967 [1952]) has taught us about the power of institutional discourse and of the colonizer's gaze to fix the colonized in a position of inferiority. For him, this is one of the most tragic legacies of colonialism, the experience of having lost one's self—as it was before colonization—and of being left wearing the masks and bearing the projections of the colonizer. The mask refers to a split self, to an inauthentic form of identification through the imago. Unlike imagination, which points to the creatively unpredictable workings of thought and experience that give rise to new forms of life and identification, the imago stands for an image that is imposed on us by someone else. It is their perception of us that becomes—once introjected—who we think we are. In Fanon's account, the colonized is turned into a Negro by the gaze of the colonizer, by the imago the colonizer had of its subjects. Thus, the imago functions more like a cage, an image into which we are interned and trapped.

The colonial self to which Fanon refers is split between multiple belongings, alliances, and identities (desired, imposed, and created). For him, the white's categories have a fixing effect that leaves no room for negotiation on the part of the colonized. While I believe similar mechanisms are at play in the practice of denuncia, I also argue that foreign women—both cultural mediators and those who file charges as victims—exhibit various degrees of maneuvering to use the law and position themselves vis-à-vis the state in order to access what is made available to them by the categories of inclusion and the subject positions constructed by institutional languages.

Thus, by highlighting certain processes through which the subject emerges and is constituted, we can see how the denuncia speaks to the issue of subjectivity more broadly. In the denuncia itself, the "I" appears fixed by the criteria defining who qualifies as "victim"; this same stable "I" conceals the fact that the subject is always the product of contradictory and multiple travelogues, inconsistencies, fragments of memory, and absences. The subject of the account and the subject of enunciation are not necessarily the same, thus revealing a form of deception. What appears as a monologue—the victim story told in the first person—is in fact a complex text populated by many voices, composed of different languages, registers, and translations. As I mentioned earlier, I approach it as a form of dialogized monologue, where assigned and willed subject positions are condensed into one stable self and various speech acts converge to form a single speech. It is dialogized in the sense that Bakhtin (1981) gives to the concept of dialogism. Unlike dialogue—commonly understood as the interaction between two people engaged in talk—dialogism points to the internal dynamic in the discourse of each single speaker. It refers to the fact that speakers' utterances and words are not merely their own, but reflect their engagement in multiple and broader ideological and linguistic worlds and situations of unbalanced power (Hanks 1996). In the denuncia the cultural mediator's ventriloquism transforms a dialogue into what sounds like a monologue. At the same time, by converting the dialogic moment of the interrogation into the denuncia account the echo of the different speakers' utterances produces a dialogized text.

In these processes of translation, I see the state's attempt to make culture monolithic and objectified, recognizable in exotic categories such as voodoo. The state recognizes the victim by making her a category wherein the other's difference can be grasped. As I mentioned in the introduction to this book, the politics of recognition imply a single world with its own categories of difference. While the state makes culture univocal and hears only the monologue—the first-person testimony—

ethno-psychiatry interferes with the state's modalities and proposes an understanding of cultural identifications as plural and in flux, and, most important, nonlinear. When I refer to the denuncia as a dialogized monologue, I urge us to listen to the various layers of practices and splinters of voices that constitute and exceed it and to acknowledge how its apparent univocality is the sign of the state's fantasy of recognition.

Promise's dilemma of having to discriminate between what can be translated and what needs to be left out points to the fact that although they are ventriloquists of the state—themselves robbed of their own individual voices—mediators have the power to use this position to various ends. As ventriloquists, they have mastered the state's language to the point that they can make their speech—and that of the woman they are translating for—coincide with it. Writing about the role of language in the colonial context, Fanon demonstrated that when the colonized were able to master the language of the colonizer, this very fact afforded them remarkable power. In his words: "A man who had a language consequently possesses the world expressed and implied by that language" (1967 [1952], 18). He means that to speak a language entails above all assuming a culture and taking on the weight of a civilization (17). In Fanon's view, this leads to the complete subjection of colonized subjects and their disappearance behind the white man's masks.

I read this part of Fanon's analysis differently. As I have illustrated, cultural mediators speaking the language of the host society—in this case, the bureaucratic jargon of legal apparatuses—suggests that they have achieved a certain degree of integration or assimilation in Italian political and social life. It also implies mastery of a powerful tool that can be used in ways that can betray the very politics of recognition instantiated by that language (Povinelli 2001). Promise, for instance, knew how the gaze of the state would produce a certain type of victim and was able to shape women's responses to fit it. While the cultural mediator's role—and power—in the police context implies making the other fit, her work differs greatly in the clinical context I describe in chapters 1 and 2. There, they are jugglers of words, and do not need to objectify practices and symbols for the sake of recognition. They create relations between multiple worlds—those of the patients and the doctors, those of dreams and death—and thus allow for the acknowledgment of multiplicity.

Many women who file criminal charges, too, use the act as a means to gain recognition and access to papers and rights; they inhabit the position of the puppet of the state without being fixed in it. Even Joy's stuttering and seeming inability to answer the cultural mediator's questions indicate a transgression of the discourse of the state, by pointing out the failure of the language to account for her experience and difference. Her stuttering speaks to her uneasiness about being framed in certain terms that comply with the categories set by the state. Silences or broken sentences are not opposed to language or to a full narrative but are another means of communication, another mode of expression that does not verbalize—or does so only partially—and does not say (Minh-ha 2011).

According to Simona Taliani, one of the Centro Fanon's therapists, Nigerian women in particular are interpellated by two "voices of authority": the law, with its investigative mode, and the voice of customary local law and its relations to families and their rules. As a therapist, Taliani (2012) argues that these two orders of the law collide on women's bodies (via symptoms, cuts, bites), and their psychological suffering is often a form of implicit criticism of the social order (see also Beneduce 2008). This is why their answers—both in the clinical and juridical contexts—are often fragmentary. They are caught in a bind where they are trying not to choose one voice of authority over the other.

Women's various and complex positions vis-à-vis the language of the rehabilitation program substantiate the state's discourse of victimhood and simultaneously question the truth claims at its core. The stories that converge in the denuncia are the result of several regimes of truth intersecting with each other; they produce a testimony that while not entirely truthful is nevertheless not a lie either.

THE SUBJECT REDEEMED

From the point of view of the law, the production of a testimony, in the form of a bureaucratic confession facilitated by someone else's voice—the cultural mediator's—allows for a second birth characterized by freedom from subjection and exploitation. The very process of the woman verbalizing her story in the text of the denuncia represents both the inscription and institution of what the state would like to believe is the truth about the other. After observing and listening to how the texts of denuncias took shape in the course of the interrogations, it occurred to me that the story produced in filing criminal charges uncannily resembled the process of religious confession, when sins are formally, but privately, admitted to the priest in order for the sinner to be redeemed. In religious confession, one tells one's story in order for sins to be remitted; in the denuncia, the woman tells her story in order to be admitted into the legal domain of society. The bureaucratic and confessional discourses overlap and create a diffuse discourse of the victim while also producing what I call a form of confessional recognition. Redemption and expiation, therefore, are central issues not only for Catholic groups involved in aid programs—as I show in depth in chapter 5—but also for the integration policies promoted by the state. Just as spiritual redemption is attained only after passing through different phases of purification—including remorse, confession, penance, acceptance of the consequences of one's sins, transformation of oneself through reform, and, finally, the forgiveness of God that washes one clean of those sins—the program of social protection and rehabilitation functions according to a logic of expiation. Filing criminal charges against one's exploiters figures as a form of social and bureaucratic confession, which is strictly connected to the will to pay one's debt to society through both penance and self-reform. The consequences women have to pay usually entail guilt, shame, and being suspended from life in the world—from work, earning money, and mastering their own everydayness. But, in the end, the state's grace is bestowed in the form of legal recognition and the testimony of the past can be erased, just as sins are washed away by God's grace.

For Foucault (1980), since the Middle Ages Western societies have established confession as one of the main techniques for the production of truth. A confessional outpouring since the nineteenth century has shaped various fields of knowledge, including justice, medicine, education, and love. Confessional technologies in modern Europe were based on the assumption that truths are hidden within the individual and, further, that revelation is purifying. The history of penance teaches us that by the very act of verbalizing sins, the individual expels them; by naming the transgression, one becomes clean of its consequences.

In a lecture at the Collège de France on Christian rituals of confession, Foucault (2003) sketched the history of the confession of sexuality by surveying the ritual of penance and the role of confession in it. Confession was not originally part of the ritual of penance; it became necessary and obligatory only in the twelfth century. In early Christianity, the remission of sins was possible only by virtue of the severity of the penalties the individual deliberately and voluntary inflicted on himself—or were publicly inflicted on him by the bishop—by adopting the status of penitent. The ritual of penance did not require private or public confessions of one's own transgressions. Starting in the sixth century, a new model of "tariffed" penance emerged. According to this new system of remission of sins—essentially based on a lay, judicial, and penal model—for every type of transgression there was a catalog of obligatory penalties. In order for the priest to apply the appropriate penance, the transgression needed to be stated, described, and recounted in all its detail, so that it could be matched with the corresponding "tariff." While this system of cataloged sins and penances marks the birth of confession as part of the ritual of penance, it also shows the secular and judicial origins of this practice, one that resembles the act of filing charges against oneself, of denouncing oneself as a sinner.

This history of confession, which illustrates the fundamental tie between legalistic approaches and sin and transgression, allows me to argue, in turn, that the religious and moral dimensions of confession (as a penalty that marks the beginning of the process of expiation) have reemerged as tools of recognition in the juridical practices of filing criminal charges and of the admission of crimes—in the denuncia. While these two practices are not the same, they still resonate with each other: a juridical logic echoes in confession, and a confessional logic echoes in the denuncia.

The act of denuncia is partly based on a form of confession during which women admit their position as "victims" of larger networks of exploitation. At the police station, women must emphasize that they were not aware they would become involved in prostitution. The dimension of "betrayal"—of having been misled and deluded by their traffickers—must emerge from the account as a proof of their innocence and unwillingness to work as prostitutes. What matters in terms of the law, what counts in order for a denuncia to be effective in obtaining a residency permit, is the intention behind the decision to migrate. If, through the narratives produced during the interrogation, a woman can prove that she did not plan to work in the sex industry, she has a better chance of qualifying as a victim. In the split between the actions performed (prostitution) and the intention behind them, the law can measure the degree of victimhood. Similarly, confession constitutes itself as an internal jurisdiction that evaluates the intentions behind actions—the inner dispositions of the individual rather than her external actions. Foucault (2003, 189) pointed out, "In the scholastic tradition it was known that not only actions but also intentions and thoughts had to be judged." Confession was aimed at stealing the desire for heresy from the subject before she even committed it.

While confession entails admitting one's own sins, the denuncia is about claiming and proving to be a victim. But the two overlap in the sense that the church needs a confession in order to make a denunciation. So the boundaries between confession and denuncia are blurred. To be recognized as a victim requires proving to be without sin, or at least showing purity of intent. Nonetheless, filing criminal charges in the context of the rehabilitation program does have a confessional connotation inasmuch as it marks the first step of a process of transformation and self-reform. The whole structure of the rehabilitation program is premised on the idea that women need to be reeducated and helped to become "autonomous and independent." This first step to a new and emancipated life seems to suggest the redemptive power of the denuncia as a first act of expiation, of the will to expel an impure act from one's life: the act of prostituting oneself. Unlike confession in the sixth century, the denuncia is not ruled by a set of penalties that meet corresponding criminal actions, primarily because women are not admitting their own crimes but someone else's. In this sense, confession and denuncia are two very different practices.

In filing criminal charges, women are exempt from responsibility: they ended up in prostitution because they were forced into it. And yet in the implementation of the rehabilitation program there is a tendency to set certain conditions, much like the penalties that ruled confession, on the women if they are to gain full access to rights and services. In other words, going through the program is a form of expiation of sins; it is the price women must pay to be recognized and accepted. They must demonstrate their full acceptance of the program, show their progress in becoming "autonomous" and capable of handling their lives away from the street, and further, they must show that they will not "relapse" into the networks of prostitution. The state, therefore, portrays the denuncia as the first step in a process of transformation, redemption, and conversion of one's lifestyle and comportment. Government officials and nuns monitor this process and have the power to judge whether it is successful.

Denuncia has a performative dimension inasmuch as it institutes the denouncer as a subject of the law by the very act of crafting the space for a specific "I" to enunciate a story.[14] In adhering to the category of the victim, foreign women are subjected to a set of rules and norms that delimit the field of both what can be said and what exceeds its limits. Certain words make things happen. In confession, too, words have a performative power. According to a confessional logic, by the very act of verbalizing sins and transgressions, the individual expels them; by naming the transgression one becomes pure and cleansed of its consequences. In this way truth is reestablished by eliminating any trace of untruthfulness, and redemption is possible. From the point of view of the state, the purpose of collecting accounts of women's experiences of migration and prostitution is mainly to unveil the "truth" of their stories, and thus to recognize them as victims rather than prostitutes. By inscribing women in the register of "the victim," the state positions them in a socially acceptable and legally commensurable category, thus making them digestible through translation. In this way, the state also produces its own legal truth.

Police officers exhibit an urge to know exactly how women became "victims" rather than "agents" of their migration destinies. They ask women pressing questions about the fake names that they used in the street, or about the expulsion papers they received while working as prostitutes. These actions point to the main purpose of the denuncia: to clear the foreign woman's story of any trace of falsehood. Just as sins are redeemed by being verbalized before the confessor, being a prostitute can be translated into victimhood—and thus lead to inclusion and recognition—by being verbalized in an official document. Both confession and denuncia represent a moment of redemption of the victim (and the prostitute) or of what is represented as such in different discursive fields. This redemptive logic at the heart of the victim rehabilitation program is one aspect of the politics of recognition through which the state translates difference into its own intelligible categories and thus redeems the other from her own untranslatable difference.

THE CONUNDRUM OF RECOGNITION

The denuncia tells a story that can be traded for recognition and inclusion. It is the inscription of a truth and a presence, both of which are partial and in tension with other truths and other ways of being present. It provides a narrative that is crafted through specific connections and chronological demands, aimed, ultimately, at forging connections between foreign women's unstable and transitory selves. My ethnography of denuncia shows that in the case of victims, the subject of the law can only be produced in translation. In the Police Department, the testimony is received in translation and becomes the pact a woman makes with the state. By means of the denuncia women provide a bureaucratic confession that, I argue, leads to a project of confessional recognition.

Inclusion is granted on the basis of an autobiographical account, the disclosure of a life that needs reformation to be fully recognized.

Yet a woman's testimony at the police station also happens by means of her own voice and language. The first phase of the testimony—when cultural mediators interrogate women—is conducted in the woman's mother tongue, but it must be translated into the state's language. Therefore, even when speaking in her native language, a layer of translation is at play. This first testimony—more fragmented and tentative—is lost in the process of making the account understandable in the bureaucratic language. This act of speech, which the institution does not hear, constitutes one order of testimony that escapes translation and exceeds the language of the law. What is said outside of translation represents a fundamental moment of enunciation and constitution of women's subjectivities. As I demonstrated in chapter 1, this part of testimony characterizes the space of the clinic more than the space of the police station.

In the text of the denuncia, testimonies are packaged and women are reduced to their stories, which, in turn, can be traded for a particular space of life. These stories are a gift; as such, they beget a counter-gift (Mauss 2000). They are consumed by the state in order to produce recognition of the other, of her difference and unfamiliarity (Agamben 1998). There is almost an ingestion of the other's stories in order to produce the counter-gift of inclusion and of access to rights and services. In the process of the objectification of the woman's story, the violence of denuncia—and of translation—reduces women to the social category of the victim.

In Fanon's analysis of the colonial situation, the colonized struggle against the colonizer's objectifying gaze and against a sovereign state apparatus, which defines the terms of the fight for recognition. He argues that the colonized are always determined from without, that their identity is the outcome of alienation, of being recognized in terms of something he is not. In other words, struggling to be recognized actually keeps the colonized marginal and alienated. Similarly, receiving countries' politics of recognition risk promising equal recognition to all—nationals and non-nationals—while defining the very terms of this inclusion by which the marginalized may be recognized. As Butler (1997) explains, the subject is bound to look for recognition of its own existence in categories that the dominant discourse has created. Such categories provide the individual with an opportunity for social intelligibility but at the price of a new form of subordination. Yet this subordination figures as

PART FOUR

Entering the Scene

The Shelter

Casa Effatà was on the first floor of a large building on a wide boulevard on the north side of the city. Unlike other shelters in Turin and elsewhere, which are located in convents, parishes, or private homes, Casa Effatà was a big, quite anonymous apartment. It had a spacious living room with a long rectangular table, some couches, and a TV set; a medium-sized kitchen; a long corridor that four bedrooms looked on to; two bathrooms; and a laundry room. The nuns had their own room and an office, which they shared with the volunteers. Although the building looked like a residential structure for families, the other apartments belonged to an organization that housed disabled people. Similar to the Immigration Office, which was located in what was once a hospice for the most marginal of the marginal, the uncanny urban planning of the shelter seemed to suggest that different kinds of "disabled" subjects should be contained together; it was a building for those in need of assistance.

When I started volunteering at Casa Effatà in September 2003, there were eight women living there. Over the course of my research, some of them moved into different kinds of shelters, one moved in with her boyfriend, others stayed longer than they had expected, and new ones moved in to start the program. I worked there two nights a week. The nuns agreed to let me volunteer and do my research at the same time. I would usually arrive at around 6:00 P.M., prepare dinner with the women, and then sit at the table to eat and converse. After dinner, we would clean up together and then watch TV or talk about different things that had happened during the day. In the morning, we would have an early breakfast and then they would go to work or attend trainings and classes. The women were somewhat aware of my position as both researcher and volunteer. I had explained to them that I was a student at an American university who was interested in their experiences as foreigners in Italy and that I was working on a book. They wondered why someone young and not a practicing Catholic would volunteer at the community. The other women doing shifts were either nuns or lay Catholic volunteers in their late fifties or early sixties, generally retired and eager to devote some of their time to community service.

Overall, my research did not interest the women much. They were much more interested in my life in America, the "dream land" for many of them. For the most part, I thought that they identified me as just another one of the volunteers at the community. At first, what distinguished me in their eyes was the fact that I was younger than the other volunteers, I smoked cigarettes with them on the balcony, I loved listening to their music, and I didn't make them pray before meals. My role was not to make them respect the rules; that was the job of the nuns and long-term volunteers. As Sister Maria framed it for me, I was "the young female presence to whom they could relate more, someone they could talk to about boyfriends and other issues they would not broach with the nuns." The nuns viewed me as marginal to their pedagogical mission because I was there for "research reasons" but felt I could still set a "good example" for the women. The nuns often lamented the fact that there were no young people who wanted to volunteer at the shelter, so they welcomed my presence. With time, the women started to ask questions about the book I was writing, and toward the end of my research, we did some formal interviews together, and some of them asked to have a copy of the recording.

I met Ana before any of the other women at the shelter. She was making lunch for the other guests when I first visited the home. I had a meeting with Sister Maria, the head of the shelter, to see if they would allow me to conduct part of my research there. Ana was not very friendly at first, but she made me an espresso and sat down at the table with me. She stared at me for a while, with an expression of defiance. "So, are you the new volunteer?" she asked. "Maybe," I answered, "if Maria agrees to it." "Do you know how to cook? It's important because all the other volunteers cook like shit and the nuns don't have a clue either." "I am okay in the kitchen. I wrote a cookbook a while ago, so I have an idea of how to make Italian food," I answered. "Ah, OK," she said, but by the time I asked whether she knew how to cook Romanian dishes she had already lost interest in our conversation. "Yeah, of course," she responded, and then she stood up and walked away. Getting the women's approval was going to be harder than getting the nuns' consent.

CHAPTER 5

Paradoxes of Redemption

*Translating Selves and Experimenting
with Conversion*

Casa Effatà housed women who were going through the second stage of
the state's rehabilitation program for victims of human trafficking.
Shelters like this provide an alternate living situation for women whose
previous residences usually are linked to networks of prostitution. As a
social worker explained to me, although Article 18 does not require
participants to live in shelters, in the actual implementation of victim
rehabilitation projects, these spaces are crucial to the "reintegration of
women into social life." Though usually funded by the Ministry of
Equal Opportunities and the municipality, shelters are often run by
Catholic associations, which tend to have easier access to additional
funding and the infrastructure to host people. This is why the associations involved in the implementation of Progetto Freedom in Turin are
largely Catholic.

The official description of Progetto Freedom—drafted for approval
by the ministry and the municipality—states its goals as (1) to emancipate victims of human trafficking from violence and exploitation; (2) to
protect them and assist in social reinsertion; (3) to help them reach
financial autonomy and psychophysical balance; and (4) to enhance the
network of associations and volunteers involved in the implementation
of the project.[1] *Accoglienza,* the practice of receiving and hosting foreign women in shelters exclusively created for their rehabilitation, is at
the core of the program and is central to the "process of emancipation
that aims to prevent the formation of other types of dependency."

The state has developed three different kinds of shelters that mirror the trajectory of the rehabilitation program, from the very first phase of "escaping from the street" to the last phase of "achieving complete autonomy."[2] The first type is known as an escape home (*casa di fuga*),[3] or house of initial intervention/reception (*casa di primo intervento/accoglienza*). Women come here as soon as they leave the street and agree to enter the program, and they usually stay for a period of from one to three months. As stated in the project description, during this period educators and women "set the foundations to build a project of social reintegration."[4] Here, women "get used to a 'normal' rhythm of life and experiment with sharing the responsibilities of the household." Volunteers or social workers accompany them to medical appointments, to file criminal charges, to apply for a residency permit, and to look for a job. Each woman also undergoes a "first assessment of her psycho-physical situation" in order to personalize the process of rehabilitation. Escape shelters tend to have strict rules: women cannot leave the house without an educator, they can only use their cell phones to call their families, and they spend most of their time inside to avoid encountering their exploiters.[5]

The second type of host community, known as "second reception," offers a more structured and stable situation. Women can stay for a longer period, usually from six months to a year. At this stage of the program, they are also required to take classes in Italian language, cooking, housekeeping, and using a computer. Those who are already trained in certain professional skills are supposed to look for a job.[6] This is when each woman's personalized project is put into practice, with the purpose of engaging her in "resocializing activities." Within the shelter, those who have been in the program for a longer period are asked to advise and orient the newcomers, introduce them to the rules of the community, and help them commit to the different household chores.

After this period, women have usually acquired a skill set that, in the logic of rehabilitation, indicates they have reached a good level of autonomy. This allows them to move to the third phase, also known as "guided living together." At this point they should have a source of income, be fluent in Italian, and know how to access services. They move into apartments, usually owned by the same associations that run the shelters. They pay rent (usually a symbolic amount) and are in charge of managing the household with very little supervision. This is the last step before complete autonomy, when they "go out into the world" and look for an apartment on their own, with little or no support from social services. The women live by themselves, in groups of two or three, and independently manage their time and activities.

According to Leopoldo Grosso, a psychologist involved in the training and supervision of nuns and lay volunteers, life at the host communities is "a rehearsal in adapting to a world that is different from the one experienced in prostitution." It is designed to be "an experience of accelerated acculturation," or a process of "learning a series of adjustments and expectations imposed by our society." Essentially, the shelter provides a stage for women to rehearse what it means to live in Italian society and to act out and personify the different roles they are expected to play, making this "play" their own. Grosso describes the months spent at the shelter as an "advanced class in learning how to engage in relations of reciprocity and interdependence, which greatly differ from the group or solitary experiences that characterized their time in prostitution." The shelter and its staff serve four fundamental functions. First, they model a different lifestyle, which "requires a radical transformation in their previous habits, both positive and negative. . . . In suggesting a change in lifestyle it is very important to function as mediators, in other words to be flexible about the cultures and people we work with; rigid models could be counterproductive." Second, they offer "containment and protection" for the women against the temptation to return to the streets. This happens through relationships with nuns, lay volunteers, and each other—particularly in dealing with the challenges of the program. Third, they support women in "defining a project about oneself aimed at reintegration in the social context." This is done by taking into account each woman's skills, qualities, and potential. In this process, "new identities are formed" based on past and current experiences, as well as actual job opportunities. Fourth, and importantly, especially during the first two phases of accoglienza, the shelter staff invests in personal relationships with the women, to show them affection and make them feel welcome. This creates trust and helps them regain self-esteem and confidence (Grosso 2003, 20–21). The shelter, then, is a space of transition where habits are abandoned, *habitus* transformed, norms redefined, and subjectivity rearticulated. The rules aim to help women disidentify from the life that they lived on the street and re-create a life that is dignified and worth living. In this process, other forms of autonomy and independence are articulated, and a new ethic, or *rapport à soi* (relationship to oneself), is incorporated (Foucault 1994a).

As stated in Article 18, victims of human trafficking are the responsibility of the state. Legislative enactments name them, define their legal status, and develop projects to rehabilitate them. The public rhetoric centers on a campaign of redemption in which foreign prostitution is portrayed as "one of the most insidious forms of contemporary slavery." Prostitutes are not seen as sex workers but as prostitut*ed*, even if they do not see themselves as victims. Furthermore, recovery is modeled on a bureaucratic rationality that conflicts with the lifeworld of the women and the multiple ruptures in their sense of self and community. The state portrays the transition from working in the streets to living in a community as a rupture that has the potential to redefine a woman's way of life and position in society. In the shelters, women are presented with new rules and modes of action that can help them form a new life in line with codes of purity and honor; they learn to live a "normal" and "good" life. These ruptures can be seen as moments wherein their own multiple subject positions are suspended, waiting to be relegitimized within the rhetoric of the victim who needs to be rescued and resocialized.

State documents portray shelters as liminal spaces that enable the performance of what resembles a transformation ritual, or the translation of a lost subject into one in need of redemption. Here, all identifications with life and work on the street are suspended, and alternative practices are encouraged in order to create a new space of individuation. "We have to help them cut all the ties with their past," is a refrain I often heard during meetings and interviews with nuns or social workers. Nonetheless, as the psychologist Grosso pointed out, disengagement with the past implies an understanding of that very past in the larger context of the woman's life story, her dreams of migration, the disenchantment that resulted from it, and the traumatic experiences she has endured. The shelter provides women with a resting place for reflection where they can gradually rearticulate their relationship to the world, where time and space are devoted to reforming one's relationship to oneself and others. One Catholic nun involved in the program once explained to me that "women are taken care of in the entirety of their being"; not only do they enter the realm of legality by acquiring a residency permit, but they are supposed to undergo a process of radical transformation of spirit, body, and mind. This transformation is the responsibility of the state, which, using the mediating role provided by Catholic associations, is in charge of "rebirthing" foreign women as socially acceptable subjects.

Catholic groups identify foreign prostitutes as "the poorest of the poor," "the most marginal of the marginalized," and therefore in need of assistance. In several conversations, nuns told me that over the past fifteen years, with the increase in illegal migration in Italy and the spread of prostitution as a phenomenon mostly affecting the female migrant population, their mission to help those in need radically shifted to victims of human trafficking. Historical and legal events in 1999 and 2000 became particularly important catalysts for Catholic associations to focus their social interventions mainly on these women. In 1999, the Regulation for the Implementation of Article 18 of the Immigration Law was released. As I explained earlier, the Immigration Law had been revised in 1998, and Article 18 was one of the changes added to the preexisting law (the Martelli Law) as a way of recognizing foreign prostitution as a real and pressing social issue. Migration, human trafficking, and foreign prostitution had been increasingly central in public debates around security and human rights over the previous ten years. In the 1990s, Italy witnessed a radical increase in the number of incoming illegal migrants, and foreign prostitution became more visible. This led to a revision of the existing law on immigration and to the creation of new categories of foreigners in need of legal recognition and protection. "Victims of human trafficking" was one of these categories. Funds started to become available for the protection of women who qualified as victims, and associations already informally involved in assisting foreign prostitutes could turn their aid projects into official programs funded by the Ministry of Equal Opportunities and the immigration offices of various municipalities.

Moreover, for Catholics, 2000 was the Holy Year of the Jubilee. Established as an important Catholic celebration in 1300 by Pope Bonifacio VIII, the Jubilee is celebrated every fifty years. Traditionally, it is a time of purification, during which seekers refresh their faith and their commitment to the church. It was on this occasion that some Catholic associations gathered to reflect on the meaning of their commitment to the church and their mission to assist the poor. The main questions they asked themselves were, "Who are today's poor? How do we make the gospel manifest in our work with the marginalized? What does it mean to carry on the mission of evangelization today?" All these questions found an answer, at least for most Catholic groups, in the victim of human trafficking. The Catholic discourse of emancipating victims overlapped and, moreover, found some resonance in human rights discourses, which identified the "poorest of the poor" as foreign prostitutes.

In this chapter I write about the encounter between Italian Catholic nuns and foreign prostitutes in the context of one of these shelters. I reflect on people's trajectories, where selves and forms of belonging are rearticulated through narratives of purification, transformation, and redemption. At issue is not just the social suffering and displacement that women face at different moments in their migration trajectories, or how these experiences are used to create and legitimize new forms of recognition on the part of the state. I also explore how, through their work with former prostitutes, Catholic nuns develop an understanding of redemption as a secular project of saving lives in line with state's projects of recognition. Nuns are also engaged in their own self-purification, as well as a project of societal transformation, that paradoxically positions the foreign woman as a confessor and necessary means of expiation. In this sense, here I approach the issue of the confessional from a different angle and bring nuns and foreign women into conversation about what it means to be free and redeemed.[7]

EFFATÀ: "OPEN YOURSELF" AND BE OPEN TO THE OTHER

When I first met with the nun in charge of Casa Effatà, she explained that they came up with the name of the community along with the women who were living there when it opened. They did not want to call it a "community" but a "home" (casa), because the nuns' purpose was not "to extend assistance to the women but to live alongside them as a family, to help and support them in their growth." "*Effatà*," Sister Maria explained, "is the imperative of the verb 'to open.'" It is an Aramaic word spoken by Jesus and appears in the account of a miracle in the Gospels (Mark 7:34). In this miracle, Jesus was wandering outside of Galilee, where he encountered a man who was deaf and dumb. People asked him to heal the man with the power of his touch. Jesus placed two fingers on his eyes and touched his tongue with some saliva. While looking at the sky, Jesus sighed and said, "Effatà!" (Open yourself). Immediately, the man's ears opened up and the knot in his tongue was released. From that moment on, he was able to hear and speak again.[8]

Run by a group of Catholic nuns with past experience assisting marginalized Italian women—mostly single mothers and former prostitutes—Casa Effatà hosted six to eight women at a time. The main rules of the house state that each guest is required to (1) follow and respect the "personal program" agreed upon by the social workers and the nuns; (2) ask for permission to go out during the day and, once a week, at night; (3) wait until having been in the program for a certain time, when mutual trust between the nuns and the woman has been established, before going on out-of-town trips; (4) go on nighttime outings only on Saturdays; (5) eat lunch and dinner at the shelter with the other guests; (6) watch TV only in free time and no later than 10:30 P.M.; (7) turn off cell phones during meals and return them to the nuns at night; (8) never give out the address or phone number of the host community, for personal safety and the protection of other guests, unless the nuns grant permission; (9) introduce a "boyfriend" to the nuns and obtain their permission before accompanying him on an outing; (10) dress simply and appropriately; (11) not use alcohol or drugs; and (12) participate in preparing the meals and cleaning the house.

As laid out in the mission statement, the main purpose of the association is to extend "social solidarity" to victims of human trafficking: "Through hospitality we give back to the women the dignity of being a capable and autonomous subject, able to integrate themselves—through educational and professional trainings—in the socio-professional life" of the country. Thus, the shelter "provides an effective response to the spreading phenomenon of prostitution by setting the example of evangelical love, social responsibility, and solidarity."[9] The rules and the mission statement are similar to those of other Catholic shelters and are in line with the guidelines and advice provided by mental health practitioners and social workers. Women's progress is measured on the basis of their ability to "cut the ties with the past," adjust to life within the community, integrate new relationships of "reciprocity" as opposed to relationships of "exploitation" within their lives, learn the language and the skills that make them ready to find a job, and, finally, reach a psychological balance within themselves.

In this domain, the discourses of law, religion, and psychology both overlap and contradict. Nuns often resort to the language of "trauma" to talk about women's experience of prostitution. To the nuns, the representation of the foreign woman as victim evokes traumatic events that have punctuated women's lives and reduced them to the condition of slaves. On the other hand, ethno-psychiatrists—to whom nuns turn for advice—argue that for most women it is not the experience of prostitution per se that represents a traumatic event but other factors such as finding out that they are HIV-positive, knowing that their families back home are threatened by their traffickers, or the lack of social networks in Italy. As I showed in chapters 1 and 2, in the clinical setting ethno-psychiatrists also collect stories of prostitution and migration, which they understand in the broader context of other histories and medical systems. A practitioner at the Centro Fanon explained to me, "Many foreign women experience sexuality differently and in discordant ways: it serves a specific end and is one of the steps in the project of migration." When ethno-psychiatrists supervise lay and religious volunteers in their work with victims, they often mediate between their understanding of the women's lives and experiences and the nuns' concepts of trauma and the rehabilitation process. In my role at the shelter, I found myself in a similar position.

LIFE AT THE SHELTERS: BECOMING "SOMEBODY" DIFFERENT

On my first day at the shelter, Ana and I ended up spending the whole afternoon together. As a way of testing my abilities as a volunteer and my motivation to help, the nuns asked me to accompany her to several dentists' offices to find out about possibilities for an internship. She wanted to be trained as a dental assistant. It was her dream job, but it was very difficult to find dentists who were interested in offering employment. "Even if you have a residency permit, they don't give you a job," she explained to me with the same expression she had when she served me coffee earlier in the morning: somewhat disenchanted and defiant. Nonetheless, we ventured to the city and stopped at a few dentists' offices to gather information. This is how we started to get to know each other. Over time I met the other women, but with Ana I developed a level of closeness that I did not have with the others. Maybe because she took me under her wing and introduced me to the other seven women in the shelter; maybe because she was older than the others and in search of an even older friend; maybe because she didn't have an Italian friend and thought I could become one; or maybe just because of the mysterious chemistry we have with some people and not with others.

At twenty-two, Ana was the oldest at the shelter and the one who had been in the program for the longest time. She had migrated from Romania one year before we met and had worked in the streets as a prostitute for approximately three months. When she left Romania, the people who helped her said she would go to work as a baby-sitter in Italy. She knew that was not true. She figured she would be a sex worker in a nightclub—just as many other Romanians had before her in Greece, Japan, and Italy—but expected to work for rich men who were more interested in company than sex. Ana thought she would do it for a month or two, make a lot of money, and then go back home. But she ended up doing it for a few more months and on the streets. One night, the police broke into her apartment and took her and her friend Rita to the police station, where she was forced to file criminal charges against her pimps. She told me that later she felt very guilty about it. "They didn't treat me badly," she explained. Even Sister Maria referred to her as a "privileged prostitute" because she had a lot of money and her exploiters treated her like "a princess." She thus entered the program of rehabilitation partly against her will. She did say that working on the streets was dangerous and tiring, but she never perceived it as a traumatic moment in her life. By the time I met her, she had decided not to go back to Romania. She just could no longer see herself returning home. While she was still working in the street, she met Michele, a client twenty years older, and she had fallen in love with him. Her dreams now were to have a family with him and to become either a dental assistant or a nurse in Italy.

Rita, Ana's friend, lived at Casa Effatà when I started to do research there, but she soon left to move in with her boyfriend. She and Ana described their relationship as a "street friendship," and they often said, "We walked the same street." This was both metaphorical and not. In Italian *fare la stessa strada* (to walk the same street) in this context means different things: metaphorically, it means, "we had the same experience, we followed the same trajectory," but it also literally meant, "we worked as prostitutes on the same street." They left Romania at the same time, and then in Italy they shared an apartment, a street corner, and pimps. The police caught them on the same night they filed criminal charges. They spent two months in an escape shelter before arriving at Casa Effatà.

Another Romanian woman at the shelter, Micaela, was nineteen years old. She was very beautiful, and very conscious of it. When the nuns described her to me they said she was "obsessive" about not gaining weight, always wore designer clothing, and went to the hairdresser every other week. She was very smart and learned to speak fluent Italian quickly. She had been in Italy for a year and in the program for four months. Like Ana, she left Romania thinking she would go back with a lot of money after a few months of work in nightclubs, only to find herself working the streets at night. She once told me she had left Romania "because all the intelligent Romanians leave in order to find a job or to study." Since she mastered Italian particularly well, she easily found a job as a cultural mediator at a municipal office that offered medical services to migrants. She made 500 Euros a month, which, she lamented, barely covered her "expenses for the hairdresser, clothes, perfumes, and some comfort food that the nuns don't provide." Although she had a job, she was not allowed to move into the third-stage community because, according to the nuns, she was still "emotionally immature and unstable, and therefore not completely autonomous." Like Ana and Rita, she had an Italian boyfriend. They had met on the street; he was a client, and they "fell in love with each other." But falling in love was forbidden by her pimps. When they found out that she was seeing one client more regularly than the others and for longer periods of time, they started to threaten and beat her. One night she escaped with the help of a client and found refuge at his house. She later went to social services and entered the program.

Fatima was from Morocco. She was also an "Article 18 woman," as nuns and social workers referred to those who qualified as victims of human trafficking, but her story was different from that of the majority of the women in the program. She had not worked as a prostitute but was involved in a network of drug dealers in the neighborhood of San Salvario, near the main train station of Porta Nuova.[10] She had been in Italy for ten years with her aunt's family but had escaped from them because they treated her "like a servant." She told me that her mother sent her to Italy to continue her studies, but once she arrived, her aunt sent her own children to school and kept her at home to help with the housekeeping. Her uncle attempted to abuse her sexually, but no one in the family ever believed her version of the story when she decided to reveal it. She found a Moroccan boyfriend and moved in with him. Through him she became involved in drug dealing. She trafficked drugs from one part of the neighborhood to the other. One day, the police caught her in a hotel room with a lot of heroin hidden in her clothes. They later caught the other people involved in the dealing, and her boyfriend declared her innocent. Thus, she qualified as victim of human trafficking. When we met, she had been in the program for two months.

Diana was from Romania, too. The other Romanians in the house referred to her as "the gypsy" because she had a Roma background. She was caught stealing from a supermarket several times, and social services put her in the rehabilitation program. Since she was not involved in prostitution, she was a different kind of victim. Through her, the police were able to trace a network of gypsies involved in "criminal activities," which qualified her to be a victim. The story that the nuns told about her involved a cousin who had brought her to Italy with the promise of finding her a job as a baby-sitter and then forced her to steal. When in Italy, she became pregnant and had a baby, Rebecca, who had been given to a foster family and was being considered for adoption.[11] When we met, Diana was working as a waitress in a pizzeria and visiting her daughter once a week. Over the course of time, the visits to the child became less frequent. The social workers and educators who observed her interactions with the child gave her negative evaluations, and the judge in charge of the case was inclined to give Rebecca up for adoption. The nuns were very supportive of Diana and told the judge that they guaranteed their support if the child could go back to live with her mother.

Varonika was from Poland. She arrived at the community a month after I started doing fieldwork there. She had been in Italy for two years and had worked as a prostitute for the same length of time. When I met her she was angry at everyone: the nuns, the social workers, the volunteers, and the other women at the community. The day she moved into Casa Effatà, Sister Maria asked me to take her for a walk because she seemed very nervous and aggressive with the other women. We walked for some time in the neighborhood, then sat on a bench in a park and smoked a cigarette. "I can't stand it! Everyone tells me what to do! It is just like being in the street with the pimps . . . there is no difference . . . and then they call it 'freedom,'" she said as she frantically smoked her cigarette, looking around in a restless attempt to focus her gaze somewhere. I asked her whether she had lived in a shelter before Casa Effatà. "Yes," she replied, "I was in that one where all the women were Nigerian, and I hated it. They smell bad, and they make a mess in the kitchen! There were mice and cockroaches everywhere. And I had fights with them. So they threw me out."

During my shifts at the shelter, the topic of conversation with the women varied. We often talked about their frustration in the program and the difficulties relating to the nuns. At night, after dinner, they would often complain about something that had happened during the day or about the shelter's rules. Quotidian happiness and discontents were the pretexts for other conversations about the hopes and disenchantments that punctuated our lives. I saw them struggling with the rules and the norms of the shelter, but sometimes they shared their experience of it "as a family" where they had found refuge. Yet on other occasions, it was "like being in a prison."

One night, during one of my shifts, we were all sitting on the couches, bored with the TV but not tired enough to go to sleep. The night before, Sister Maria had called a house meeting with all the women during which they discussed rules, new and old, and how they were not being respected. I was there, taking notes and sitting on the margins of the group. I noticed that the women who were newer to the shelter were more resistant to the rules, while the ones who had spent more time there had almost become the gatekeepers of norms and conducts. There was nothing particularly original in my observation, but I wondered how they would talk about rules in the absence of the nuns. So I posed the question later. How did they feel about the rules? Were they fair? Did they help in the process of transformation that the rehabilitation program was supposed to produce in their lives? What was it like to live at the shelter? I was trying to understand whether they thought the program prepared them for the outside world, as the state expected, and if or how they felt transformed after living at the shelter. Did they really feel the need to change or to be rescued at all? An animated conversation followed. Here are some moments of it.

> *Micaela:* In the beginning it is difficult, it is like being in prison. It is difficult for people like Ana and Rita who did it for pleasure. They had to denounce their own friends and knew what they were going to do here in Italy. They were treated well, taken to the beach for the weekend, had nice clothes, beauty treatments, went dancing at night, had a good time. For me too it was difficult, but I wanted to leave my pimps. . . . Sister Maria stresses me out like they stressed me out when I was on the street. She is violent when she asks you to do things. Then there is the rule of going to the shrink when you get into the shelter, for five sessions. But she is the one who needs to go to the shrink. She's the one who needs to change, not me. She orders me around. It is like when I was in the street when they forced me to do things I didn't want to do.

> *Cristiana:* Did it become easier to follow rules with time?

> *Micaela:* Yes. In the beginning I didn't know how to cook, wash my clothes, iron, clean the house. I was like a little animal. I didn't know how to wash my underwear, so I would throw a pair of panties away every day. Because there are rules, now I feel better, I know how to do all these things and I feel calmer than before. Even if it feels like a prison sometimes, the rules are good . . . if you want to get on the right track. . . . Being a prostitute is easy. You make a lot of money, sometimes without having sex. It is easy money. Entering a normal life is ten thousand times more difficult. You need to have rules for that.

> *Varonika:* When I entered the shelter, the most difficult thing was not having money! I couldn't stand it. I had everything in the shelter, but I felt like it was a shitty life. The first two weeks they didn't let me go out by myself because they thought I was still going to beat the street. They didn't let me use my cell phone and I couldn't live without it. They would give it to me only to speak to my mother.

> *Ana:* I felt that the escape home had many more rules than here. There you could never use the cell phone, you could go out one or two hours a day,

always accompanied by a volunteer. It was shitty! I felt so bad there. I used a cell phone secretly. Yes, because it was like being in jail, if you want something, you can always get it secretly. You want cigarette, and there is someone who smuggles them in the jail. It is the same. I had a hidden cell phone that I used from inside the closet so that no one could hear me. We were also forced to speak Italian: "If you don't speak Italian you go to your room!" But here [meaning at Casa Effatà] it is like being in a family and the other women are like sisters. Sister Maria, she is like a manager. I don't know why she has become a nun.

Micaela: Because she likes power!

The issue of power came up in other conversations. Ana once shared that when she worked on the street it was tiring and dangerous, but she also had fun because she had a lot of money, and "there was nothing that I could not afford to buy or do." Power also implied the possibility of choosing clients and what services they would perform. Power, even for those who had very difficult and traumatic prostitution experiences, meant that they were able to send money to their families back home. This is what emancipation meant to them: emancipation from poverty, from families who had been implicated in sending their daughters to Europe in search of success while knowing—or not—that it would involve working in the sex industry. Also, emancipation involved imagining where money and power could take them or what it could get them: wealth and the possibility of improving one's status back home, or in Italy; and acquiring certain things that had been objects of their desire even before they left home. Moreover, power characterized the experience with other women in the street: it determined who controlled one block, who was the leader or madam of the street, and how those relationships changed over time, allowing the old timers to move up in the hierarchy of the street.

In the shelter, they had no access to money, men, buying, or selling. Those who had been in the program for a while said that their bodies did not display that power any longer. I asked them what they meant by that. Ana responded one day by taking me to her bedroom and pulling out a pair of black, pointy, high-heeled boots. She placed them in the middle of the room and announced, "This was Ana when she used to work in the street." Then she took out a pair of hiking boots that she had recently bought at the neighborhood market for work (at the time she worked as a cleaning lady at a convent), "And this is Ana now!" I smiled at her sense of humor. Then she took out her nail polish. I had asked her if she would give me a manicure, and she had agreed. She displayed several expensive brands of nail polish, perfumes, and makeup: Christian Dior, Chanel, Armani. I was impressed. She had a disenchanted expression and said, "I don't use these things anymore. I don't remember the last time I did my nails." "Why don't you do your nails anymore?" I asked. "For who? For the nuns?! I clean the floors now, and my nails get snagged easily." She continued, "I was beautiful when I was a prostitute; I was skinnier, I walked sexily, I was always made up, had beautiful clothes. Look at me now! I am fat, I walk like a hiker, and I wear jeans and T-shirts all the time."

I had this kind of conversation with other women in the program, too. Micaela often complained about not having the money to take care of her body. She was very careful about not gaining weight and always managed to look elegant and made up. But she could no longer afford massages, the hairdresser, and pedicures. Both Micaela and Ana also lamented that although they felt more beautiful as prostitutes, their bodies were constantly at risk. They felt sorry for their bodies. "You risk and expose your body for what? Luckily we haven't caught any diseases," one of them said. Other women had very violent experiences while they worked in prostitution. Their bodies were beaten and used, and the power of seduction that it might have exercised on the clients was not enough to make them feel powerful and in control. They wanted to leave the street, and yet the sense of empowerment that money gave them had a strong hold on them. As undocumented prostitutes, they were no one and invisible to the state, but they had the means to help their families and make money for themselves. They were "visible" in other ways—to clients, to other women with whom they would compete for the territory, to their madams. They felt empowered vis-à-vis their families. Now they were being turned into "somebody" more acceptable in Italian society, but they often felt powerless, unable to face their families and reveal their current situations. I was struck by how dissonant some of their perceptions of emancipation were from the state's definition of freedom, and how their sense of autonomy could be simultaneously enhanced and reduced by the program. They translated the state's project into their own experiences in ambivalent ways.

In some cases, family members were not aware of their ties with prostitution. Ana and Micaela told their families that they worked as baby-sitters. Other women told different stories in order to cover up their work on the streets. In some cases, as I explained in chapter 4, family members were involved in the decision itself. In either case, coming out of prostitution meant not having money to send home. This often resulted in feelings of guilt and shame for being unable to pursue dreams of emancipation for themselves and their families. Relations with home became unbearable. Family pressure for help, the inability to fulfill this request, and the frustration of "having failed" often led the women to stop communicating with home.

The ambivalence of this relationship to their homes is also what makes telling stories about them difficult. The nuns often lament that they do not know enough about the women's pasts, while ethno-psychiatrists attempt to create a clinical space that facilitates telling these stories. Women are frequently caught between the desire to forget and the desire to tell a story that they can own. The nuns try to provide a space for this tension to play out.

DIVINE PROVIDENCE AND RECOGNITION

And forgive our trespasses, as we forgive those who trespass against us. And lead us not into temptation, but deliver us from evil.
—The Our Father

The nuns at Casa Effatà explained to me that the first type of community—the escape home—served the same function as an emergency room. They described it as a place where educators and volunteers should not ask women questions about their past but instead develop a relationship of trust that would sustain them later as they go through the program. It is also the time to start the education process in which, as a sister stated, women learn that "the night is for sleep and the day is for work." Women must acquire new habits and routines and, most important, prove that they have "real intentions" to enter the program. Once this is assessed, they can move into a shelter of second reception, like Casa Effatà. Four nuns and four lay Catholic volunteers rotate shifts in the community to make sure that the women are supervised twenty-four hours a day, although none of them reside permanently there.

Unlike at the escape house, the nuns described the time spent at the second reception shelter as a moment not only for rehabilitation but also for reflection and self-inquiry, to contemplate one's true purpose in life and come to terms with the past. For the nuns, prostitution is an unexpected outcome of migration, something that disrupted an otherwise linear and transparent project. Sister Chiara, who had long experience in working in this domain, described the women's first few months in the program as the most challenging time, in which they need to be "remodeled, reset, remotivated" (*rimodellate, reimpostate, rimotivate*). In the words of Petra, a young Franciscan nun, shelters provide the space and time for women to "re-own their past." She thought that women who prostituted themselves were "complete slaves, with no freedom of choice." Thus, it is only by recuperating a narrative that gives meaning to that moment in the larger context of their lives that they can start a process of healing and reeducation.

Sister Maria, head of Casa Effatà, described the psychological conditions of women who have just entered the program as damaged: "They are twisted inside; they have a wound that hasn't healed. Until they heal it and take responsibility for it, you can't put anything on them because it hurts. Only then can we start to teach them something." In the same conversation, she told me about an illness she had suffered for many years that forced her to revisit her whole life in light of her condition as a sick person: "Being ill taught me a lot; it taught me that I was not in control of myself and my life. I had to come to terms with it and take responsibility for it, re-own my life in light of my sickness. It was a form of redemption." Having often heard the nuns raise the question of redemption in relation to the process women needed to undergo in order to emancipate themselves, I asked her what she meant by it. She answered that it was not about moral redemption but about "taking responsibility for the moments of suffering and looking at what positive learning they have brought to you." I began to understand Maria's statements as her way of explaining a wounded self that opens up to new forms of identification. She recognized that a traumatic event can have a blocking effect on the self, and she made sense of this blockage by translating it into her experience of illness. Redemption here is not used strictly in a spiritual sense, but as a bodily transformation of the self, a rearticulation of subjectivity that takes place through physical changes.[12]

At other times the question of redemption was raised more specifically in relation to the issue of freedom. Nuns would evoke this term to point out the need to come to terms with the experience of exploitation. They meant redemption from subjugation, from victimhood, from enslavement. In the words of Sister Romana: "We must help women re-own their dreams of migration, their project of emancipation, and show them that they can be the agent of it." In the nuns' perspective, this would lead to autonomy, which, as part of the migration trajectory, certainly did not correlate with the will to work as a prostitute. In listening to their conceptions of redemption, I noted an interesting parallel between the nuns's idea that the victim cannot have agreed to her own slavery and the state's discourse. For the juridical apparatus, it is tantamount that the victim had purity of intention and that there is no proof of her complicity in prostitution. Any allusion to the contrary needs to be effaced in the testimony deposed at the police station. Both religious and juridical discourses function through the logic of purity of intention, thus fixing the subject in the victim/agent dichotomy and making redemption the accomplishment of the subject who has taken responsibility for her own life.

The nuns resist believing that women might have been aware of the prospect of working in prostitution before leaving their countries. For them, these women are victims on many different levels. By considering them as such, they spare them the burden of being "sinners." On several occasions, I asked about the relationship between sin and redemption. For me, there could not be redemption unless one had committed a sin, and therefore the logic of the victim and redemption was paradoxical and at odds in the nuns' narratives. While the possibility of retaining purity despite prostitution is inherent in the rhetoric of the victim—who was forced to sell her body and sexual services—the nuns' practices and conceptions of the rehabilitation program revolve around the issue of transforming the victim not only into an agent of her own life but also into a person who is "better fitted" to society and cleansed of her past deeds. In this sense, the nuns' project coincides with the state's secularized aim at confession and moral expiation of the victim. Although she is a victim, she is simultaneously treated as a sinner in need of redemption. "What do you think of women who make the decision to work as prostitutes? Do you think they are sinners?" I once asked Sister Paola, one of the nuns in charge of an escape home. She was a young nun who belonged to a newly formed Franciscan order. She always struck me as a very progressive and politically engaged person, very informal in her demeanor, and open to talking about different issues related to women's sexuality. Shortly before having this conversation, she had told me about women in the program who wanted to have abortions and how, although the question was very troubling to her, she found ways to support them. On other occasions, we had talked about the issue of condoms and how she encouraged women to use them with their boyfriends, although this question raised contradictory feelings in her. On the particular question about the relationship between sin and prostitution, she answered with no hesitation: "I don't think a woman who is mentally healthy can make such a conscious decision. Even those who say they want to work as prostitutes must have some psychological problems. So I think they too are victims of some sort and have no control over their lives." She went on to explain that several Catholic groups would answer my question differently: "Some of my co-sisters see all the women in the program as sinners who need to expiate their sins. I personally believe they are slaves who have nothing to expiate but only freedom to regain." Sister Paola's words reinforce the issue of purity of intention and show how the religious paradigm does not allow her to see beyond the victim/agent categories of recognition; one cannot be simultaneously a victim and an agent, a sinner and mentally ill, without contradicting oneself.

In the nuns' narratives, women are spared from the status of sinner but nonetheless must undergo a process of radical self-transformation to become autonomous subjects. They are slaves and need to be reeducated in order to become agents of their lives. They pass through a process that includes being disciplined in how to dress, eat, cook, speak, work, and relate to others as well as to oneself. They should also explore forgiveness for the harm that has been inflicted on them and find paths of redemption. The shelter provides a space where, at first, time is suspended and women can focus on introspection and exploring new forms of life. This near-monastic life suspends the time and power of the state, which requires that women be rehabilitated on a specific schedule. Thus, the nuns are in some way suspending the cannibalistic function of the state that I explore in the previous chapter, offering women protection from the outside world. Nonetheless, when women are disciplined in bodily and moral practices in order to be transformed into independent subjects, it becomes clear how the nuns' practices are also inscribed in the state's biopolitical project of redeeming lives. In this sense, the nuns use the state's categories to accomplish the task of rehabilitation. In their work with the women, the nuns recognize the redemptive aspect of state power and turn redemption into a secular project of saving lives. In this political form of redemption, saving lives occurs by assigning state categories of recognition—victim, agent, prostitute, migrant—that make all lives translatable into one form of life, one that needs to be redeemed, rehabilitated, and converted. Therefore, it is not just the state that takes up a confessional logic in its project of saving victims. Religious institutions are equally influenced by the juridical apparatus and its urge to define what the good life is, and which life is worth living and redeeming. It is through the shelter's discipline and rules that the processes of rehabilitation and secular redemption initiated by the bureaucratic confession of denuncia can finally be realized.

THE VICTIM: AN EXPERIMENT WITH REDEMPTION

In my conversations with the women at the shelter, we often discussed the question of power and the meaning women assigned to the shelter's rules. Initially, I thought it was important to understand why a society would delegate the task of re-educating foreign prostitutes to religious women. How could these disparate worlds relate? At the same time, I had in mind what the psychologist Carl Gustav Jung had theorized about the shadow.[13] So, one of the first questions that emerged for me from the encounter between nuns and former prostitutes was if they symbolically function as shadows of one another? In their radically opposite ways of experiencing sexuality and femininity, are they on an unconscious level projecting onto one another, or do they want to resemble one another?

When I explicitly asked the women for their opinions about the fact that shelters for former prostitutes were run by Catholic nuns, and if that was a problem for them, Micaela responded:

> Yes and no. Yes because in a way they live in another century. They want you to be on time, to speak properly, to go out with your boyfriend one night a week, and then they are surprised if you tell them that you sleep with him. "Oh, you had sex with him!?" What do they think? Wake up! I am a whore . . . or at least I was. Or if I stay out late at night they complain. But I used to live at night and sleep in the day. They want you to behave like a virgin. They can teach you how to be innocent and to follow rules, but they don't know how to prepare you for the world as it is today, they are incapable of telling you of the risks of falling in love, if you lose yourself for a man. But it is also good that the nuns are running the shelter because other people, normal women who have a family, a husband who maybe sleeps with prostitutes, they might treat you with no respect. I think that the nun always has a lot of power over the prostitute.

"In what sense?" I asked.

"In the sense of respect."

"Whose respect? You have respect for them, or they have respect for you?" I pushed, to which she responded:

> Both. Sometimes in front of a nun you don't want to use a certain language, like, "Fuck off, you don't fucking understand anything." You restrain yourself. While with some of the volunteers who are normal women, you want to say, "Fuck you, you cook like shit, don't come and do volunteer work here!" I don't understand the volunteers who want to help us. At least the nuns, they have sacrificed themselves to take the evil away from the world, so they accept working with us, it is their mission. Also, I think it is best that nuns run the community because with a normal woman you may feel jealous for the kind of life she has. With the nun, what do you have to be jealous of?

Varonika added, "When I heard that I was going to live with nuns I was scared. They scared the shit out of me."

During the supervisions at the Centro Fanon, when nuns talked to ethno-psychiatrists about the difficulties of relating to the women's sexuality, they argued that having lay volunteers would create a balance in the shelter. People with families could provide an alternative model of morality for the women. I remember listening to the comments of one ethno-psychiatrist on this issue. He agreed that if nuns were the only gatekeepers of morality and sexuality—the only role model that women had for what it meant to "transform oneself" through the rehabilitation program—chances were that reorienting themselves in Italy, in a different cultural environment, could become a very disorienting experience.

The women voiced their ambivalence to their interactions with the nuns. On the one hand, it is easier to confront a consecrated woman than a married one because, as Micaela put it, "there is nothing to be jealous of with a nun." Although some of the women I met at shelters for victims had developed a fantasy of becoming nuns in order to purify themselves from their past (and therefore had associated the power of redemption with the image of the nun), for many of them, the nun represented a figure to both respect and disrespect. Micaela said, "Nuns have nothing to teach us about real life, they cannot prepare us for that." They are distant, and yet so close to the women. They end up representing a mirror that only partially reflects back. They are more like a repository of authority, the gatekeepers of rules and norms. Micaela's reference to the nuns' inability to understand falling in love with a man points to a desexualized vision of the nuns. Yet de Certeau (1996) has shown the opposite: the whole discourse of the nunnery is precisely about how to lose oneself for a man (Jesus, embodied in his deputies—the confessor, the director, etc.). In this sense, Jung's idea of the shadow reinforces de Certeau's argument about the sexual desire at the heart of the nuns' longing for a union with Christ, and it teaches us how nuns and women may be reflecting sexualities that are more similar than they appear at first glance.

The lay volunteers, on the other hand, can become dangerous mirrors that reflect an image of what women want for themselves: a family, a job, financial security, and so on. The women who volunteer at the shelter may also feel threatened by the image of the prostitute, by the phantasm of betrayal, and may use this projection to harm the women themselves. I once asked Fatima about her take on the program and, in particular, on the volunteers. She answered, "We are only an experiment, this is what we are to them. They only come here to feel clean inside, or because they have nothing better to do." The lucidity of this statement stayed with me for a long time. It reminded me of some childhood experiences in the Catholic milieu and my early reactions to the underlying morality of fixing people's lives, making people better, helping, assisting. Most of the time, I sympathized with the women and their reactions to the nuns. At the same time, I was intrigued by how the nuns, too, were experimenting with what redemption could become when approached as a secular project of turning victims into agents, prostitutes into autonomous subjects. I began to understand the nuns' approach to this secular form of redemption as yet another practice of recognition that fits women into categories that religious and juridical institutions can understand so that difference can be made familiar.

CONVERSION: ANOTHER PRACTICE OF TRANSLATION

Although never addressed explicitly, the logic of conversion emerges from the central practices of the program aimed at supporting women's independence. This same logic—and its implications for questions of purity and redemption—constitutes the heart of the church's mission of evangelization. How do nuns rearticulate this universalizing mission in their work with foreign women? What happens to the urge to convert souls to Catholicism at this particular historical juncture? What does it mean to "accept" the other as culturally different? The entire discourse on conversion is questioned by the presence of the foreigner, and the nuns articulate the meanings of conversion and evangelization today through seemingly ambivalent logics. The discourse on multiculturalism and tolerance overlaps with the Catholic discourse of acceptance and provides a different language in which to talk about the relationship to the migrant other. Instead of talking about religious conversion, the nuns invoke the logic of reform and emancipation, of facilitating the women's integration into Italian society. In a way, just as with redemption, they translate their project of conversion into a secular process of transformation of the self that maps onto biopolitical categories provided by the state.

In our conversations, the nuns evoked two levels of conversion: conversion of the other and conversion of themselves as servants of God. In questioning their mission of converting souls, they seem to find the meaning of Christ's teaching in "welcoming the Christ in the other without any discrimination of color or religion." Therefore, they encourage women to pursue their own confessions by pushing them to attend the mosque, the Orthodox church, or African Pentecostal churches, according to their respective beliefs. Women's spirituality is very important for the nuns. They believe that they should take care of women "in their wholeness," considering both the need to receive legal recognition and the need to pursue a spiritual life as essential. This does not necessarily translate into the desire to convert souls to Catholicism, although the process of rehabilitation can reflect a similar logic of conversion and reformation of the body and the soul.

At a meeting in Turin organized by several groups involved in the program—including educators, social workers, and lay volunteers—to discuss the spiritual implications of rehabilitation, Sister Carla said, "We don't only take care of the legal aspect of their lives, in other words, of the residency permit, but we provide them with food, clothes, shelter, and we should also provide some spiritual nourishment." Her statement was responding to a more general reflection precisely on the role of conversion and evangelization in the work with foreign women. This conversation was part of a larger debate among religious and secular organizations on the role of cultural difference and tolerance in their work with migrants. Ethno-psychiatrists from the Centro Fanon were present at this meeting, offering their own perspective on difference and mental health and on how to approach the work of victim rehabilitation from an angle that took culture and history seriously. What does difference mean, and how should it be dealt with? If foreigners are to be rehabilitated, how to draw the line between what could be changed and what has to be changed without being disrespectful of difference and what is "cultural" and therefore irreducible to any transformation encouraged by the receiving society? Although this meeting resembled many of the ones I attended at the Immigration Office (see chapter 3), it did focus specifically on the spiritual dimension of the rehabilitation of victims. It also represented a very important moment in my understanding of the frictions, paradoxes, and discrepancies of nuns' experiences and thoughts about the question of cultural difference.

What emerged was that, on the one hand, some nuns suspended their mission to convert people to Catholicism by invoking cultural and spiritual difference as heritage, which has meaning in and of itself and must be respected as such. As long as women attended a church or mosque, the nuns supported their spiritual practices. The manifestation of their faiths may be different, but nuns recognized in them the universality of believing in God. "I have complete respect for those who believe in a superior being, because in it my own God certainly exists. If they are Muslims, Christian Orthodox, or Pentecostal, I respect them all as long as they believe in something," said Sister Anna. In this view, all human beings have a spiritual side, and the nuns were mostly concerned about it being sustained in the women's lives. In the words of another nun at the meeting:

> It is true, there are girls who only want the residency permit. But then the person comes into the picture. It is obvious that that is the excuse, but then a new path of life starts. And here my situation as a consecrated woman comes into play. This doesn't mean that I ask them to come to mass, but by my very presence the girl asks herself certain questions and a relationship can start. To me, it is a personal challenge to let their spirituality find a way to express itself. Because it is there. I believe that in each person there is spirituality. It can express itself in doing voluntary work, loving nature, being vegetarian. There is a force of human spirit. My concern is that it gets expressed. . . . I would feel very frustrated just giving her a residency permit. I am interested in seeing the person come out complete.

Thus, conversion does not happen through proselytism but by setting a good example. This is supposed to inspire women to resort to their own faiths and confessions, which are immanent in all human beings. The rehabilitation program is supposed to spark, or rekindle, spiritual longing. Only this can make the person whole. The pedagogical process inherent in rehabilitation cannot run its course if the spiritual component of a woman's life is not addressed. On more than one occasion, I asked nuns whether they encouraged women to attend mass. Sister Maria told me that in the past she had invited some of them to accompany her to the Sunday service, "but they all seemed allergic to it." She continued by saying that they refused to go because when they worked as prostitutes they had sex with priests, and now they did not want anything to do with the church. She could not blame them for that, she concluded.

At this same meeting, another nun shared the story of an Albanian woman who was once taken to mass. During communion, she put the Eucharist in her pocket, not knowing what to do with it. Others shared experiences of women who became interested in going to church after a few months in the program and others who wanted to become nuns. The general agreement among the participants was that Nigerian women's spirituality was much more vibrant, alive, and profound than that of Eastern European women. The latter had endured the spiritual dryness of communism and had come out of it often "with no human values" to grasp. One nun said:

> Girls from the East don't have a sense of religiosity; therefore, you have to work in order to recuperate their basic human ethical values. Albanian girls are empty. They are a people without soul. Helping them recognize basic values is spiritual work because it means reconstructing the person. Nigerian women, on the contrary, are a more fertile terrain because they are concerned with religion, they know the Bible, it is easy to talk about spiritual topics, they go to their Pentecostal churches, and they pray. Romanians go to their church, too.

Nigerian women are considered a more "fertile terrain" than Eastern Europeans because they have a closer relationship to spirituality. The nuns often referred to "African spirituality" as rich and profound. The history of missionary work and the encounter with "the African" often resonated in the nuns' narratives. Although Nigerian women's spirituality is also associated with "voodoo rituals," which are mostly considered to be superstition, it nonetheless points to "a spiritual longing" and is the sign of "a seed of spirituality." This seed is lacking in Eastern European women, who, on the contrary, "are attached to money and material belongings and don't care about anything else." They are often considered "amoral," as opposed to immoral. I was reminded of the logics guiding the drafting of denuncias. In that process, the state uses the belief in magic and proof of women's participation in voodoo rituals to accomplish the transformation/translation of the subject from victim to agent. What was different in the nuns' approach to the belief in magic was that they saw it as a potential point of entry for Christian belief and ethos. It proved the truth in the universality of spiritual life.

Another parallel that I noted at this meeting was that, similar to what happened at the Immigration Office where bureaucrats and volunteers involved in Progetto Freedom translated women's differences into patterns of cultural conduct and typologies of "cultural suffering" (chapter 3), the nuns tended to identify patterns of spiritual behavior and reproduced distinctions among the women that recognized different nationalities as more or less capable of attaining a spiritual life. Once again, I was observing an instance in which difference was translated into familiar categories that made the other recognizable and digestible. According to those distinctions, Eastern Europeans must be taught basic human values. This teaching, though, happens on a terrain that is dry and more difficult to "sow."

This image of a terrain in need of domestication evokes a missionary scenario and the practices of conversion embedded in it. During the history of colonization, missions often played a central role in reconfiguring the geographic space by conquering "nature" with "civilization," and by establishing new systems of relations, new notions of time, space, and personhood (Leenhardt 1979 [1947]; Comaroff and Comaroff 1988). In other words, discourses of colonization and missionary work have often appealed to the image of undomesticated terrain that needs to be cultivated. There are traces of this discourse in the integration of new migrants into receiving countries in Europe. In part, it was in this context that I listened to the nun's words about women's relationships to spirituality and morality and to what the nuns understood as their culture.

"Evangelization does not only happen through words," Sister Chiara told me. "It happens through your very deeds and your life; my condition as a consecrated woman raises questions in them that doing catechism would not bring up." I interpreted her words as a way of emphasizing the fact that there are different forms of evangelization and that spreading God's word is not the only way to touch and transform people's lives. Catechism—understood as the practice of teaching the principles of Christian religion through question and answer and therefore through verbalization—is not how the nuns approached foreign women pedagogically. Thus, I interpreted the nuns' efforts to distance themselves from an explicit discourse of conversion and their attempt to be more culturally sensitive to women's difference as a way of conforming to discourses on multiculturalism and the importance of welcoming difference instead of reducing it to sameness. Different discourses are at play in the nuns' words, and a complex overlapping of logics makes their practices ambivalent, constantly at odds with each other: logics of domination and conversion, on the one hand, and logics of tolerance and respect of difference, on the other. As I point out throughout this book, the state is caught in these same ambivalent discourses. What state and religious institutions portray as a project of integrating foreign others is, though, often close to a process of converting and translating difference within categories of recognition. It may thus resemble conversion more than one would think at first glance.

On the same issue of evangelization, Sister Maria used the example of Jesus, who never imposed prayer on his disciples. Instead, he waited until they asked him to teach them how to address the Lord. "He set an example; just as we nuns must set an example for the women through our lifestyles." Moreover, in this particular field of rehabilitation, the nuns take up the state's guidelines and translate the pedagogical project inherent in all forms of evangelization into a project of disciplining the body, behaviors, desires, and aspirations of the women. Although not in the sphere of women's spiritual practices, the logic of conversion nonetheless informs the nuns' ways of engaging with the women and their mission of emancipation. After all, the image of Mary Magdalene, the prostitute who became a saint after coming into contact with Jesus, remains central to the collective Western consciousness and influences practices aimed at rescuing the marginal.

Nuns function through a logic that is both universalistic and relativist. It is universalistic insofar as they recognize the universal value of spirituality and the importance of recognizing Christ in each and every person, regardless of their cultural background. On some fundamental level we are all Christ's children and therefore worthy of respect. On another level, women present a difference that is incommensurable and cannot be reduced to the same faith. Their own spiritual paths are worthy of respect. Women must be encouraged to pursue them. This line of thinking echoes discourses on multiculturalism and the issue of cohabitation and questions the very idea of missionary work and evangelization.

By turning to anthropology and ethno-psychiatry to make sense of the unsettling experience of cultural difference, nuns attempt to reformulate their roles within contemporary Italy in a language that mirrors and reproduces the discourse on tolerance produced by mainstream politics of recognition. Implicit in the state discourse of recognition is also the idea of a hierarchical organization of different forms of spirituality. On the one hand, recognizing women's different religious affiliations can be interpreted as a way of questioning the centrality of evangelization in Catholic practices of assisting marginalized others and acknowledging that the main purpose of their missionary work is shifting. On the other hand, nuns may function through an implicit belief that there is a hierarchy among different religious paths according to which some faiths are better than others. In this case, at the bottom of the ladder would be practices that the nuns consider "superstitious."

As I showed in chapter 3, when nuns turned to the Centro Fanon's ethno-psychiatrists with questions concerning the women in the program, they often brought up possession, which concerned Nigerian women in particular and their affiliations with the worship of Mami Wata. To the nuns, cults such as Mami Wata belonged to the order of superstition and did not count as a form of spirituality they could support. If, in addition to being devotees of the goddess of water, women also attended a Pentecostal church, then the nuns would recognize their faith in God as a truer expression of spirituality. This implicit tendency to identify what counts as spiritual as an expression of the universal longing to believe in a god points to a compulsion to commensurate, to reduce to what is familiar, rather than to acknowledge difference. It is a translation that finds equivalence between the other language and the one we know best.

CONVERTING THEIR MISSION, CONVERTING THEMSELVES

That the nuns are engaged in practices of recognition similar to the state's projects does not mean that their work with foreign women does not produce frictions or transformation. In fact, while the question of how nuns convert victims into dignified subjects is important to me, I further ask how, through the rhetoric of salvation and liberation, the nuns engage in projects of self-purification as well. Conversion of oneself is a transformation the nuns personally experience time and again in the course of their encounters with women in the shelter. For them, relating to women who are different is redemptive in and of itself, and it raises questions about one's own way of intervening. Sister Maria once told me about her personal turning point in her work with prostitutes. She referred to it as "the culmination of my conversion." At the beginning of her service at shelters for former prostitutes, she mostly worked with Italian women. Her conviction was that those who chose sex work were fundamentally sinners, even though she recognized that they all came from disadvantaged backgrounds. One day, social services sent over a woman who had worked in the sex industry by choice for several years. She had AIDS and other major health problems, and, Maria said, "It did show on her face." This is how Sister Maria described the "redemptive moment" triggered by this encounter:

> I used to treat her very well, or at least this is what I thought. She didn't think so. Unconsciously I thought that since she had chosen that work she must have deserved all the illnesses she suffered. I felt as if I was schizophrenic myself: on the one hand, I treated her very well and, on the other, in my thoughts I punished her. She used to rebel against everything I would say or ask her to do. One day, I told her, "I treat you with kid gloves, and you are always so rude to me; why?" She answered, "You treat me with kid gloves because you are disgusted by me." I didn't know what to say. Then I realized that she was right. My disgust was unconscious, but she perceived it. So, from that moment on, I started to treat her less well, but I felt more sincere and transparent.

For Sister Maria, this was a transformative moment that allowed her to accept the other. She realized the meaning of acceptance: "I understood that we must accept them as they are. When we work with migrant women, we as nuns must put our morality aside. This is a form of sacrifice. We must be prepared to sacrifice ourselves for them."

In Maria's account, the prostitute becomes the means of purification and sacrifice. She mirrors the nun's unconscious disgust and judgment. The woman's difference provides for a moment of catharsis, of expiation. In this encounter, the nun's prejudices vis-à-vis the other's sexuality and morality are surrendered and sacrificed. This sacrifice benefits both the nun and the woman, or at least this is how Sister Maria experienced it.

Similarly, Sister Rosaria summarized how through her work with the prostitutes she was able to let the shame of prejudice come to the surface to be expelled.

> I consider myself lucky because some of my cultural prejudices that were lying dormant in me, such as racism, have come to the surface again. I was able to experience a catharsis of my personal purification. I was able to see again a lot of mental and cultural schemas. Living with those who are different serves the purpose of personal growth.

While in chapter 4 I argued that women who file criminal charges as victims of human trafficking are caught in the state's confessional logic inasmuch as they agree (or are made to agree) to enter a program aimed at reeducating and transforming them into autonomous and independent subjects, here I propose to turn the confessional logic upside down. While in the case of the denuncia I interpret the state as a form of confessor that sets the criteria for redemption and inclusion of the foreign woman, in the shelter the women themselves become confessors for the nuns, who, as Sisters Rosaria and Maria expressed, experience a form of purification through them. This is the opposite of Foucault's (1980) confessional power. The power comes from the women, from the way in which they experience the body and sexuality. Through them, the nuns learn the anatomy of the body and of desire; they can imagine bodily pleasures, even though they interpret them in the register of the sin. The nuns also recognize that working with former prostitutes can have the spiritual outcome of overcoming prejudice, discrimination, and judgment. They can improve themselves by understanding their disgust for the prostitute. In this cathartic process, the nuns bring the sublimation of their own desire to yet another level that can be read not only through the lens of their spiritual vows, but of their civic and political engagement.

By "confessor," I am referring to someone who has been invested (formally or informally) with the authority and power to hear confessions and to guide the "sinner" in the process of converting her shortcomings into opportunities for spiritual growth. On the one hand, the women are given this role by the nuns, who experience them as a means for their own expiation of sins. On the other hand, the nuns, inasmuch as they are engaged in the implementation of the state's integration policies, become the gatekeepers of state rules and the mediators for the women. In this sense, they themselves occupy the position of a particular kind of confessor that embodies spiritual, moral, and political power to convert and transform the other.

The sacrificial aspect of the nuns' activities is also inscribed in their desire to "commit an act of justice." Maria told me, "We wanted to scream against the injustice of the world." Paola, the young Franciscan nun, once shared that what most transformed her spiritually was going out at night in the areas of the city where women were waiting for clients and then approaching them to tell them about the rehabilitation program.[14] "I felt I was getting in touch with the reality of the world, with the reality of their lives, and I realized I was doing it as a simple act of justice and not because I was a 'good girl.'" For her, the reality of the women's lives meant a state of enslavement but also the recognition that behind the facade of their unruly sexuality they wanted to share a moment of prayer with the nuns in the street. The nuns would suggest that they pray together, or, as Sister Paola explained to me, the women would initiate a prayer sometimes. "It is extraordinary to be in the street with a half-naked woman who says 'Please pray with me.' The intensity of the prayer is incredible," she said.

For the nuns, working to rehabilitate victims of human trafficking conjures a sense of reciprocity, a give-and-take that occurs between them and the women. Sister Tina once put it in these words: "I help you go through it, and you help me purify myself. While you purify yourself from your previous life, I purify myself of prejudice." "This is the teaching of the Gospels," Maria once told me. "I support you, and you support me." Moreover, this is the gift and aim of the program: to show women that outside of the logic of exploitation, other kinds of relationships are possible. For the nuns, reciprocity stands as a synonym for emancipation and the opposite of, as well as antidote to, enslavement. Learning to establish relationships of reciprocity is, in the nuns' eyes, a sign of the women's progress. In this context, reciprocity also applies to the logic of conversion: through the transformation of socially unacceptable subjects into autonomous beings, the nuns undergo a similar process of emancipation and purification, and, more broadly, society's sins are expiated. I interpret what the nuns call reciprocity as the reverse of the confessional, where women are seen as holding the power to transform the nuns' subjectivity and posture in the world, just as the nuns can help them free themselves from victimhood.

PARADOXES OF FREEDOM AND CONVERSION

As for the women, conversion and transformation through the rehabilitation program have different connotations. While they often act as if the shelter were a "good family" and the nuns the mothers of the family, at the same time they privately say that they are using it in order to obtain legal status in Italy so they will not be repatriated. Even so, though the rhetoric of self-transformation belongs to the nuns, it does gradually creep into the women's narratives as they spend more time at the shelter. Nuns, government officials, and psychologists understand the experience of life at the shelter as an alternative anchor for identification. Through it, a socially unacceptable identity is translated into a commensurable subjectivity. The women often refer to their experience in this community as "being in prison" or being forced to follow rules that are just as alienating as the ones they had to follow when they worked the streets. Women often experience what the state and religious groups refer to as "a process of liberation from victimhood" as another form of subjugation.

Rarely, though, do women enter the program with the intention of transforming themselves. Katia, a young woman from Poland, once told me, "I have decided to live in the shelter because I want to get the residency permit. Once I get it I will be ready to leave." Or they experience this stage of their lives as a failure to fulfill their desire to work, to earn money, to have a relationship, to have a house of their own, and, further, as proof that they do not yet have a respected status vis-à-vis the receiving society and their own families back home. They often express frustration at the nuns for deciding what they should wear and eat, whom they should see outside of the community, and what jobs to accept. Often, this space becomes another impasse in their lives, another form of disguised exclusion and infantilization. This is the case for many women who enter the program and are never able to find a so-called normal job, so they go back to working as prostitutes during the day and sleeping at the nuns' shelter at night. As I discuss in chapters 3 and 4, the state's logic of inclusion has a double facade: as it includes, it also excludes; as it grants access to rights, it also constricts women's choices.

When I asked the women whether they felt changed after going through the program, I received very different responses. As I mentioned above, some of them adopted the language of the rehabilitation program and stated that they have changed for the better, that they did not know who they were before and feel more "independent" now. They agreed with the nuns that following the rules of the shelter and learning to live together have made them better people, ready to face life in the world again, freed from relationships of subjugation. For some of them, the whole apparatus of the rehabilitation for victims has provided real support and opened up opportunities for their future in Italy.

Other women responded differently. Micaela told me that once she entered the program, she did not feel like herself anymore. She did not recognize the new way she related to others and to herself. This left her with a sense of disconnection from her previous self. When she told the nuns about it, their response was, "You are more mature now." This answer seemed to convince her, and she told me that it had been worth going through the program and the sacrifice of reforming herself.

Ana, on the other hand, gave yet another answer to the question about her transformation:

> I haven't changed; I didn't need to change. When I entered the shelter I was not like other women who were so shy they couldn't speak a word of Italian. They needed to change. I wanted the residency permit, and this has changed. Let me think . . . what else has changed? Oh, I have a job now, even if I hate it. I have to clean the nuns' convent. Ah, and I have a boyfriend! And I also have learned to be patient, so patient, that if they ask me to be patient again I will kill them!

Jokes aside, she added that she did not regret entering the program after all.

Amen, a Nigerian woman who lived in a different shelter, once approached one of the social workers and said, "You are the slave, not me when I was a prostitute. Do you know how much money I made back then? In four days I made the equivalent of what you make in a month!" When the social worker told me about this conversation, she admitted that it left her speechless. It made her think about what emancipation and freedom actually meant to the women. At the crux of many women's experiences was the economic need to turn to prostitution; thus, becoming a normal independent subject as defined by the institutions may actually lead to being unable to support themselves and their families back home.

In this chapter, I have broached the question of coexisting subjectivities and definitions of what it means to be free and redeemed. I have also explored what is at stake in life at the shelter as a mode of being in the world, suspended from the past—often figured as traumatic—and from an imaginary dream of capitalist success (the power and money tied to work in the streets). Both the nuns and the former prostitutes seemed to work toward a different organization of their lives and to share an underlying neoliberal idea of the self according to which autonomy and freedom are the unquestioned goals of life. Yet when they came into contact with one another they also felt their respective ideals of freedom were threatened. The women posed freedom as having access to money and the ability to support family members in their countries, or to consume certain objects, while for the nuns freedom was linked to God's will and their pious work of rescuing women from the street to turn them into real "free" subjects. The nuns also strived to be free from prejudice, something the women helped them do.

The encounter between these groups of women forced them to feel dis-ease. They each tried to come to terms with this discomfort by stating that the other group is lacking something. From the nuns' perspective, the women lack a sense of morality, or are psychologically vulnerable, or are not equipped to live autonomously in the world. From the women's points of view, the nuns lack a sense of the real world, of what it means to have a family, a normal job, and the everyday difficulties of life. The nuns are subjected to the order to which they belong and their vows of obedience to the church. Does this count as freedom? For the nuns it does: it is an exercise of "free will." But this kind of will is, nonetheless, a response to God's call, which the nuns must obey.

Women's responses to the program were not simply a sign of resistance to change but rather their expressions of different concepts of the self, emancipation, and what it means to be an autonomous subject. Similarly, the nuns' inability to understand prostitution as a choice was a way to protect their idea of what it means to be free and pure. The ways in which they offered redemption mirrored their own "free" choices and notion of purity. They tended to translate ethno-psychiatrists' advice on how to approach the larger political and historical contexts of women's experiences into categories that reduced difference to the familiar rather than acknowledge it. They partially missed out on ethno-psychiatry's challenge.

PART FIVE

Reentering the Scene

The Centro

"I am here for an appointment with Doctor Fanon," said the woman who entered the main office at the Centro Fanon on the first day of my work there. She must have been in her mid-forties, and was from Romania. The Immigration Office had referred her to the center for a consultation. She held a small piece of paper with the name and address of the center written on it, and she handed it over to Sara, the trainee at the desk. Sara smiled and told her that she probably had an appointment with another doctor; "Fanon" was the name of the center. She later told me that it was not the first time people asked for Doctor Fanon. He was, apparently, very popular at the Centro.

A black-and-white photo of Fanon—young, fierce, and looking away from the camera—hung in a simple all-glass frame on the wall of the main office (fig. 6). It greeted you as you entered the Centro, and it was one of the first things I noticed. "Of course," I thought, "how could it be missing in a clinic named after him?" When the Centro moved to another location, the photo moved with it, and found its place again on one of the walls of the main office where patients were welcomed, appointments made, staff meetings held, and most of the life of the center outside of therapy sessions occurred. In the second location, the photo was hanging over a bookshelf, at least for a little while. I sometimes thought that the shelf gave that corner of the wall a sacred aura; it was an intellectual altar to someone who had deeply inspired the practices and thinking at the clinic. For me, his photo was a statement

FIGURE 6. Photo of Frantz Fanon on the walls of the Centro, 2002. Photo by author.

that the clinical work done there was most of all a political engagement with the issues of suffering and care.

I often experienced the Centro as a space populated by many voices, presences, spirits, shadows, and ghosts. Like the iconic images of exotic others painted on the walls of the Centro's corridors that, although painted over in white, retained a ghostly presence—a reminder of the power of images to reduce difference to its stereotypes—Fanon's photo was a presence and a reminder as well. His image called on us to remember that representations and stereotypes become masks, imagos that can fix and trap us, and others; that representations efface people, objects, practices, and experiences.

His photo was also a gesture to the fact that in clinical work there can be care without cure, that cure—in the sense of remedy or successful treatment of a disease and its causes—often forecloses the possibility of care. When we are caught in institutional time and the demands of biomedical treatment, the time for listening to the enigmas of history and the unconscious, to the blurring of life and death, is suffocated. Fanon opened up a time for listening, for caring without necessarily curing, or, as Donald W. Winnicott (1986a) once framed it, for a "care-cure"—a relation not punctuated by diagnoses and the eradication of disease but by a presence and a holding, an acknowledgment that others have their own words that need to be spoken and heard and their own timing to be cared for.

Tragic Translations

"I am afraid of falling. Speak well of me,
speak well for me"

> *Afërdita:* Every time I come to the Centro I am afraid of getting lost.
>
> *Cristiana:* What are you afraid of?
>
> *Afërdita:* I am afraid that no one will ever find me.

On the bench outside the consultation rooms, she sat and waited. Afërdita had gotten into the habit of arriving early, sometimes an hour before her appointment. In Albanian her name means something like "close to the light," and almost as a respectful bow to it she would often dress in light blue, pink, and cream, which made her pale complexion appear even paler. Afërdita would sit and look down at the floor, a sad look, while frantically tearing at a Kleenex she held in her hands. Sometimes she had tears in her eyes, which she dried with what remained of the Kleenex. She would bite her nails and offer a melancholy smile to anyone who walked past the bench.

This is what I saw the first time I met her in the corridors of the Centro. When I first joined the group of practitioners to do my fieldwork, Afërdita was one of the patients they often discussed during case conferences or informally. Her therapist and the cultural mediator were not the only ones concerned about her situation; the whole staff would often comment on her recent hospitalization at the mental health facilities, her relationship with the Catholic nuns at the shelter where she lived at the time, her children in foster care, and her endless issues with the social worker in charge of them. Something about her suffering and the way she expressed it exceeded the walls of the consultation room and made itself heard. When she was in a session, her lamenting and sobbing echoed throughout the Centro. There was also something endearing about her and the way she would ask you how your day was going and how your family was doing each time she saw you. She had a generous, yet desperate, expression on her face when she would lean toward you in conversation, almost as if she wanted to make sure she heard everything. That engagement could also disappear suddenly, and she would be pulled back into the depths of despair. She had already been a patient at the Centro for over a year when I was invited to join in her therapy sessions with Dr. Z and Ilir, the cultural mediator. She never missed a single one of her weekly appointments at the Centro over the two years that I knew her.

Like most stories we stumble upon as anthropologists, I encountered this one during its unfolding. When we met, Afërdita lived in the shelter run by Sister Carla, who also attended the Centro, once every other week, to consult with her therapist on how to best help Afërdita in the program that social services had designed for her. I participated in these meetings and visited Sister Carla's shelter on several occasions. Afërdita and I often conversed in the corridor during the long waits that preceded her appointments and at the shelter when I visited. I also learned about Afërdita from the Centro's psychologists and psychiatrists, from the various reports produced by social services, the Tribunal for Minors, and other mental health practitioners involved in her case. Her story was often presented as a "case," and as such her life was recounted in the genre of a story that was out of the ordinary and thus required explanation (Berlant 2007, 666). In the language of a case, the story is represented as a coherent whole, with a plot and singular narrative that must hold meaning. The format of the case makes confused narratives and contradictory experiences intelligible and analyzable. In line with the politics of recognition that I have explored in this book, the case can also be interpreted as a way to translate the enigmas and chaos of life into an ordered account. The form of the case can have the effect of generalizing norms and therefore lead to a loss of singularity. In this sense, it parallels the state's categorizations and the practice of denuncia (see chapters 3 and 4, respectively). Of course, this can prove very useful in the context of rehabilitation and integration projects for foreigners because it provides a framework where past, present, and future are linked and projected into the desired outcome. Yet if a life story is turned into a case, it is also because it is exemplary of something; it has conundrums that seek an opening and a resolution. This is particularly true for the etymology of the Italian word *caso,* which does not merely point to the general rule of the bureaucratic example, but also to the mysterious and unknown aspects of an investigation. In a way, it reintroduces incommensurability into the discourse.

While I attend to the various versions of Afërdita's stories as they were produced by the institutions involved in her case, my purpose here is also to pay attention to those instances when her words, dreams, cries, and laments cannot be heard in that register. I mostly knew her in the context of her therapy at the Centro, where ethno-psychiatrists only used the format and temporality of the "case" when they discussed her course of treatment. For the most part, though, the space of the clinic allows memories to emerge not in the coherent form of a story but in the elusiveness of dreams, in the interruptions of narratives, in the repetition of symptoms, all instances that escape linear narration and time. Hence, while clinical language determined the general terms of the case, her singularity inscribed something untranslatable into her case, thus preventing any sequential narrative.

In this chapter, I examine several reports that social workers, doctors, and judges wrote and put them into conversation with what emerged of Afërdita's life in the ethno-psychiatric space. Multiple institutional gazes produce different narratives about Afërdita that are cumulative, and they produce written accounts and spoken assessments of her that have the power to fix her in the temporalities of institutional bureaucracy and represent her through what I call a theater of classifications. But Afërdita mostly speaks from a space of loss and death that does not correspond to institutional time or the rigor of narrative. For the most part, her speech disrupts the linearity of institutional scripts. By focusing on how ethno-psychiatrists turned to a phenomenological analysis of Afërdita's experience—and did not necessarily identify "culture" as therapeutic—I show the potential of this clinical listening to interrupt the time of the state. Instead, dreams, desires, fears, and cries provided an alternative language to approach experience and difference outside of the debates on culture and recognition. Although in this chapter I also focus on the ways in which therapists discuss Afërdita as a case, I see this kind of operation as different from the genre of the case that the judge, social worker, and nuns produced. I read ethno-psychiatrists' formulation of the "clinical case" as a necessary moment of analysis—a strategic reification, similar to the one created through clinical work discussed in chapter 1. This, somewhat fictionally or artificially, reconstitutes a momentary narrative linearity out of unconscious material that the therapists themselves know can only be approached obliquely, as fragmented and elusive. Afërdita's sessions at the Centro, her silences and words, accounts or lack thereof, are not translated into diagnoses or heard as missed narratives but collected as testimonies in and of themselves. To listen outside of the structure of diagnoses and case histories is a form of acknowledgment that, I argue, counters the modality of recognition that biomedical diagnostic criteria provide and that the state offers through multicultural projects. The ethno-psychiatrists practiced a phenomenological suspension of diagnosis and pathologization to refute the violence of institutions. Once the diagnostic and institutional approaches to the case have been set aside, what emerges is, as Franco Basaglia argues, the problem of diversity as the problem of life (cited in Venturini 1979, 246).

I decided to write about Afërdita because she articulates a malaise larger than her own. She gestures toward and echoes the loss and melancholia that accompany the experience of crossing borders—not just national ones but those between life and death, pathology and health. Here I attempt to show what it means to learn to reoccupy a space—political, social, and existential—that is constantly threatened by the crisis of presence (de Martino 1956). By this I mean that this story and its discrepant versions show what it means to rearticulate one's sense of self when faced with the ambivalent task of learning to reoccupy life according to the shifting norms and expectations of the receiving society. This challenge constantly puts one at risk of losing oneself in the labyrinth of what is often experienced as an unintelligible order (the law, institutions, and discourses on health and illness). This chapter locates the individual in political and historical contexts that produce symptoms and forms of suffering. It thus becomes possible to understand symptoms as stories, simultaneously individual and collective, and not necessarily coherent in their narratives. Inconsistency in stories has a logic of its own that the politics of recognition considers pathological. I argue, however, that inconsistencies signal what cannot be fully understood and thus beg for acknowledgment.

CARE, CURE, AND EXISTENCE

It was an early April afternoon, one of those that make you feel like summer is coming. It was warm and humid outside, but in the Department of Mental Health's basement where the Centro was located the temperature was fresh if damp. I had been participating in Afërdita's sessions for over two months when her therapist, Dr. Z, called a special meeting to discuss her case.[1] The issue at stake was urgent. The Tribunal for Minors had requested that Dr. Z write a report on the course of Afërdita's treatment, because her children had been in foster care for a while and were now being considered for adoption. Afërdita had a seven-year-old daughter, Mailinda, and a one-year-old son, Marcello; she had lost another son, Pietro, who died when he was two years old. Dr. Z was in her early thirties, around the same age as Afërdita and me at the time. Unlike the other practitioners at the Centro, Dr. Z did not have a formal background in ethno-psychiatry or anthropology. As she explained to me, she had acquired her training in ethno-psychiatry "by osmosis," working with the other practitioners. She had joined the Centro two years before I began my research, and she was also a clinical psychologist in public services. At this moment in her work with Afërdita, she was struggling with how to communicate the course of her progress in therapy to other institutions that were evaluating whether she was a fit mother. She called on the experience and advice of other practitioners at the center to discuss and reflect on Afërdita in an attempt to understand her position vis-à-vis the various institutional gazes scrutinizing her competence as a parent.

We gathered several chairs and formed a circle in the main room of the center, where the photo of Fanon hung on the wall. Besides Dr. Z and me, the participants at the meeting included a staff psychologist (Dr. N), a psychiatrist (Dr. L), three trainees, and one educator.[2] Dr. N was also an anthropologist by training who had done long-term research on mental health in Morocco; he was also one of the founders of the Centro in the mid-1990s. The voice of the psychiatrist is that of Dr. L, senior psychiatrist and medical anthropologist, a central figure at the clinic. All of the cultural mediators worked in other services and were unavailable to come to the meeting.

In this meeting, the practitioners struggled to help Dr. Z frame a report for the Tribunal that would counter the other institutional interpretations of Afërdita, which represented her as an unfit parent who is pathological and manipulative. Because case conferences are precisely that, organized around a "case," that is how Afërdita is represented here. However, in this situation the point is not so much to standardize her story as to show how her experiences cannot be translated into the language of the state and religious institutions, which are more interested in curing than caring for her. The ethno-psychiatric approach, on the contrary, attempts to acknowledge her suffering and provide some care.

In what follows, I try to capture the theatricality of this ethnographic moment by maintaining the dialogic structure of the case conference. I want to suggest that Afërdita's stories speak generally to the experience of being caught within the benevolent and violent power of institutions that define what constitutes life versus death, pathology versus normality, and legality versus illegality. I signal the institutional roles of the participants in the meeting (psychiatrist, staff psychologist, and anthropologist) to highlight the scriptlike aspect of the various institutional narratives that populate this book. The web of institutional representations that frame Afërdita's experience could ensnare anyone. We could all, potentially, at different moments of our lives, go mad or experience a "crisis of presence."

The case conference unfolded as follows:

Dr. Z (Afërdita's psychologist): Today I want to discuss the case of Afërdita, Albanian, who has been reported to the Tribunal for Minors for not being able to take care of her children. Afërdita is thirty-three years old. She arrived in Italy two years ago, eight months pregnant, with her husband and a seven-year-old daughter, Mailinda. They arrived in Rome, where they stayed with a cousin who lived in a shantytown in the outskirts of the city. After a few days, the husband decided to return to Albania. She continued the journey alone and decided to move to Turin with her daughter because she knew someone from her country there. The woman she stayed with was a prostitute, and Afërdita did not feel safe living with her. Through the help of social services, she was placed at a shelter for foreign women in the periphery of the city.

In September 2001, she was sent to the Centro Fanon by the shelter's social workers. According to them, she was often very sad, couldn't sleep at night, had strong headaches, and struggled with the children. She was unable to contain her anxiety and would complain to her daughter and rely on her for support. I started seeing her with Ilir, the Albanian cultural mediator, in January 2002, once a week for over a year. The symptomatology was that she was always very tired, a depressive state that didn't let her get up in the morning. She cried a lot. We consulted with our psychiatrist and decided to prescribe an antidepressant and a sleeping pill.

Social services had a project to help her become independent. They found her a job as a house cleaner, which she did for a while. The message they sent her was, "Now that you have found a job, in a few months you can look for an apartment and maybe get a residency permit." I think she became scared because she was going through a lot of anxiety at that time. She needed support with the children. Moreover, there was another Albanian woman at the shelter with whom Afërdita had a fight because, apparently, she had an affair with her husband; they accused each other of various things. These episodes are not clear to me. There was also a rumor that this woman's teenage sons had tried to rape Afërdita's daughter. I heard contradictory stories from both Afërdita and the social workers. Moreover, Afërdita had hysterical crises during which she cried, tried to tear her hair out, hit her head on the wall, and said she couldn't handle this woman's presence any longer. The social workers decided to move her from the shelter, although we at the Centro did not agree with their decision. They decided behind our back in the sense that they asked a psychiatrist from outside the Centro to write a certificate to hospitalize her the day after she had yet another argument with the same woman. There was no need to hospitalize her at that point. . . . I must add an important detail: this shelter used to specialize in the rehabilitation of ex-alcoholics and drug addicts.

Dr. N (staff psychologist): Yes, and it has recently been converted into a shelter for immigrants, but the staff is new. Some of the current social workers and educators are former patrons of the shelter itself, former drug users. The staff is not specially trained to work with immigrants, and they are ambivalent about it.

Dr. Z: When Afërdita lived there, she mentioned several times that she wanted to die. One night, she walked into the garden where there was a well and tried to open it. The following morning they asked her why she did it. "Because I wanted to throw myself in it," she answered. When we heard this story, we told the social workers to come and talk to us about her suicide attempt. They never bothered to come and decided to hospitalize her instead. She was in the hospital for three months, not because she needed treatment for the entire time, but because social services didn't know where to house her since she didn't have a residency permit. Otherwise the hospital psychiatrists would have discharged her after three weeks.

While she was at the hospital, the children stayed at the shelter, but the staff started to say that they couldn't look after them without the mother. So they reported her case to the Immigration Office, which in turn reported it to the Tribunal for Minors.[3] From that moment on, the children were separated and transferred to two different shelters because they were in two different age groups. These places were at the two opposite ends of the city. Social services asked the mother to sign a document to give consent. They explained to her that the children couldn't stay at the shelter where they used to live together. She had no choice but to sign it. At the hospital, the diagnosis was "acute psychotic episode." On these premises, the request to transfer the children to other housing situations was soon translated into a request to maybe consider them for adoption. Meanwhile, Afërdita made herself at home at the hospital and made friends. Then she was moved to another shelter for immigrants and later to a shelter run by Catholic nuns, where she has now been for the last seven months.

The Tribunal has scheduled her visits with the children. Afërdita has met with the judge who told her that they don't want to take the children away from her, but they will put them in foster care with another family while she gets better. Her ability to be a mother is in question. In the report that I had to write for the Tribunal, I underlined the fact that since she was discharged from the hospital, she has made some progress, although now she is doing poorly again. But she never misses a single visit with the children. The social workers say that she really cares about them.

According to the judge, Afërdita can receive a residency permit because she is a mother of two minors who reside in Italy. This kind of permit, though, will prevent her from working and possibly from renewing it in the future. She can only have short training contracts but not a regular job. After two years she might have to leave the country.

Dr. L (psychiatrist): We have to cure her by the end of the second year, then!

Afërdita's story is another instance of the ambivalence at the heart of state power. On the one hand, the state wants to cure her, so it hospitalizes her; on the other hand, this curative approach then deprives her of any rights that she might have as an economic migrant. Also, the imperative to cure her quickly and at all costs comes with a price. Dr. L's sarcastic remark about having to cure Afërdita in a specific time frame alluded to the paradoxical urgency and timing of the institutions that demanded to see proof of her progress. I had several conversations with practitioners at the Centro about the question of time. Each experienced frustration dealing with the different time line of their institutional counterparts. To them, suspending a diagnosis also meant giving patients the time to orient themselves in the new country, within institutional cultures that were often unintelligible. The time it takes to cure and heal is at odds with the expectations of social services, the hospital, the Tribunal, the school, and the Immigration Office. Moreover, in ethno-psychiatry different temporalities come together in the therapeutic space: Western psychological techniques, healing approaches from the patient's background, and therapeutic practices that emerge when etiologies encounter curing practices. Each system of medical knowledge assumes a different relation to time and space. For example, when spirits and otherworldly presences take part in the cure, what time do they follow? Is this time the same as in psychoanalytic or psychiatric approaches to symptoms? How can the temporalities of unconscious memory, spirits, and bureaucracy coexist? Bureaucratic care is characterized by a kind of indifference for those who are cared for (Stevenson 2012), and for the different temporalities they occupy.

These are some of the questions that came to mind as I listened to the practitioners discuss Afërdita.

> *Dr Z:* There was a misunderstanding regarding the residency permit. Since the second child was born in Italy, they could have requested a permit for her on this very basis. But none of the people at the first shelter did anything about it, and Afërdita had no idea of how things worked. The people at the Immigration Office, who later took on Afërdita, are resentful because they now have to deal with the legal difficulties of regularizing a woman with a history of hospitalization and who is considered an unfit mother. . . .
>
> I find it difficult to help Afërdita cope with her relationship with the nun, Sister Carla, who runs the shelter where she currently lives. Sister Carla is very strict but seems to become softer and more understanding with time. Also, Afërdita has difficulties with the social worker, who she perceives as very aggressive. I have the impression that the social worker is manipulative when it comes to Afërdita. Every time I report about Afërdita's progress, she turns it into a negative element. She says, "I do things in the children's interest, I try to help her as much as possible, but she always cries. I tell her not to cry." Or she says things like, "I do this for her, but she doesn't respond; she doesn't do what I tell her to do." The message she conveys to Afërdita is, "Please pretend to be well."
>
> When Afërdita was called before the judge, she started crying and talking about the dead people in her family. They told her again not to cry, not to talk about the deaths in her family. Many different people evaluate her: the nuns at the shelter, the social worker, the people who observe her interactions with the children during her visits, the children's psychologists. They all write reports on her for the Tribunal. I have the impression that they all tell her, "Don't suffer; it is not proper." When she comes here she is relieved because she can finally cry and talk freely. She says she tries hard not to cry before the judge, the social worker, but then she can't help it, she feels too anxious and worried.
>
> *Dr. L:* Something important seems to be coming back in Afërdita's story, like a refrain, which can be helpful in reading her relationships to other people. Everyone seems to tell her, "You mustn't cry before the judge, you mustn't cry before the children, you mustn't cry before me because we cannot cope with it, we don't tolerate your pain. We can't witness your suffering any longer. We can't stand the ways in which you express your pain." No one seems to be at ease with this woman's crying.
>
> *Dr. Z:* The nuns always tell her, "Please go and cry in your room and stop saying that you want to throw yourself from the window." It seems like they are all saying, "Do not suffer! It is not allowed!"
>
> *Dr. L:* Or rather, they seem to be saying, "Suffer in a better way!" I also think that many of the problems that Afërdita had in the first shelter where she lived with her children were caused by the staff's inability to cope with the intensity of her suffering. They couldn't handle her signs of anxiety and despair.

Dr. N: I remember that during the supervisions we did with the staff back then, their anxiety was stronger than Afërdita's. Even though we tried to show them what was behind her dramatic gestures and words, they remained attached to the literal meaning of her actions, such as getting closer to the well as if she was actually going to throw herself in it.

Dr L: I might sound banal, but it is hell for a parent to make appointments to see her children, like making an appointment to go to the dentist. We have to take this into account in our evaluations because it is a very stressful situation. I don't know how many of us would put up with it.

Dr. N: Only a sick person would put up with it.

In these exchanges, I heard the practitioners commenting on the fact that various institutional figures and languages do not authorize Afërdita to exist. She is not legitimized as a suffering mother. Being undocumented, her situation makes her emblematic of other foreigners' experiences. The host society often represents the undocumented other through the discourse of "absence," "lack," and "non-being." As Achille Mbembe points out with regard to the relationship between the West and Africa, "Here is a principle of language and classificatory systems in which *to differ* from something or somebody is not simply *not to be like* (in the sense of being non-identical or being-other); it is also *not to be at all* (non-being). More, it is *being nothing* (nothingness)" (Mbembe 2001, 4; original emphasis). The experience of being judged by the institutions—as a good mother, a deserving citizen, a good woman, an autonomous subject—is intrinsic to the experience of crossing borders and being subjected to the nation-state's criteria of belonging. This entails the possibility of being reduced to nonbeing, to a nonperson (Dal Lago 1999). As I have asserted throughout this book, the gaze of institutions has both enabling and annihilating effects.

In this meeting the practitioners are critiquing the other institutions' demands on Afërdita. By interpreting her crying not as something that needs containment but as an expression of her existence, the ethnopsychiatrists are acknowledging Afërdita's experience outside of diagnoses. What I saw taking shape in this meeting was also a distinction between the way various institutions wanted to cure Afërdita to make her qualify as a competent parent and the care—maybe without cure—that ethno-psychiatric listening provides. I thus began to understand the difference between cure and care through the lens of what in this book I have framed as recognition and acknowledgment. While in order to cure her, the state and the nuns translate her experiences into pathologies and behaviors that need to be rectified ("Do not cry in front of the judge"), the space of care suspends institutional languages and listens to that cry. This type of care affirms Aferdita's expression of emotion as a speech that in and of itself discloses her existential predicament and has the potential to reveal a different understanding of the threshold between life and death, normality and pathology.

> Dr. Z: She is very good at doing introspective work. At times, she says that she doesn't want to see the children because it is torture to be with them for just an hour. She is aware of how difficult it is to be a mother in these circumstances. She asks herself, "Even if they come back and live with me, will I be able to be a mother again?"
>
> There is a history of depression in her family that runs through the women. Her mother suffered from depression and committed suicide, possibly by throwing herself into a well. Afërdita took care of her while her sisters and brother went to school. She dropped out of school and stayed at home. The mother would tell her, "You will become just like me, but don't think about it now." Therefore, a prophecy is coming true. Afërdita seems to think that her mother died of cancer, although they never did an autopsy. At other times, she thinks that she killed herself by jumping into the water, either in a well or in a lake. The story is confused. Apparently, her grandmother was diagnosed with brain cancer and suffered from depression, too. Afërdita never met her grandmother but has heard stories about her. Afërdita took care of other old people with cancer who died while she was with them: her mother- and father-in-law and her grandfather. She often says that she is afraid of having brain cancer and she obsessively wants to be tested, even when the doctors say she is healthy.
>
> Dr. N: It is easier for her to identify with these deadly events, with death and illness, with suffering and cancer, than with nothing at all.
>
> Dr. L: . . . She has turned into an attendant of death.
>
> Dr. N: In this sense, living becomes an impossible task.
>
> Dr. Z: She has always had a very close, too close, relationship with death. Since the age of twelve she has been surrounded by death.
>
> Dr. L: Now it becomes clear how ridiculous it is to tell her, "Come on, don't cry." By telling her not to talk about death we inevitably hit a wall and there is nothing therapeutic about it.
>
> Dr. Z: The social workers tell her to think about her children, to be well for them, not for herself.
>
> Dr. L: This is something that people often say to depressed mothers. It is a paradoxical invitation because it increases the sense of guilt. . . . Given the pressure that the institutions put on us, we need to think about how we can help shift the attitude of the people who work closely with her, like Sister Carla. This should be part of our strategy; otherwise, the therapeutic work we do with Afërdita might not be enough.

Dr. N: She talks about the thing we fear most—death—as an everyday aspect of her existence. She talks about the possibility of dying, of dead people in her family, her own fear of dying. Death has become her lexicon, her language. I wonder how we could work with this constant mourning and find ways in which she can still think about life from within this language. It sounds paradoxical, but can we find ways in which death for Afërdita is not incompatible with life? Did she attend the funerals of all the people she took care of?

Dr. Z: Yes. Ilir [the cultural mediator] explained to me that in Albania, especially in the north where she is from, during the funeral people gather around the coffin in the courtyard of the deceased's house. Several rituals are performed: people kiss the dead body, then later get together to talk about the dead person and what she or he had done in life. The doors of the house are kept open for several days after the funeral.

Dr. L: In Afërdita's case, this cultural dimension of death, usually aimed at creating a space for mourning and for detaching oneself from the dead, does not seem to have been effective. Quite the contrary. These events of death have been translated into a pathological mourning. Life has turned into mourning, to the point that there is no clear boundary between life and death. She moves in between these two dimensions as if they were the same. Hence, her attempt to open the well. If she stopped talking about the dead people in her life, she probably wouldn't have much to talk about. The question for us is how not to be annihilated by her constant reference to death. How to tie her back to life through vital relationships, not only the ones with her children? I think it's important to start from the fact that these dead people are her life and not a way to talk about death.

Cristiana: A couple of weeks ago, during a consultation, she talked about the time when her in-laws died, and they kept the corpses in the house for a few days. Her husband had disappeared for several days and she was afraid of being alone with the dead bodies. She said that she was afraid because people continue to do things, even as corpses.

Dr. Z: This is also a popular belief, according to which the spirit of the dead goes back to the house where he used to live. The doors are kept open for several days after the funeral so that the spirits can enter and exit the house. According to our Albanian cultural mediator, this is a positive and protective quality of the dead, but Afërdita is afraid of it. She feels safer in Italy, because, she said, "that [the presence of the spirits after death] is an Albanian thing."

Dr. L: These corpses are vital. How can we prevent her from being too at ease with them and from identifying too easily with illness and death?

Cristiana: She doesn't talk about dead people a lot during the consultations here. She talks more about the fact that she can't sleep and doesn't know how to answer her daughter's question: "When will we be together again?"

Dr. L: It means that here she is able to talk about her present without constantly referencing the past. We represent, as Centro Fanon, a more dynamic relationship of help. How can we transform this into an anchor for her? How can we help her take back the "blood of life"? Because this is what she lacks. If she is not capable of answering her daughter with a half-truth, with some lies, using her imagination, or putting off an answer, it means that she knows that something needs to be said but she is not strong enough to do it. If she could only recuperate some vitality and communicate it to the children, be more present with her body, a body that has a gaze, the children would respond in vital ways, and she would benefit from it.

Dr. Z: I thought I would work on her needs and desires. She often says that, in different circumstances, she would like to ask questions but she doesn't dare to. For instance, her daughter is going on a trip with the school, and the teachers asked for Afërdita's signature. She wanted to ask where they were going, for how long, but she couldn't find the courage to do it. Her daughter was upset about it. Also, she doesn't ask the social worker if she could see the children more often. I think these are vital desires.

Dr. L: Even before recognizing the desires, one needs to authorize her as a desiring subject, as a subject of desire. I think she doesn't see this possibility yet.

Cristiana: I remember she once told me that when she went to see her son—who is now one and a half—she noticed that he was still wearing diapers. She would have liked to point this out to the educator, but then she thought, "Maybe they want to wait until the summer when it gets warmer, and then they will stop the diapers." As a mother, she knows that you stop using diapers at a certain age. She has done it before, but now she does not dare to say it. Here she is able to voice herself as a mother, but outside she is dispossessed of the children and of her desire to take care of them.

Dr. L: Outside she is in a constant state of castration. She doesn't seem to be able to "exercise her existence," to quote the African author Achille Mbembe. Therefore, it is the exercise of her existence that needs to be suggested to her. She needs to be supported as a mother who asks, "Where is my daughter going?" You need to support her as a desiring subject. This support will help her exist. This is what existence is all about. We wouldn't be who we are if we weren't able to desire, to express an opinion, to assert our difference vis-à-vis the other. In this way we resist non-being.

In *On the Postcolony,* Mbembe discusses the relationship between subjectivity and temporality and describes subjectivity itself as temporality. Each time and age, he says, has a distinctive "spirit" (zeitgeist) that is "constituted by a set of material practices, signs, figures, superstitions, images, and fictions that, because they are available to individuals' imagination and intelligence and actually experienced, form what might be called 'languages of life.' This 'life world' is not only the field where individuals' existence unfolds in practice; it is where they exercise existence—that is, live their lives out and confront the very forms of their death" (Mbembe 2001, 15). Although Mbembe refers to historical ages—and specifically to the postcolony—the psychiatrist used the same idea of exercising existence to understand Afërdita's experience. This analysis can be extended to the experience of crossing borders more broadly. What is the temporality of exercising existence and of crossing borders? These two experiences resemble each other, because to locate subjectivity as temporality is to place it in the here and now, in the nothingness that is inherent to existence. Both experiences involve a confrontation with nothingness and various forms of death, and both are shaped by the time of the institutions (Binswanger and Foucault 1986). Moreover, Afërdita's case forces the question of what it means to exercise one's existence in a culture other than your own. How does one desire in another culture? If we understand desire/wanting as something that is shaped by social and political categories and is thus contingent on a specific time and space, then Afërdita did not know what to desire, how to desire, or if desiring was appropriate.

> *Dr. Z:* The desire for a man is another issue she brings up with us.
>
> *Dr. L:* Yes, and in this case it is better that Sister Carla is not the only one who sets the rules and their meanings. If Afërdita is able to express herself more as a mother, maybe she won't feel the same need to look for a mother in the nun, which is what complicates her relationship with Sister Carla.
>
> *Dr. Z:* We talked to Sister Carla about this. She always talks about the women at the shelter as "my girls." So I told her that it sounded as if she was a mother who had many teenage daughters, and Afërdita was the most demanding one. I tried to explain that if Afërdita transgresses rules, it is also to test her, to see how much attention she can get. On the one hand, Sister Carla seems flattered to play the role of the mother, and on the other, she insists that Afërdita can't stay in the shelter for much longer because they need to respect the time line of the shelter, which doesn't allow women to stay for more than six months.
>
> *Dr. L:* When they start to talk about rules and the time of the institutions it means they are uneasy about someone.
>
> *Cristiana:* Sister Carla longs to wean Afërdita!

Everyone laughed. The metaphor of Sister Carla weaning Afërdita refers to the paradoxical lifeworld staged at the shelters—that of the family—where nuns come to personify mothers who raise unruly girls in need of discipline and containment. The rules Sister Carla applies are supposed to discipline Afërdita and help her cure. Those rules are imposed by the state's integration programs, which determine how long a cure is supposed to take. The meeting at the Centro shows once again that the time it would take to cure Afërdita and the time it takes to care for her are at odds. The cure that the shelter provides is in line with the logic of recognition, according to which Afërdita is either compliant with the program or sick. Curing, in this context, implies translating dis-ease into ease, pathology into normality. Caring for her, on the other hand, means surrendering these categories and paying attention to her transgression of the rules—not as something in need of redress, but rather as her active response to the institution's failure to hear and attend to her despair.

> *Dr. L:* Afërdita's symptom is not that she looks for a maternal figure but that the lack of a mother is still her main issue. Maybe you [addressing Dr. Z, her primary therapist] can help her reflect on the fact that she doesn't have a mother, and she never will. This is the most difficult aspect to work on, especially with someone who did have a mother who pulled back from the relationships with her children. The fact that her mother committed suicide and that when she was alive she was unavailable constitutes the shadow in which Afërdita is looking for maternal figures. This search is symptomatic because it prevents her from coming to terms with the loss. To start with, it would be good to work on the situations in which she feels inappropriate and misrecognized as a mother, since the Tribunal has put her on hold and suspended the decision about the children.

> *Cristiana:* In many ways, she needs to reinvent what it means to be here, which is not the same as being in Albania. She is faced with so many different institutional cultures, and she is asking herself, "What is a mother supposed to do in Italy?" She is trying to test the boundaries of what is legitimate and allowed. She is lost and trying to reinvent herself as a mother and as a woman. It is as if she were learning a new grammar to fit into this specific form of life, or rather these multiple forms of life that institutions represent.

> *Dr. L:* All the tribunal procedures are based on implicit assumptions, like what a good parent is or what a reliable mother does. Afërdita's case is different from other cases of parents whose children have been taken into custody by social services. She does not abuse her children or forget them at the market. In her case, her illness is the cause of her inadequacy. Therefore, the knowledge she would need to acquire in order to become a "good mother" does not exist. It is like telling a crippled man, "You are not a good enough father because you are crippled." This is a paradoxical message.

I agree with you [referring to me] that the Albanian culture is no longer available to her. Italian culture, on the other hand, is a big mess if it is all about Sister Carla's rules, the Tribunal's and the judge's decrees, the social workers' projects. She finds herself in a labyrinth. It is understandable if she at times feels lost, disoriented, and inert. It is precisely the reaction of those who find themselves in a cultural labyrinth, more than in a different culture.

Dr. Z: Even when she walks around the city she always questions whether it is a good thing to walk alone or not. Apparently where she lived in Albania it is not good for a woman to walk by herself in the streets. Especially when it gets dark, she is afraid of people's gaze, of what they might think of her: "Maybe they think I am a prostitute, that I am an easy woman."

Dr. L: Let's do a theoretical and anthropological reflection. If culture is meant to guide us in understanding how to feel and how to be at ease, this had not happened to her in either Albania or here. She still doesn't know how to behave and feel. She doesn't know how people see her actions and whether she is doing fine or not. She doesn't know if she feels happy walking alone at night in the city. She needs to reinvent a way to feel, something that the culture of her group doesn't seem to have taught her. But what she encounters here are simulacra of culture, because the Tribunal for Minors is not a culture but a simulacrum of juridical culture; the nun and the shelter are simulacra of family life; the social worker is a simulacrum of human solidarity. They are all simulacra, and none of them is suited to teach her how to feel and behave. So the work on being a mother is part of a broader issue: What does she feel, and how? Can she go out? Can she desire? Can she look? Can she be looked at?

In Dr. L's words, the hospital, the Tribunal, and social services enact "simulacra of culture." As such, they risk having no referent or reality except their own. Baudrillard (1983) has taught us that when signs are separated from their referents, the distinction between object and representation does not hold any longer, and a new configuration of the world emerges—one that is made of models, copies of copies, or simulacra that have no referent to reality.

Cristiana: She is testing the limits of what is allowed by always exceeding it.

Dr. Z: She often complains that she gets tired by doing nothing. When I ask her to describe what her day looks like, she lists the things she does: she gets up at 6:00 A.M., cleans the room, goes to language school in the morning, comes back home, has a quick lunch, then goes out again to visit the children, and gets home when it is dark. So I tell her that she is tired because she does do a lot. But she keeps saying that she doesn't do anything, meaning that she doesn't have a real job.

Dr. L: It is important to appreciate and value what she does, says, and thinks because she was probably never appreciated for her work. If all she did in her life was look after sick people who eventually died, it is easy to believe that she received very little approval. In her life she probably took care of things no one else in the family would have, so this must have created a certain degree of discouragement, which needs to be changed in the therapy. It is important that she understands that she is tired because she does a lot of things, that learning a new language is tiring and difficult.

Dr. Z: Her father used to undermine her suffering by saying things like, "Don't worry, don't think about it and it will pass." So her suffering was not valued either; it was treated as something unimportant.

Cristiana: She often mentions the fact that when she lived in Albania with her family, she was ashamed of eating in front of other people and of asking for more food if she was still hungry.

Dr. Z: This also happened at the first shelter where she lived. They would forget to give her the medicines, and she wouldn't ask; she was afraid of asking for more food and other things she needed. She always brings a lot of food to the children. It's her way of showing that she is a good mother.

Dr. L: If it is true that her mother was absent because she was depressed, we can only imagine that she was deprived of food and that she would have liked to receive more. But she didn't ask for it because she was afraid of not getting it anyway. This is why she is also so afraid of losing the few relationships she has at the moment and is so hesitant to ask for what she needs. Her needs as a child were never attended to. . . . I think she has great expectations of the work she is doing with you [referring to Dr. Z and me]. I see it in her eyes that are charged with expectation. It is important that you reassure her about it.

ON THE TIME OF DREAMING

In the space of the clinic, the world of dreams came to life for Afërdita. She dreamed a lot and took to writing down her dreams in a journal. Together with Dr. Z, she attended and listened to her dreams as important moments of her life. The dream space was a different world from Albania and Italy. It allowed her to live in multiple worlds simultaneously; she did not have to cross from one to another but could rest in between here and there, life and death. She did not have to leave death behind in her dreams, as she was asked to do before the judge. She could be alive in the midst of death. Ludwig Binswanger (1963) identifies the dream as the space where we can ask what it means to be a human being. For him, dreams, like language, are our way of being-in-the-world. Something fundamentally central to existence is dramatized in dreams: the hovering of human existence, which does not necessarily move in a downward direction, but "can also signify liberation and the possibility of ascending" (83). Binswanger brings dreams back to their existential dimension; images are not indexes pointing to some other hidden meanings but are themselves manifestations of Being. A joyous image and the happiness experienced through it and a sad image and the sadness that accompanies it are one and the same. Who is dreaming, and what is the place of the individual in both the dream and its interpretation? Dreaming and life are bound together, and the dream is the moment when existence happens in its translation into the dream's images. Dreams are thus a moment that can only be acknowledged and that relieve the subject of the pressure of institutional languages and their urge to translate difference and existence into categories. In this sense, the therapeutic space allowed Afërdita to be in the midst of death and loss. This kind of attention to and engagement with her dreams is an illustration of the listening that ethno-psychiatry does.

One night Afërdita had a dream. The next day, she arrived at the Centro for her session, early as usual. When she entered the room she sat on the chair next to Dr. Z and asked me to sit close to her, so that she could be between us. She was smiling and slightly covering her face with one hand, almost as a sign of shyness. Then she touched her hands, started biting her nails, and turned serious. Here is how she recounted the dream:

> I am in Albania with my mother who is still alive. She holds my son, Pietro, who is still alive, and tells me not to worry, she is looking after him. I hold my other son, Marcello, and worry that my mother is there to take both sons away. In another part of the dream, my mother runs after me and wants to take me away, too. I run fast, and when I awake I have fear in my heart. Every time I dream of my mother, something bad happens. The next morning, Marcello was sick with the flu.

"My deepest wish is to heal, to feel better," she said, with an imploring expression. "But I am afraid of dying, of having brain cancer, something bad in my brain." Dr. Z reminded her that the last medical check did not show any problem in her brain and that lately she had even reduced the dosage of the antidepressant because she was feeling better. "Sometimes we are afraid of healing, of getting better," Dr. Z suggested. Afërdita went back to the dream. She was afraid of dreaming of her mother because it made her fear for her and her children's lives. Dr. Z commented that dreaming about her mother reminded her of what Afërdita had heard when she was a teenager taking care of mother: "You will become like me, but don't worry about it now." The dream was almost like another prophecy, her therapist remarked.

These dreams haunted Afërdita, even in Italy, far from Albania and her family. She also shared that in her dreams Italy figured as a place of light and hope, whereas Albania stood for the darkness of the night and for the house of the dead where mourners kiss corpses as a sign of a final departure. Afërdita was never able to kiss her mother's corpse, so her mother's returns in her dreams scare her. She often spoke of dreams. She recalled them vividly. As stories she told to herself, she took them seriously and described them with care, with the expectation of a revelation. She was a good storyteller. Dr. Z and I listened to what happened in Afërdita's dreams and learned to inhabit them with her. The dreams allowed her to experience fear, death, and life, without having to hide them or translate them in a way that would be digestible for the institutions.

This is another dream that Afërdita recounted to us:

> I am in Albania in my in-law's house. The house is empty; everyone has either gone away or died. My husband's parents have just died. I am getting ready to leave. The darkness of the time of illness is gone, the windows are open, the curtains flutter in the wind, and there is air and light coming into the rooms. My father-in-law comes back because he wants to see me. He gives me a bag full of black clothes because someone has just died, and 400 euros. I am happy about the gift but hesitate to take the money. He tells me to eat good food and then to leave but not to take the path that cuts through the bushes. I would ruin my new clothes. I saved myself by taking the path he showed me.

When she awoke from the dream, she was happy. As she told us about it, she smiled and said, "It is good luck to dream about a dead person who gives you a present." She does not dream about life very often. As we talked about this dream, she explained it as her father-in-law's blessing to migrate, to go toward the light. "Maybe he has helped you take the right path," I suggested. "Yes, and maybe it means that I can have the children back," replied Afërdita. "Were you happy to take the path he showed you in the dream?" I asked. "Yes, definitely," she replied enthusiastically. But then her eyes became sad, and she said, "Maybe, had I stayed in Albania, I could have kept my children. They would have never been taken them away from me." She had reentered the world where rules and categories turned her experience into pathology in need of a cure.

ON THE TIME OF MELANCHOLIA

Afërdita often said that she was afraid of getting lost in the city, of losing her fixed and familiar trajectories. When I first started participating in the consultations, she kept telling me how devastating it was when the bus she was taking to go visit her daughter had to take a detour from the usual route to avoid construction. She panicked and did not know what to do. When I related this to Dr. L, he replied, "Two things happen in the labyrinth: you get lost, and no one can find you. These two possibilities are symmetrical."

Afërdita spoke from a space of loss and death. Loss was the experience she associated with Albania, but moving to Italy marked a different kind of loss: the loss of her husband, her children, and the sense of who she was as a woman and a mother. Her tragic attempt to defend herself to the judge in the custody hearing was a measure of the difficulties she encountered reoccupying the world in the context of Italy and in making sense of the norms and rules that regulated social order. She searched for ways to exercise her existence in the various institutional languages whose codes she did not know how to interpret and follow. The past would seep into her attempts to represent herself as a "healthy and good mother" before the law, a domain that demanded certain evidence in order to grant her recognition and the right to be a parent.

But to speak of her as a migrant and to interpret her suffering only in the context of her migration could produce yet another kind of alienation and silencing. The immigrant story that various institutional figures attempted to trace in order to understand her present substitutes a more painful and horrific history. In the ethno-psychiatric setting, her various stories were heard as both a testimony of her crossing borders and, simultaneously, as symptoms of what Dr. L described as coming from afar. When the group at the Centro reflected on Afërdita's urge to talk about dead people every time she was called before the judge, what emerged was the transgenerational dimension of her suffering, an unresolved and unclaimed trauma that was passed on and never fully claimed and mourned (Freud 1981 [1917]; Faimberg 2005; Caruth 1996).

In "Mourning and Melancholia" Freud writes, "Mourning is regularly the reaction to the loss of a loved person, or to the loss of some abstraction which has taken the place of one, such as one's country, liberty, an ideal" (1981 [1917], 243). Over time, the mourner undergoes a psychic process that allows her to work through the sorrow and grief produced by the loss and restore meaning to life and the world. Melancholia, on the other hand, turns mourning into an endless process. Freud adds, "Melancholia too may be the reaction to the loss of a loved object," but in this case, "The object has not perhaps actually died, but has been lost as an object of love" (245). Thus, it is not clear what is actually lost in melancholia: one knows *whom* one has lost but not *what* one has lost in them (245). In mourning there is nothing unconscious about the loss, whereas in melancholia the lost object is somewhat withdrawn from consciousness. In Freud's work, melancholia constantly blurs into mourning, and vice versa, but one clear difference between the two is that "in mourning it is the world which has become poor and empty; in melancholia it is the ego itself" (246). In melancholia the relationship with the lost object is never fully severed, but it is a relationship that depletes the ego and makes it feel empty. This produces an eternal loss, something that functions as an open wound that hurts endlessly.

For Freud, melancholia is a pathological disposition of the subject. Judith Butler's (1997, 167) reading of Freud's essay provides an opening onto the possibility of understanding melancholia "as an account of how psychic and social domains are produced in relation to one another." Butler identifies melancholia as an experience that can offer insight into the workings of social boundaries and how they affect the psychic life of subjects. We can thus understand forms of subjectivity that emerge in the crossing of boundaries, or in the context of personal and collective trauma, as melancholia (Garcia 2010).[4] Here the temporality that constitutes subjectivity is experienced as a frozen past that can no longer be presented or made present (Benjamin 2009). However, as Benjamin has shown in his praise of baroque reason, this past is part of existence. But this past is experienced as mourning for something that will no longer return and for which one has to be responsible. Incorporating mourning into one's existence is not the same as going mad forever; rather, it makes accessing existence a possibility. One could say with Benjamin and Julia Kristeva (1992) that the melancholic subject of migration bears the potentiality of emancipation, precisely because it has consumed all roots of the past.

In listening to the Centro's therapists interpret Afërdita, I began to understand her experience in light of Freud's idea of melancholia and its fundamental—maybe even unchangeable—effects on the psychic life of the subject through generations. Contrary to what the institutional figures thought, her constant references to death were her way of talking about life. She embodied the language of death and loss to the point that she did not have anything else on which to build her voice. Her crying became louder and repetitive, unbearable to listen to for some, because she did not feel heard. Through the psychiatrist's reflections and the several hours spent in sessions with her, I began to understand that Afërdita's wound was old and fresh at the same time, and also timeless. I joined the therapists at the Centro in listening to her refrains about death and dying as a form of speech, as a life story turned into a death story. In this context, death and life were evoked simultaneously. What made her story disturbing for the judge, the social workers, and the nuns was that it forced the question of whether it is possible to live with death and to understand this experience outside the register of pathology. Is a cure possible? If not, would the care provided by a different listening be enough? Furthermore, death is not cherished in late liberalism; it is life that takes center stage—the life worth living and the life that reproduces itself (Povinelli 2011). Death tends to be abandoned or pushed to the margins.

In the months following the discussion of her case, Afërdita often lamented the fact that she could only see her children twice a week in a "neutral place," where a psychologist and a social worker observed their interactions. During these visits she was not allowed to speak in Albanian to the children because the observers could not understand them. During one consultation, she expressed her concern about this: "My son, who is only one and a half, is forgetting all the words in Albanian that I taught him. How will he be able to communicate with his sister when they see each other?" She often felt anxious about being exiled from her mother tongue and not being able to speak it with her children. I heard this as yet another loss, of her mother tongue, which was being silenced and erased from her relationship with the children. At times, though, she also lamented that in therapy sessions she preferred to speak Italian even in the presence of the Albanian cultural mediator (a man her age) because she wanted to talk about "female problems," as she put it, only in the presence of women—her therapist and me—and neither of us spoke Albanian.

This is one paradox of the institutional apparatus that is supposed to test her ability to be a "good mother" but in doing so denies her access to her mother tongue. She experienced this as a violent form of censorship, and of severing the ties between her, Albania, and the children. At the Centro, she could speak her mother tongue and explore the trajectories of memory that this entailed. Yet this experience seemed at moments unbearable. Afërdita did not always accept the invitations on the part of the therapist and cultural mediator to evoke familiar terms, phrases that resonated with her life in Albania, practices, images of her childhood spelled out in the grammar of her mother tongue—something that could be understood as "culture." She resorted to Albanian only when Italian words eluded her. Language, too, became a lost object that she could not mourn. I understood this loss as complex. It was produced by social norms and by Afërdita's inability to creatively engage with the language of the mother. In the ethno-psychiatric setting, the patient's mother tongue is used as a sign of recognition and as a tool that the subject can use to access speech. In Afërdita's case, though, this language may have had deadly, rather than vital, qualities. In fact, she associated death with the mother—and with being a mother herself— and thus the mother tongue as well was inscribed in the experience of death. In this case, how does one make death speak?

The stories that Afërdita told in the consultations were punctuated by different refrains that while accounting again and again for some event inevitably also eluded it. If a traumatic experience is not fully assimilated as it occurred, we cannot know it by asking a straightforward question. Rather, the language that can speak it always defies the traumatic experience even as it attempts to put it into words (Caruth 1996). Afërdita's refrains were the stories of the dead, of her mother's prophecy ("You will become just like me, but don't think about it now"), of her fear of having a brain tumor, of not being able to escape the prophecy, of her shame in asking for more food when she was hungry, of her fear of getting lost in the city, and of walking by herself in the streets, feeling like a prostitute. I heard them as moments that exceeded the verbalization of a story that cannot be contained in a coherent narrative. In a way, these refrains appeared as symptoms, as ways to relate to the world and others.

One day during a consultation, she was particularly anxious. The judge in charge of her case at the Tribunal had requested a series of reports from the different people involved in assisting her (the social worker, Sister Carla, and the psychologist at the Centro). She asked them to assess her psychological state and general progress, and he would use this information to make a final decision on the children's custody. Afërdita was aware of this procedure and was very nervous about the outcome. She also had to be evaluated by a psychiatrist and a psychologist chosen by the Tribunal for a second opinion. She was scheduled to meet with the judge to discuss her situation after a week. As soon as she walked into the therapy session, she started crying. "What worries you?" asked Dr. Z. "I have to meet the judge to discuss the situation with the children, and I am afraid of falling," she replied. I asked what she meant by "falling." "I am afraid of losing myself as I talk to the judge and that I will fall again." "Do you mean that you will start crying and won't be able to answer the judge's questions?" asked the therapist.

"Maybe I should take stronger medicine because I am afraid of falling, and this is what the judge wants," answered Afërdita. "I don't think the judge wants you to fall; she is trying to make the best decision for the children," remarked Dr. Z. "I want to take more sleeping pills; I can't wait to go to sleep so that I don't feel anything," she said.

Dr. Z pointed out that this was a difficult moment for her, and it required a lot of strength and courage for her to face all the different institutional figures appointed to evaluate her progress. She continued crying and said, "You will help me, won't you? Will you write well about me for the judge, right? You must tell me what to do, how to behave; you must teach me all that I am supposed to do." Dr. Z was hesitant to make any promises and told Afërdita that her report for the Tribunal was only one perspective on her situation and that others would write different reports. "But you know me well, you can tell my story better than me," Afërdita insisted. "You can tell them about my love for the children, that now I am doing better, that I am in good spirits, that I fear losing the children. Please write well for the judge! Speak well of me, speak well for me."

I thought that she was afraid of losing herself in the midst of the stories about her that different actors collected and crafted. Which story would allow her to exist as a mother? What testimony would allow her to exercise her existence in general? Was she getting lost in the labyrinth of stories that were presented about her? Afërdita feared falling before the judge, and she looked for something to grasp in the story that took form in the therapeutic setting. Yet, for her, this story could hold only if someone else told it on her behalf. It was almost as if she asked, "Would you pretend for me, because I don't exist, I am not." There was something tragic in this request for a *porte parole*, for someone who could convey her words in a way that institutions would hear. It was a request for mediation, for someone to be a word bearer (or word carrier) for her. It was tragic because it sounded ancient and yet present. Her mother could not function as a mediator between the coded symbolic system of the social order and Afërdita's use, as a child, of symbols in the outer and inner world (Glassgold 2010). In the context of her present, she still sought a mediator like this that would help her orient herself in the social world while supporting her being alive.

I heard her plea for a porte parole not as a lack of voice. Rather, I understood it as a fear that death would permeate her speech to the point of annihilating her. I wondered whether Afërdita was asking Dr. Z and me to pretend before the judge that she was alive, while at some existential level she was not. Her fear of falling also resonated with de Martino's (1956) crisis of presence: the existential fear of being effaced by situations that challenge one's ability to handle external and internal realities. Falling, thus, stands for losing contact with the world and, at an experiential and emotional level, dying. Afërdita knew that the space she spoke from exceeded and disrupted what the institutions demanded of her. She could not be recognized as a competent mother because her speech could only be translated into pathology and hence what she called "falling before the judge," which I also interpret as a form of misrecognition. To her, letting someone else speak on her behalf meant having a chance to be spoken of in a language that could be recognized and thus could legitimize her as a mother.

THE THEATER OF CLASSIFICATIONS

When Dr. L described the different institutional cultures and their doubling effect as simulacra of family life (the shelter), human solidarity (social services), and juridical culture (the Tribunal), I started to see more clearly how his approach to this particular story was departing from what I have referred to in this book as practices of recognition, approximating instead what I have called acknowledgment. The ethnopsychiatrist's attempts to provide a different kind of listening as a form of care conflicted with other ways in which Afërdita's story was framed and made intelligible. I call these other renderings of her "theaters of classification," because by portraying her as pathological, incompetent, and unfit as a mother, these accounts simultaneously open up and shut down possible scenarios for her and the children. After reading the various institutional reports about Afërdita, these words never sounded truer to me: "Nobody is the author or producer of his own life story" (cited in Merkell 2003, 13). I would only add that we have as many life stories as the number of authors who craft them for us. Each story enables a world, a play, a plot, and an outcome. As simulacra, they always linger over the threshold of truth and fiction. In the particular instance of the accounts produced by the nuns, the Tribunal, and social services, what emerges is a genre that represents Afërdita as a known object who is either possible or impossible to cure.

As I mentioned in the introduction, practices of recognition ground sovereignty in the knowledge of who one is and what categories can best locate her in the larger community. These reports do not see the enigmas in Afërdita's experiences. Or, rather, their aim is to solve and explain away those enigmas, instead of trying to learn other truths about her from them. Her stories come from a past that cannot fit into the institutions' time frames because it is always already misunderstood. A comparison of the accounts produced by the Catholic nun in charge of the shelter where Afërdita lived, the reports by the Tribunal's mental health practitioners, and the interpretations of the ethno-psychiatrists at the Centro shows that while the institutions insist on a cure, the clinic opens up a space of care whose structure and time are incommensurable with those of the institutions.

The Nun

It was hard to give Sister Carla an age. She could have been in her early fifties, or mid-forties, or neither. She had a round face, a pale complexion, and blue eyes, and she always wore her gray habit and matching veil. She was not very talkative, maybe a little shy even; she blushed often when the topic of concern made her uncomfortable. She was the head of the shelter where Afërdita lived and came to the Centro twice a month to speak to the therapeutic team about her work with Afërdita. The sister's main concern was that Afërdita demanded a lot of attention and constantly complained about not receiving enough: "She has her crisis, says she wants to throw herself from the window or hits her head against the wall. . . . She always looks for an audience; she has her crisis in the TV room in front of the other guests and then complains that I don't love her as much as I love the others." She would often tell Afërdita, "If you stay in bed the whole day and don't eat at mealtime, I will take you back to the hospital because sick people cannot live here." At other times, according to Sister Carla, she transgressed the rules by bringing men into the shelter, where they were not allowed. She wanted to introduce them to Sister Carla but was seeking an approval she would never receive. Sister Carla felt none of them were reliable, responsible, or suited to take care of her or, eventually, her children. "She is very worried that I will judge her as an easy woman," Sister Carla reported.

During one supervision, Sister Carla said, "As a nun, who is unmarried and a virgin, I think my role questions Afërdita as a woman and maybe this makes her feel that there is something wrong with her." The psychiatrist, Dr. L, who was present at this meeting, suggested that Afërdita had a *transfert* on the nun. In other words, she projected the role of the moral judge onto the nun. She was testing the boundaries of her sexuality and morality and asked the nun to do it for her. For this reason, she would bring men to the shelter. He also suggested that there was a dialectic between the nun and Afërdita, between a woman who embodies the law and one who transgresses it:

> Afërdita insists on finding out what she is allowed to do and what she isn't; but this search is not only of the order of the moral. It has to do with her psychological survival. She . . . is trying to define her possibility of being a subject. Her request is not so much, "What can I do," but rather, "What am I?" She is asking you, Sister Carla. Her suffering is very complex and comes from afar. We need to move from the moral sphere to the constitutive sphere of subjectivity.

Afërdita was trying to substitute her old reference points, which no longer held, with new ones. For Dr. Z, her therapist, this was a therapeutic moment in which Afërdita attempted to hold two parallel worlds together: her life in Albania and her life in Italy. But these two worlds were also collapsed into one because it was impossible to bridge them. Any attempt to invoke the temporality of Albania clashed with the frozen time of dead people. In Afërdita's imagination, Sister Carla became the gatekeeper of meaning and therefore an example of motherhood and femininity that she could follow in her attempt to bring her different worlds together. But the nun only presented her with rules that limited her exercise of existence. Sister Carla also contributed to the construction of a simulacrum of family and the mother-daughter relationship: she referred to the guests at the shelter as "my girls," a role that Afërdita resorted to, both in moments of loss when she could not hold onto any reference point around her and in moments of anger when she did not know what the different institutions expected of her.

The Centro's practitioners suggested that Sister Carla could help her have an active role as a mother to her children. After all, pointed out the psychiatrist, Afërdita had been affected by her mother's prophecy-turned-curse: "You will become just like me, but don't think about it now." The nun did not perceive Afërdita's behavior as a request to be rescued from this prophecy but as manipulative and in need of attention that she could not provide. The nun thought, just like other institutional figures, that if she could not follow the shelter's rules she could not be a good mother to her children.

Enter The Tribunal's Experts: The Verdict

Nine months after I first joined Afërdita's sessions, the Tribunal for Minors appointed a psychologist and a psychiatrist to evaluate hers and the children's psychological conditions. The purpose was to gain an outsider's point of view and have "an objective perspective on the case." The Consulenza Tecnica d'Ufficio (Technical Office Consultation [assessment of psychological competency]) is another competing account about Afërdita. This is the Tribunal's procedure for assessing parents' competence to take care of their children. It is often referred to as CTU. The Tribunal took into account other evaluations, such as the reports by Centro Fanon's therapist, Afërdita's social worker, Sister Carla, the daughter's therapist, the educators at the children's shelters, and the observers of her encounters with her children.[5]

Drafting the CTU took approximately three months, during which the mental health practitioners appointed by the Tribunal had to accomplish the following tasks: (1) identify whether Afërdita was affected by psychiatric disorders, and if so, of what nature and entity; (2) describe the symptoms and their consequences for her parental role; (3) describe the possible development of the disorder; (4) describe the quality of her relationship with her children. The Tribunal's mental health experts referred to the DSM IV for diagnostic purposes. After a series of consultations, they produced the following diagnosis: "Depressive nucleus of a persecutory nature; . . . the psychotic state has chronic and stable connotations, but it is not completely disabling in her social and environmental functions." They confirmed the diagnosis made during her previous hospitalization in Italy: "Major Recurrent Depressive Disorder according to the DSM IV." In phenomenological psychiatry, the document continues, this kind of depression is also defined as "unipolar," as opposed to "bipolar."[6]

During her consultations with the Tribunal's mental health practitioners, Afërdita recounted her story again, starting from her mother's death. I learned new things about her when I read the report. For example, she recalled being hospitalized in Albania six months after getting married. She was seventeen when she got married, and her husband used to drink and have sex with other women. Afërdita stayed at home to take care of her in-laws, both of whom were dying from cancer. Six months after her wedding, she and her mother-in-law had come upon a well filled with water. As soon as she approached the well, she felt paralyzed and began to scream uncontrollably. They took her to the hospital, where she stayed for a month and a half. The diagnosis was "depression with delirious episodes."

After six years of marriage, Afërdita learned she was pregnant. Her first pregnancy was easy. Her daughter, Mailinda, was born with a hip problem that was later resolved with a surgical procedure. After two and a half years, her second child, Pietro, was born. The second pregnancy was more difficult. Pietro was born in Albania with "a problem in his ears," which turned out to be a form of meningitis. He died there when he was two, after several failed attempts to restore his health. When this happened, Afërdita was hospitalized a second time with a similar diagnosis of depression. She told the Tribunal's mental health practitioners that she had been unable to overcome the loss of her second child, even after her third son was born. She was afraid that her dead son would come back and visit her at night, in her dreams. His presence in her memories threatened her.

The CTU document was strictly formulated around the depression diagnosis. In one section, it refers to the psychological work Afërdita underwent at the Centro Fanon. The document says that the diagnosis of depression was "completely ignored in the current project for Mrs. Afërdita at the Centro Fanon, where they don't respect the guidelines of treatment outlined by the APA [American Psychiatric Association]." According to the document, social services had not noticed any progress since she had been in psychotherapy at the Centro. Furthermore, "The Centro Fanon has a protective and supportive attitude with a tendency to underestimate Afërdita's depressive tendency." According to the CTU document, Afërdita's therapist does not formulate "a psychopathological diagnostic hypothesis, and instead explains her distress as the consequence of the lack of maternal care and little emotional containment" that she experienced as a child. The Centro's therapist, it continued, interprets Afërdita's case as a form of "reactive depression to the environment, with a neurotic frame." The document concluded that the children needed to find "a stable and solid situation within an adoptive family as soon as possible."

Unlike other accounts about Afërdita, the Tribunal's version contained a verdict. This document followed the guidelines of the law aimed at protecting children; according to it, Afërdita was a psychologically incompetent parent. The law's purpose is to provide guardianship to minors in cases of abuse or when a parent is considered emotionally incompetent. In Afërdita's case, the CTU declared her a sick mother.

The verdict was not lifted even when, months later, Afërdita started a relationship with Carlo, a man in his late forties who was divorced and had a good job. He was very devoted to her and provided her with great stability. They moved in together, and Carlo was open to adopting the children. Even Afërdita's sister and brother, who had migrated to Italy, were available to help with the adoption by providing a family network that the state should have recognized as suitable for the children. Afërdita found a lawyer who followed the case closely and tried hard to convince the Tribunal not only of Afërdita's improved state but also of the suitable family network she now had. Nothing worked to her advantage. The children were still given up for adoption. It felt like a Kafkaesque trial: the more rules she tried to comply with, the more trapped in the system she became, and the more her situation turned into what Dr. L once described as "a case of epistemic violence that screams for justice because it was never heard."

The Center at the Margins

The verdict not only affected Afërdita. In fact, the different reports about Afërdita clearly show the tensions between the institutions and their competing gazes. The Tribunal's document positions the Centro Fanon in a marginal position vis-à-vis other institutions that have more power in making final decisions. Over the course of my research at the Centro, I read two reports that Dr. Z wrote to the judge in charge of Afërdita's children.[7] The reports noted her steady progress in therapy. Dr. Z explained that Afërdita was facing her big life conflict: being abandoned by her mother, who committed suicide. This experience was now exacerbated by the fact that her children were in foster care and being considered for adoption. She was reliving the separation and abandonment from her own mother. Dr. Z explained how Afërdita felt powerless and frustrated because she did not know how to reassure her children when she visited them. She often asked for advice on how to be a "good mother" because she felt constantly questioned by various institutional figures. Overall, Dr. Z's report documented Afërdita's ability to reflect on herself, her greater awareness of her limits and strengths, "which can lead to strengthening her motherly function." These reports did not mention curing Afërdita—at all costs and according to the institutions' schedule—because that is the state's agenda, not the Centro's. This tension echoes Franco Basaglia's struggle against the mental hospital and its focus on control and custody (chapter 2). Cure does not fit with the ethno-psychiatric notion of care, which does not depend on translating suffering into diagnoses.

When I later compared these reports with the CTU, I realized that while ethno-psychiatry's suspension of psychiatric categories has an impact on dominant apparatuses of power that turn to ethno-psychiatrics for an expert opinion on cultural competence and mental health, it is still at the margins of that power. Ethno-psychiatrists are frustrated by that powerlessness. For them, working with various institutions in charge of integrating foreigners into Italian society often felt like tilting at windmills. Institutions such as the Tribunal can silence or dismiss the Centro's approach to care and cure precisely because ethno-psychiatry brackets diagnostic criteria and acknowledges other etiologies and healing techniques. It is in part from this marginal space that the Centro can exercise the power of disagreement and interruption with the state and its practices of recognition, but this can also become a powerless position. In their report on Afërdita's psychological competence, the Tribunal's mental health practitioners implied that the Centro could possibly produce a "misdiagnosis." I thought it was interesting that suspending a psychiatric diagnosis automatically equaled, in the Tribunal's culture, a misdiagnosis. The possibility of there being other interpretations—or listening—outside of diagnostic categories was not even an option. Their psychological assessment of Afërdita thus shows the complex overlap and intersection of juridical and diagnostic apparatuses that reaffirm their centrality by locating ethno-psychiatry at the margins. Was the Centro, then, perceived as "indigestible" by the state and its apparatuses because it produced an excessive discourse about difference that broke with existing medical and juridical discourses? Was it being marginalized just like the clientele it represented?

STUMBLING TEMPORALITIES

From the perspective of the Centro's therapists, suspending a diagnosis implied suspending the temporality of biomedical reasoning and the linear logic that assigns symptoms to a diagnosis, a diagnosis to a course of treatment, and a treatment to a cure. The ethno-psychiatric setting—much like a psychoanalytic one, at least in Afërdita's case—makes room for the temporality of the unconscious to present itself. What I mean by this is that Afërdita's memories and language followed a paradoxical temporality; they emerged as stuttered accounts, fragments of stories, and repetitions that stumbled upon each other. In other words, in this therapeutic setting, multiple temporalities can coexist: the time of dreaming, of mourning and melancholia, of regression, and of repetition. The time of the unannounced—those words that should not be spoken in other institutional times and spaces but are nonetheless uttered, like Afërdita's insistence on speaking of the dead—has a place in the time of the clinic, too. There is also the time of political and collective violence that emerges on patients' bodies as symptoms or broken sentences, as in the case of the women involved in prostitution or people applying for political asylum. These temporalities have no definite boundaries, and what makes the therapeutic encounter complex is that they overlap and intertwine. And then there is the time of transgenerational trauma, with its silences and dangerous prophecies, where history seems to be frozen and unaccessible and signification breaks down. The time of dreaming becomes a moment where what cannot be said in words is experienced on the screen of the unconscious in the form of images. In dreams, Afërdita speaks about the ghost of her mother and the sense of hope in leaving the dead behind. The relationship between Afërdita's language and her suffering, what she says and what it signifies, points to the fact that her speech can only be heard indirectly, obliquely. It cannot be translated literally into the language of medicine or the courtroom. Language fails her before the judge, the nun, and the social worker, who can only listen to its literality and translate it into a form of pathology or deviance that must either be cured or rehabilitated. Her repetitions create a discomfort because their referential meaning—her continuous mention of death—points to something institutions recognize as "depression" of various degrees and seriousness. In these institutional roles, Afërdita is constantly betrayed by language—her own and the one she tries to master in order to be recognized as a fit mother. In her accounts, language becomes a symptom and as such needs to be attended to differently. In the clinical space, however, it is not translated into a diagnosis, nor is it recognized only as a sign of illness. Here, it is acknowledged as pointing to pathways of memories that do not lead to the archive of the state institutions; it produces a different kind of knowledge where uncertainty and opaqueness are not explained away, where life is not the opposite of death (Desjarlais 2012), and suffering can be contemporaneous to life and health. Here I am reminded of Veena Das's (1996, 70) words: "Pain . . . is not that inexpressible something that destroys communication or marks an exit from one's existence in language. Instead, it makes a claim asking for acknowledgement, which may be given or denied. In either case, it is not a referential statement that is simply pointing to an inner object."

Afërdita's words did not necessarily express what they formulated. All institutional figures involved in her "case" had to struggle with the disorienting question of how to listen to her speech. The Tribunal's report, like the reports provided by social services and the nuns, attempted to interpret her speech as pathological and as a sign of her incompetence as a mother. Her behaviors and words were translated into the language of pathology, thus making her intimacy with death intelligible and, to some extent, manageable in terms of deciding her children's future. The uncertainty of pain and suffering, of life and death so fiercely voiced beyond the power of her words, cannot be known through categories and diagnoses; it begs for acknowledgment (Das 1996), for a form of knowing that can only be acquired through experience and by suspending categories. In the case of ethno-psychiatry, experience comes from listening as care and from cure not as treatment but as yet another kind of care. Acknowledgment blurs any easy distinction between health and pathology, between a dream and reality, and thus puts epistemology as a modality of knowing to rest.

By suspending diagnostic and cultural categories, the ethno-psychiatrists heard Afërdita's cry as coming from afar. The tone of her melancholia was acknowledged, and the accounts about death were heard as symptoms that carried her life story. This listening provided a form of care in which her difference and pain were not necessarily "recognized" as something else. Through acknowledgment, one can move from the politics of treatment, which translates difference into diagnostic or social categories, to a different kind of politics of life and care, beyond the logics of understanding and sovereignty and the time of the state. The very linear, singular, and predefined time of the state, which subscribes to the *telos* of progress and development, decides and erases all the other temporalities and is thus challenged by the Centro's assessment of Afërdita's progress in therapy. The ethno-psychiatric approach provides an example of acknowledgment akin to the way that critical medical anthropology attends to the relationship between language and the body, or language and the unconscious, as experiences that do not fit within definite categories. It is this kind of attention, rather than recognition, that allows for a different politics of life that can rest in the uncertainty of experience.

This story and clinical case leads me to make a broader argument about the kind of politics of therapeutics and difference that ethno-psychiatry proposes and that challenges state projects of recognition. As a clinical practice, it opens up a political space, in the sense Jacques Rancière (1999) gives to the political. For Rancière, political action is about changing the social order, creating a form of *dissensus* that changes the meaning of political engagement and redefines what can be said and what is visible within a given community. As I explained in the introduction, he distinguishes between political acts and policing practices: the former refer to those actions that disrupt preexisting discourses and make space for new forms of social existence; the latter refer to the management of given social roles and places that are rearranged but do not change. Ethno-psychiatry's bracketing of diagnostic categories and attendance to the multiple temporalities of trauma and of experience create an interruption, a disagreement, with the discourses and temporalities imposed by other institutions. It is in this space of interruption—in all those moments when Afërdita's narrative was heard beyond her words, as a form of grief that clings to her language and body, in friction with the expectations, demands, and hopes of other institutions—that I see ethno-psychiatry attending to difference without necessarily wanting to know it or translate it into something known. In resting in the unknown of someone else's experience, it proposes the acknowledgment of difference rather than recognition and care over cure as ways to rethink the politics of difference. Cure always allows the state to exercise its control on the body of the other, to take care of her while simultaneously depriving her of economic rights, or, in Afërdita's case, of custody of her children. The politics of care, on the other hand, challenges the ambivalent logics of cure and by listening to difference opens it up to its multiple temporalities without taking away the right to exercise one's own existence. Afërdita's story illustrates the possibility of receiving care but not cure, where the coexistence with loss became her life, where trauma, instead of being heard as a missed narrative or a deadly narrative, was held as an account in and of itself, received in the fullness of its holes and stuttering.

matter what form, can only recognize us *as* such and such, that is, as something which we fundamentally are *not*."[1] In Pirandello's play, the characters are haunted by the absence of an author, but when they find one in the theater's director they feel misrepresented by the actors' personification. They, too, are recognized as something they are not.

In what other scenes, outside of institutional settings and their scripts, is life negotiated in ways that rupture practices of recognition? Here I am thinking of possible heterotopias. These are spaces of radical otherness that disturb shared discourses, where categories no longer hold and institutional languages are shattered and unable to name experiences (Foucault 1994b, xviii). Heterotopias are radical worlds that emerge in the interstices of institutions and that contest and reverse their hegemony. Because they turn the established order upside down, these spaces do not fit into common categories; often they remain unrecognized. For these reasons, though, they have the potential to create new forms of life.

In 2008, in Castel Volturno, a town in the south of Italy near Naples, the Camorra, the powerful local mafia, killed six African seasonal construction workers. Between 2008 and 2010, in the town of Rosarno, African migrants took to the streets to protest organized crime after the local mob murdered several migrants. In these places, criminal organizations control everything—from jobs, wages, and housing to immigration documents. Local mafias tolerate foreigners because they provide cheap labor; in this way, they often provide the recognition and protection that, especially in the south, the state is incapable of offering. This is a lawless kind of recognition that originates from unrecognized rights and operates with merciless violence. It has a profound impact on foreigners who come to Italy in search of jobs and who do not qualify as "political refugees" or "victims of human trafficking." Despite this reality and even though they were reacting to the poor living conditions and slave hours imposed on them, the rioters were portrayed as criminals by the media. These uprisings were not about attacking the law but finding a space to live within the interstices created by state law and the law of organized crime. By standing up to the mafia, foreigners were, in fact, creating a new space where they could defend their rights and those that Italians are too afraid to stand up for. In a way, they had nothing to lose; they had the drive to fight that the local population lacked (Saviano 2009). In the past several years, the most important marches against organized crime in the south have been led by groups of Africans shouting, "Ora basta!" (Enough is enough!). I see this moment of revolt as a possible heterotopia, where a group of migrant seasonal workers has found a way to exercise existence in a space created by institutional logics but outside of and in disagreement with it.

A similar space is occupied by the women who went through the rehabilitation program for victims of human trafficking, were granted documents and legal residence, and later went back to work in the sex industry. I met several of them. Some women were disappointed with the state's promises because they could not find a good job or they struggled to keep regular employment. Others knew they could make more money in the sex industry, especially now that they were not tied to a madam. Because prostitution is legal in Italy, they were no longer afraid of being deported; they could just show their residency permit when the police stopped them. Still others became madams themselves and found ways to avoid getting caught. Even if they did get arrested, after a year or two in jail they went back to managing prostitution networks. If the state provides only a few categories of recognition, people find spaces outside of and in between those categories to invent a different life, because of and despite those very categories.

In the years following the conclusion of my research, the Centro Fanon has also come to occupy a space of radical rupture with other institutions. In fall 2012, I spoke with Roberto Beneduce. He told me about the increasing difficulties the Centro's practitioners were having working with institutional actors. He reminded me that during my fieldwork (2002–4), they were privileged interlocutors for several institutions involved in aid programs for foreigners. Although mostly in disagreement with these institutions' practices, they were considered experts whose input made a difference. Over time, however, local administrations changed their political agendas, and the Centro started to receive less funding from the municipality and the regional government. The latter has been ruled by the right-wing Lega Nord for the past four years, which has increasingly promulgated radical anti-immigrant propaganda. Despite the fact that at the municipality level the city of Turin is ruled by a coalition of the left, funds for integration programs for foreigners have either been cut or dispersed among a growing number of new NGOs interested in social projects for migrants.

In this new scenario, ethno-psychiatrists faced new difficulties. On the one hand, they had to start collaborating with organizations that were completely without experience working with migrant populations; on the other, they felt that the new political atmosphere did not recognize their expertise as crucial to working with foreigners and encouraged or justified more racism on the part of the institutions. This new situation made the work of ethno-psychiatrists more arduous and con-flicted. Moreover, in 2009, Roberto Maroni, Lega Nord's deputy, passed a decree that called foreign migration an "emergency," estab-lished regular roundups to secure the safety of the territory, and pro-longed the detention period of undocumented foreigners in the Center for Identification and Expulsion (CIE). This juridical change encour-aged social workers, bureaucrats, and volunteers to adopt a more dis-criminatory approach toward foreigners in general. The ethno-psychia-trists were perceived as even more disturbing interlocutors than before, and the funding stopped.

Beneduce explained that some of the new NGOs that competed with the Centro for funding in the field of psychosocial support for foreign-ers used a phone service instead of cultural mediation to help translate between patients and doctors. This minimized the importance of the clinical encounter and of what it means for patients and doctors to inhabit the space of the clinic, where multiple languages, body prac-tices, and symbols coexist. Most important, he lamented the fact that their work as state consultants had reached an impasse: their expertise could no longer be translated into the practices of social workers and bureaucrats. "They never loved us because we had always been critical of state practices, but eventually our approach was overlooked," he told me. He explained to me how he would go out of his way to consult with state bureaucrats and Catholic nuns on the clinical and cultural aspects of specific cases, to later find out that some of the women were hospitalized if the nuns or social workers thought they were feeding their children in a weird way or combing their hair strangely. After years of ambivalent collaborations with state institutions, the Centro's ethno-psychiatrists no longer wanted their patients to identify them with the very institutions that were adopting restrictive and discrimina-tory measures. Thus, they decided to cut ties with religious groups, the immigration offices, social services, and other institutions for which they consulted, turning exclusively to their clinical work. From that rupture, the clinical work of ethno-psychiatry continues to pose critical challenges to state apparatuses and biomedicine. Ethno-psychiatry has now become a heterotopia because its practice does not fit in the space of the state or of biomedicine. Ethno-psychiatry has come to occupy a space that eludes power, that is not recognizable, but that can produce an alternative place for patients to find life and acknowledgment.

While ethno-psychiatrists use their clinical work to make a radical break from the institutions, the African rioters in the south destabilize the boundaries of what is licit and illicit by literally lighting this distinction on fire and thus generating new possibilities for existence. In the end, it is in these liminal spaces, where the risk of being annihilated is higher, that existence can be exercised once again in ways that can break with dominant discourses.

Notes

1. Throughout this book I use pseudonyms to ensure confidentiality and protect people's identities. In the case of doctors, I have used initials that do not necessarily correspond to their real names. In the case of Nigerian women, I have used names that are common among them. These are Christian names such as Mary, Joy, Grace, Promise, Favor, Prudence, Charity, Amen, and others. Their African names are usually used as second names and do not always appear in official documents.

2. "Victim of human trafficking" is the expression used in immigration law to define those who have been physically abused and forced into forms of exploitation. This ethnography takes a critical approach to the categories "victim" and "trafficking," showing how the lived experiences of those labeled "victims" exceed the terms of the law in their complexities and ambivalence.

3. I use the term *prostitute* to talk about foreign women who worked in the sex industry and later entered the program of rehabilitation for "victims of human trafficking" because this is the ethnographically appropriate term. Members of the Italian Committee for the Civil Rights of Prostitutes such as Pia Covre use this term to talk about sex work. Although I am aware of the different connotations of terms such as *prostitute* and *sex worker*, I also argue that they point to a dichotomy that my work attempts to question. On the one hand, the term *sex worker* situates sexual labor as work that has been consciously chosen as a source of income. In this context, sex work is not represented as merely exploitative, and women are agents of their decisions. The term *prostitute*, on the other hand, alludes to the condition of victimhood and exploitation to which women are subjugated. My ethnography shows how the agent versus victim representation of sexual labor is not always appropriate and does not

capture the ambivalence that foreign women experience in being involved in it. The complexities of their experiences, the coexistence of different kinds of reasons—conscious and unconscious—for their migration plans, are often erased by the terms that describe sex labor. For these reasons, I have decided to use the term that most of my interlocutors in the field used.

4. Geneva, International Seminar on Co-operation and Social Exclusion, June 27, 2000. See full document at www.lucciole.org/content/view/4/3/, on the website of the Italian Committee for the Civil Rights of Prostitutes.

5. By "recognition," I also refer to the projects of citizen making that many scholars have studied (Petryna 2002; Ong 2003; Nguyen 2010; Rose and Novas 2005; Ticktin 2011; Muehlebach 2012).

6. In some ways, ethno-psychiatry resonates with the notion of cultural competence in medicine, social services, and other institutions that regularly encounter difference. As Laurence Kirmayer (2012, 149) notes, "cultural competence" is a movement that places knowledge of the other at the center of clinical practice and denotes "a variety of strategies to address the challenge [that] cultural diversity" poses to healthcare providers. In many different mainstreams of medicine and social services, these challenges are described as "barriers to care" (see Betancourt et al. 2003). Yet in an increasing number of "culturally competent" medical practices, culture is seen as a tool of care rather than a barrier to its effective delivery. Today, culture is deployed in a multitude of practices, from addiction treatment in Native American communities to the rising interest in identifying "protective factors" in specific cultures and identities (see Mossakowski 2003). Ethno-psychiatry proposes a more radical approach to the question of competence in clinical practices by being critical of the very concept of culture and its therapeutic application.

7. For in-depth explanations of the field of phenomenological psychiatry, see Binswanger 1958; Minkowski 1970; Basaglia 1981; Jaspers 1997; Callieri 2001. Phenomenological psychiatry does not rule out the study of drives and patterns of behaviors, but these dynamics can only be understood as occurring at a given moment in space and time, which allows for certain conditions of existence and for the emergence of the subject.

8. Many patients who cycle through the clinic only come for short periods of time or go to sessions irregularly; in other cases, they move and never come back. Others, however, have been patients for years.

9. When the Italian kingdom was unified in 1861, state builders of the northern region of Piedmont sought to promote a secular and rational government as the conditions of modernity, while poverty in the south endured. At this time, Italy's internal social and cultural division emerged even more markedly than before. Industrial workers failed to understand that the northern belief in the innate backwardness and biological inferiority of the southerner was the ruling class's way of reinforcing their hegemony (Gramsci 1978). Italian unification marked a period of internal colonialism.

10. In 1992, the members of the European Community signed a treaty in the town of Maastricht, the Netherlands, which went into effect on November 1, 1993. The treaty created the European Union and led to the creation of the euro, the common European currency.

11. There has been in Italian popular memory, and continues to be, an almost radical repression of Italy's colonial past—its crimes and genocides. The myth of "Italiani brava gente" (Italians as kinder colonizers) is the only memory of the colonial past that has been consistently passed on from one generation to the other. This almost complete absence of debate over colonialism—due in part to the fact that the archives of the Ministry of Foreign Affairs were not accessible until the late 1970s—has not only impeded a critical revision of it but also silenced a possible reflection about the encounter with the other in the context of colonial relations of power and of contemporary migrations to Italy (Palumbo 2003).

12. Pamela Ballinger (2007) has also documented how at that time, within national boundaries, ethnic minorities in the border regions of Valle d'Aosta, Venezia Giulia, and Istria had to speak Italian in order to be recognized as Italian. In the 1947 Peace Treaty, a note from the Ministry of Foreign Affairs to the Border Commission stated that Italian residents abroad who had been born in the ceded territories could preserve citizenship if the language of daily use was Italian.

13. In 1985, Belgium, France, Luxembourg, West Germany, and the Netherlands signed an agreement near the town of Schengen (Luxembourg) that led to the creation of Europe's borderless area, the Schengen Area. The five member-states of the European Economic Union proposed the abolition of border controls and a common visa policy. Today the Schengen Area includes twenty-six member-states of the European Union.

14. NGOs recognized by the state gain credibility with the police when they adapt to its praxis. In these cases, NGOs receive "favors" that would otherwise be unimaginable and are able to obtain residency permits for their clients outside of the set norms for acquiring legal status (Palidda 2000).

15. On migration to Italy, see Carter 1997; Merrill 2006; Cole and Booth 2007; Napolitano 2007.

CHAPTER 1

1. Winnicott (1986b, 2) used the term *cultural experience* as an extension of the idea of transitional objects, which is an "intermediate area of experiencing, to which inner reality and external life both contribute." By "culture," he means "the inherited tradition"; he claims that " it is not possible to be original except on a basis of tradition" (1967, 370). It is in the interplay of these two dimensions, and between the individual and the environment, that experience and life occur.

2. In 1979 Tobie Nathan established the first clinic in ethno-psychiatry together with Georges Devereux. Later, in 1988, he founded the Centre Georges Devereux, an ethno-psychiatric center for foreigners linked to the Université Paris VII in Saint-Denis, on the outskirts of Paris. He named the Center after his teacher, Georges Devereux, from whom he had distanced himself, both theoretically and clinically.

3. In psychiatric diagnoses, as in all diagnoses, the patient's symptoms are reinterpreted and translated as signs of a particular disease. Experience is

decoded in biomedical terms. As Arthur Kleinman (1988, 8) notes, "A psychiatric diagnosis implies a tacit categorization of some forms of human misery as medical problems."

4. Roberto Beneduce practiced for many years as a psychiatrist in the public health care system and founded the Center in 1996 as a space of mediation between foreign patients and Italian institutions. He also trained in medical anthropology and joined the Department of Anthropology at the University of Turin. He conducts field research in Mali and Cameroon, has consulted for international organizations and NGOs in Africa, the Middle East, and Cuba. He also practices as an ethno-psychiatrist at the Centro Fanon. Other clinicians and medical anthropologists who have been engaged in debates about ethno-psychiatry and transcultural psychiatry in Italy are Mariella Pandolfi (1990; Pandolfi and Bibeau 2005), Tullio Seppilli (1989), Pino Schirripa (2005), Giuseppe Cardamone (1990), Salvatore Inglese and Cesare Peccarisi (1997), Piero Coppo (2005), Simona Taliani (Taliani and Vacchiano 2006), Francesco Vacchiano (2007), Pompeo Martelli (2009), Natale Losi (2000), Alfredo Ancora (1997), Goffredo Bartocci and Ray Price (1998), and Luigi Frighi (1992).

5. On this aspect of ethno-psychiatric practice, Beneduce (2007, 252) writes, "Inner ruptures, regrets, conflictual relationships between the 'culture of origin' on the one hand, and new experiences on the other, point to a tormented territory: the ethno-psychiatry of migration is for the most part a 'clinic of ambivalence'" (my translation).

6. From an interview conducted in Turin, June 21, 2004.

7. There is a burgeoning anthropological and psychoanalytic literature about memory, post-traumatic experience, and the "missed narrative" of trauma. On the relationship between trauma and testimony, arguing that traumatic experiences produce a crisis of representation, see Caruth 1996; Pandolfo 1997b; Das 1996, 2003; Fellman 2002; Kidron 2003; Feldman 2004; Robben 2005; Beneduce 2010. On trauma as a discursive construct that has taken the central stage in late-twentieth-century Western culture, see these anthropology studies: McKinney 2007; Fassin and Rechtman 2009; Young 1995. On the universal paradigm of trauma that medicalizes and pathologizes experiences that are first and foremost political and social in nature, thus requiring a context-specific approach, see Summerfield 1999; Foxen 2000; Pupavac 2004; Kirmayer, Lemelson, and Barad 2007; Zarowski 2004.

8. According to the anthropologist Misty Bastian (1997), in southern Nigeria, Mami Wata is a water spirit found in the western coastal regions and central Africa. She has a fair complexion and is interested in contemporary objects, including perfume, sunglasses, and Coca-Cola. Sometimes Mami Wata is considered a metaphor for modern African conditions: she knows about global wealth and wants to consume on a large scale but lacks the resources to participate in global capitalism.

9. From an interview conducted in Turin, October 6, 2003.

10. Stefania Pandolfo (2008) reflects on madness and the search for meaning in a Moroccan psychiatric hospital, where patients inevitably resort to and are described by different vocabularies of healing.

11. See Davis 2012 on how *culture* works as a cipher for difference in the interactions between psychiatrists and those "cultural minorities" that populate Greece's borderlands.

CHAPTER 2

1. These questions are at the heart of contemporary Italian debates on difference and mental health discussed in a series of journals. Among these, *I Fogli di ORISS* emerged as part of the work of the Organizzazione Interdisciplinare Sviluppo e Salute (Interdisciplinary Organization for Development and Health, www.oriss.org), a nonprofit founded in 1990 by a group of researchers and practitioners interested in the intersections of anthropology, medicine, psychiatry, and psychology and engaged in development projects in Italy and abroad. See also *Antropologia Medica,* the journal tied to the activities of the Italian Medical Anthropology Society (SIAM) founded in the late 1980s (www.antropologiamedica.it/am.html).

2. Here I do not focus on the specificity of ethno-psychiatric treatment of torture victims and refugees at the Centro Fanon. My reflections are on the use of culture as a therapeutic trigger in the treatment of foreign patients in general. On the specificities in the practice and theoretical approach of ethno-psychiatric treatment with people who have experienced political violence and torture, see Beneduce 2008, 2010; Taliani and Vacchiano 2006.

3. This theoretical issue emerged earlier, in 1984, in the School of Psychiatry at the University of Rome, where Mariella Pandolfi and others founded the first Society of Transcultural Psychiatry as part of the Italian Psychiatric Society. Around the same time, in the context of the international conference of the Psychiatric Association, Pandolfi organized a workshop on transcultural therapies that gathered scholars and practitioners from different parts of the world, introducing them to the work of Ellen Corin, Gilles Bibeau, Byron Good, and Tobie Nathan, among others. Over the years, they had a great impact on the debates on difference and therapeutic treatment.

4. Although Basaglia was one of the main leaders of the Italian anti-psychiatric movement and Trieste was the cultural and political center from which he operated, the anti-institutional movement within democratic psychiatry was very active in other Italian cities, including Varese, Parma, Arezzo, Perugia, Nocera, and Rome.

5. From an interview conducted in Turin, Italy, October 6, 2003.

6. On the use of the mother tongue in a psychiatric setting, see Pandolfo 2008. For a reflection on the persecutory aspects of cultural references in the ethno-psychiatric setting, see Benslama 2000; Beneduce 2007; and Giordano 2008. On the use of the language of voodoo in ethno-psychiatric work, see Taliani 2012.

7. In the past twenty years, especially in the literature on nursing, alternatives to the concept of cultural competence in clinical settings have emerged, including "cultural responsiveness," "cultural humility," "cultural safety," and "structural competence." For a comprehensive review of these debates, see Kirmayer 2012. For an overview of the concept of structural competency, see http://structuralcompetency.org/.

8. The anti-psychiatry movement, and Basaglia in particular, had a complex relationship with the Italian Communist Party (Giannichedda 2005, 23). Although Basaglia's political alliances within the party played an important role in the reform of the mental health system, he also interpreted the relationship between reality, ideology, and utopia in a way that differed from a certain revolutionary culture of leftist movements and from the Communist Party's program of reform itself (xxx).

9. Over the past ten years, the changing political scene in Italy has taken a much different approach on issues of mental illness and deviancy. During my fieldwork (2002–4), the reform draft sponsored by the center-right Forza Italia's deputy Maria Burani Procaccini during the Berlusconi right-wing government in 2001–5 essentially promoted a discourse that described mentally ill patients as subjects dangerous to themselves and to society, and in need of control and discipline. For an account of the state of mental health services in Italy and Basaglia's legacy, see Martelli 2006. During the same period, other draft reforms of Law 180 took a similar approach to mental illness. The most recent, sponsored by Deputy Carlo Ciccioli from the right-wing PdL, advocates for the medicalization of mental illness and a general return to hospitalization. None of these drafts has passed, but they are a measure of the counter-debates to the Basaglia Law. See also www.triestesalutementale.it/welcome.asp, and psichiatriademocratica.com.

10. This and the following quotes from Beneduce are from interviews conducted in Turin, Italy, March 21 and July 3, 2003.

11. Fanon's book *The Wretched of the Earth* was published in 1961 and Basaglia's *L'istituzione negata* in 1968.

12. Basaglia's legacy also informs the treatment of foreign patients in the Departments of Mental Health in Trieste.

13. In 1970, Guattari wrote a review of Basaglia's *L'istituzione negata,* in which he applauds his ability to refuse any medical alibis while facing the reality of psychiatric problems and relating them to larger political and socioeconomic conditions. Guattari argues that Basaglia's experiments ended not because of theoretical dogmatism but because they failed to take madness on its own terms and reduced it to social alienation.

14. From a seminar on global health organized in the anthropology department at University of California, Davis, October 22, 2012.

15. De Martino's interest in subaltern forms of medical and magic-religious knowledge had its roots in Italian medical history. In the nineteenth century, doctors working in the public system started to develop an interest in medical representations and practices in different parts of Italy. Their attempts to collect forms of medical knowledge and practice showed the coexistence of the official system of health care and alternative, more local etiologies and therapies (Zanetti 1978 [1892]; Pitré 1896). At the time of Italian unification (1861), these "local medicines" were considered forms of superstition that threatened the hegemony of scientific knowledge as well as the political unification of the peninsula (Pandolfi and Bibeau 2005).

16. Ironically, a similar critique has been made of Nathan's ethno-psychiatry and his clinical use of culture as a therapeutic trigger that functions as a womb.

Nathan's approach has been read as a static way of interpreting the patient's ever-changing ways of identifying with cultural interpretations in the context of displacement, migration, and exile (Corin 1997).

17. Interview conducted in Novara, Italy, September 4, 2010.

18. In the same interview with Ellen Rooney, Spivak (1993, 3) explains, "Strategy works through a persistent (de)constructive critique of the theoretical." Since the 1980s, Spivak has distanced herself from the idea of strategic essentialism.

19. Giovanni Jervis participated in Basaglia's movement and was involved in de Martino's research, which led to the publication of *La terra del rimorso* (de Martino 1961). Bruno Callieri (2001), a psychiatrist and psychoanalyst himself, influenced de Martino's idea of crisis of presence and utilized it in his own work on psychopathology.

20. These studies were mostly conducted in Africa because it symbolized the most accessible and exotic expression of alterity. See Fassin and Rechtman 2005.

21. John Colin Dixon Carothers worked as a psychiatrist in Nairobi, Kenya, in the early 1950s. He was involved in the treatment of African and European patients and in the study of local political and military revolts against the colonial power in order to define effective strategies of control. He published *The African Mind in Health and Disease* (1953) and *The Psychology of Mau Mau* (1954). See also Keller 2007; Collignon 2002; and Vaughan 1991.

22. See the introduction to Mannoni 1990 [1950].

23. See also Roudinesco 2005; Cole 2001.

24. Ethnographic reflections on colonialism have shown how colonial encounters produced a "crisis of understanding" and modes of forgetting (Mbembe 1997; Cole 2001; Peel 2003; Obeyesekere 2005; Beneduce 2008).

25. In the chapter "The Negro and Psychopathology," Fanon refers to Lacan's theory of the mirror stage to discuss the relationship of alienation between the white man and the black man (1967 [1952], 161).

26. In *Black Skin, White Masks*, Fanon links the formation of black identity in a colonial and postcolonial context to the power of the language used to address the black man. His reflections echo Althusser's (1971) idea of interpellation.

27. In his later political essays, such as *Towards the African Revolution* (1967 [1964]), Fanon seems to take a more complex position vis-à-vis the past's role in providing tools to face the revolution and the process of emancipation from colonial domination.

28. The practitioners in Nathan's clinical work are usually trained in Western psychology and mental health and/or anthropology and come from the countries of origins of the patients or from neighboring countries. They are not traditional healers but are familiar with healing techniques that resonate with patients and their cultural backgrounds (Nathan 2003, 68).

29. From an interview conducted in Novara, Italy, September 4, 2010.

30. Rosalba Terranova-Cecchini, M.D. and neuropsychiatrist, is one of the founders of Italian transcultural psychiatry. She was also one of the first Italian psychiatrists with an interest in medicine applied to anthropology and

collaborated with international development projects abroad (Guatemala, Madagascar). In Milan, she founded the Istituto di Studi Transculturali (Institute of Transcultural Studies), where, among other activities, she organizes training in transcultural psychology for mental health practitioners.

PART TWO. ENTERING THE SCENE

1. In Dante's *Divine Comedy* both Hell and Purgatory are divided into nine circles (*gironi*). In Hell the circles descend toward Lucifer's circle, while in Purgatory they ascend, increasingly approaching the doors to heaven. Each *girone* hosts a different category of sinners. In Hell, they are sentenced and condemned; in Purgatory, they aspire to redemption.

CHAPTER 3

1. See Fanon 1967 [1952], chap. 2.

2. Douglas Ficek (2011) has devoted an essay to the issue of "petrification" in Fanon's work.

3. Several activists in Turin remember that the minister of Equal Opportunities, Livia Turco, paid numerous visits to Turin to see how the different associations and services were dealing with the issue of foreign prostitution at the time when the immigration law was being revised (1997–98) and that her exchanges with them had influenced the drafting of Article 18. Turin was identified as one of the most advanced Italian cities as far as the discussion and implementation of immigration policies and programs of integration were concerned.

4. In the course of my research, I spoke with the president of a nonprofit that oversees the implementation of the program in Novara, a town in Piedmont near Turin. He explained to me that in 2000, the year Article 18 became effective, it was extremely easy to receive funding from both the Ministry of Equal Opportunities and local government agencies. With time, though, funds began to be dispersed among too many groups.

5. In 2000, the U.S. government passed the Trafficking Victims' Protection Act. Unlike in Italy, the act distinguishes between two types of trafficking: (1) victims of trafficking and (2) victims of severe trafficking. Under this legislation only the latter are eligible for assistance and support from the government. Thus, the law is designed to assist the authorities in shutting down trafficking networks, rather than provide assistance to victims (Chapkis 2003).

6. The debates stressing the ambivalence of this piece of legislation refer to the antecedent to Article 18, a decree introduced in 1995–96 in the first comprehensive immigration law instituted in 1990 (Law 39). According to this decree, the foreign national who decides to cooperate with legal authorities to denounce criminal actions related to illegal immigration may be granted a residency permit (for one year with no possibility for renewal) for social protection on the conditions that she or he would be in danger for having filed criminal charges against traffickers, that she or he could not safely be repatriated, and that her or his testimony had made a substantial contribution to police investigations

against the illegal trafficking. Before Article 18, foreign illegal women who worked in the sex trade and wanted to obtain legal status could only cooperate with the police in this way. The kind of permit they would receive did not grant them the right to work. Article 18, on the contrary, grants a residency permit that is renewable after six months and allows foreign residents to work; it therefore represents a way to establish, in time, permanent residency.

7. In *Questa è la legge . . . Art. 18 e dintorni,* special issue of *Pagine: Il sociale da fare e pensare,* no. 2 (2001), Gruppo Abele, Turin, 5. Luigi Ciotti is the founder and president of the nonprofit organization Gruppo Abele, based in Turin. It is involved in several projects of support for different categories of the marginalized: the homeless, drug addicts, migrant prostitutes, and HIV/AIDS patients. It is also involved in projects in Africa and Latin America. Lorenzo Trucco is president of the Associazione Studi Giuridici sull'Immigrazione (Association of Juridical Studies on Immigration).

8. Interview conducted in Novara, Italy, September 5, 2010.

9. Alleanza Nazionale is the party that grew from what remained of the fascist Movimento Sociale Italiano (Italian Social Movement).

10. See Vincenzo Castelli, in *Articolo 18: Tutela delle vittima del traffico di esseri umani e lotta alla criminalità (l'Italia e gli scenari europei),* Rapporto di ricerca, (Martinsicuro: On the Road Edizioni, 2002), 25.

11. The Lega Nord's main concerns are establishing regional autonomy and denouncing the corruption and inefficiency of the government. Animated by strong antisoutherner and antimigrant sentiments, Umberto Bossi's political project was aimed at proclaiming a Repubblica del Nord (Republic of the North), which would ideally exclude all the regions south of Emilia Romagna and expel from Italy all migrants who are not legally employed.

12. This protocol was a supplement to the Palermo Accord (the Convention against Transnational Organized Crime) that was adopted by the General Assembly of the United Nations on November 20, 2000. States that ratified this convention commit themselves to taking a series of measures against transnational organized crime, though this is not legally binding (Winterdyk and Reichel 2010). In 2003, 117 countries signed the protocol and thus committed to prosecuting traffickers, protecting and assisting victims through law enforcement, witness protection, social benefits, repatriation, border control, and international cooperation with sending countries (Gajic-Veljanoski and Stewart 2007).

13. This definition is a compromise between various contradictory terminologies that attempt to capture a complex experience (Gozdziak and Collett 2005; Schauer and Wheaton 2006; Agustin 2007). A general lack of consensus regarding the term *trafficking* has made statistics difficult to collect (Musto 2009; Doezema 2010). The large numbers that are usually attached to it are arbitrary and imprecise, according to the International Organization for Migration (IOM 2000). Still, no matter how sophisticated naming human rights abuses like trafficking has become, it cannot translate modes of suffering—psychological, structural, systemic—into political strategies that prevent their emergence (Musto 2009, 286).

14. Articolo 18, 35. Available at www.camera.it/parlam/leggi/980401.htm.

15. Laura Agustin (2005, 8), referring to the work of Francesco Carchedi et al. (2003), suggests three categories of prostitution: autonomous, semiautonomous or semivoluntary, and coerced and/or slavelike.

16. Here I draw from sociological literature on the therapeutic state in order to retrace some of the specific features of the therapeutic ethic when it takes on institutionalized forms. See Rieff 1966; Reddy 2002. Renteln (2004) has also written a detailed study of the use of the "cultural defense" in American criminal courts.

PART THREE. ENTERING THE SCENE

1. Juventus is the football team owned by the Agnelli family and therefore linked to the Fiat industry in Turin. Historically, it is the team that most working-class and southern Italian migrants support.

CHAPTER 4

1. This was my main ethnographic site of the practice of filing criminal charges. The denuncias drafted here were later filed at the police station.

2. The concept of bonifica played an important role during the fascist period in Italy. According to Ruth Ben-Ghiat (2001, 4), "Initially the term referred to the conversion of swamp-land into arable soil. . . . The campaigns for agricultural reclamation (bonifica agricola), human reclamation (bonifica umana), and cultural reclamation (bonifica della cultura), together with the anti-Jewish laws, [were] different facets and phases of a comprehensive project to combat degeneration and radically renew Italian society by pulling up the bad weeds and cleaning up the soil." Engineering, medicine, and science provided the paradigms of this fascist approach to governance. In fact, Mussolini used to refer to himself as a "clinician" (5).

3. These centers—also known as Centers of Temporary Permanence (CPT) and, more recently, Centers of Identification and Expulsion (CIE)—have been at the heart of current debates on immigration policy. Inspections by EU and UN officials have denounced their inhumane conditions.

4. In most cases, foreign women hear about these types of NGOs and associations from others who have gone through the program. In other cases, women's clients become their saviors and refer them to the associations. In addition, volunteers and social workers do outreach in the streets.

5. In his work on the scriptural economy, Michel de Certeau (1984) reflects on the relationship between the emergence of a scriptural system (inseparable from the development of printing), modernity, and the destiny of the voice. He argues that there is no "'pure' voice, because it is always determined [and codified] by a system" (132), yet there is a degree of pleasure in "being recognized (but one does not know by whom), of becoming an identifiable and legible word in a social language, . . . of being inscribed in a symbolic order that has neither owner nor author" (140).

6. Saba Mahmood's (2005) work on the grassroots women's piety movement in the mosques of Cairo, Egypt, challenges some of the key feminist assumptions about free will, agency, and subjectivity.

7. Prior to January 2002, the lira was the Italian currency. The amounts cited above corresponded to approximately $590, $320, and $55.

8. At the national level, 54,559 people reached out to rehabilitation projects for victims between 2000 and 2007. Of this number, 13,517 filed criminal charges and entered the rehabilitation program. Only 6,435 found employment after finishing the program. Nigerians make up the majority of those served by these programs, followed by Romanians, Moldavians, Albanians, and Ukrainians. Of the number of denuncias filed each year, between 75 percent and 85 percent result in residency permits. The number of permits issued tends to increase 2 to 10 percent each year (Barberi 2008).

9. For Nigerian women, the linguistic dimension of cultural mediation is more complex. Although the majority of women are from Benin City and their mother tongue is Edo, others speak Yoruba or Igbo, and they are not necessarily fluent in English or pidgin English.

10. Rijk van Dijk (2001) writes about the trafficking of young Nigerian girls for the Dutch sex industry and the role of voodoo in the girls' submission to Dutch male desires. The discovery of this translational trafficking gave rise to what he calls a "voodoo scare," resulting in a special police task force, the "Voodoo team."

11. When the drafting of the denuncia takes place at NGOs the setting and process can be very different. The interrogation often takes the form of a an informal conversation between the cultural mediator and the woman denouncing her exploiters. The denuncia is drafted over the course of several meetings, providing, as one volunteer described it, "a less intimidating environment."

12. On the subject of migrants' access to legality by means of official documents and testimonies, see Fassin and D'Halluin 2005.

13. On the relationship between magic, reification, and power in the constitution of state politics of recognition, see Gordillo 2006. On the state as a form of fiction that creates the idea of being a separate and autonomous rational entity that has power, see Abrams 1988; Coronil 1997; Pietz 1993; Taussig 1997.

14. This kind of speech has to do with what Austin (1962) called the "performative." For a critique of Austin's theory of performativity, see Bourdieu 1991.

CHAPTER 5

1. A. Allegato and D. Allegato, "Modulo per la presentazione del progetto." This is the report that the municipality of Turin wrote to justify Ministry of Equal Opportunities funding. It presents the project's mission statement, along with a list of associations involved in it.

2. Ibid.

3. In Italian casa means "home," or "house." In this context I translate it as "shelter."

4. "Progetto Postituzione e Tratta. Dati Bilancio Sociale 2003," published by Gruppo Abele (Turin), one of the major Catholic associations involved in the implementation of Article 18 and victim rehabilitation programs. This is the end-of-year report (2003) in which the lines of praxis are outlined.

5. Ibid.

6. Generally, parishes or the municipality organize the trainings to teach foreign women to take care of the elderly, keep house, and cook. When women are in the rehabilitation program the jobs they find are usually temporary and often include caretaking, waiting tables, baby-sitting, or working in retail.

7. During my fieldwork, I encountered representatives of several associations—for the most part Catholic but also lay ones—involved in the implementation of the victim rehabilitation programs. They were all engaged in the practice of accoglienza, and their main purpose was to manage the shelters. The ethnographic material in this chapter was collected mostly among nuns and women residents in this shelter community but not exclusively. I also draw from interviews and conversations with nuns who work for other associations and with women in the program who lived in other shelters.

8. *Effatà* is also an Arabic word, *Al-fatah*, meaning "opening," and appears in the opening surah of the Koran.

9. In "Certificato di Costituzione dell'Associazione Utopia 2000," February 2000. Copy in possession of author.

10. San Salvario is a very popular neighborhood in Turin with a high concentration of migrants.

11. *A rischio di adozione* (at risk of adoption) is the technical expression in Italian to describe the status of the relationship of the child vis-à-vis his/her family of origin and the possible adoptive family. A family takes custody of a child while the tribunal evaluates the situation of the biological family. The expression refers to the risk that the child might not be better off with its own parent or family. In that case, the whole procedure results in adoption.

12. In her study of Catholic postulants in a Mexican convent, Rebecca Lester (2005) explores the intersections of theories of the self with theories of the body.

13. In Jung's psychology, the shadow represents one part of the unconscious. Although relatively close to the conscious mind, this is the part of one's original self that is superseded and repressed in early childhood. For Jung, the individual deals with the shadow in four ways: denial, projection, integration, and/or transmutation (Jung and Stone 1953).

14. Some NGOs involved in aid programs for victims of human trafficking also make night rounds to find prostitutes in the streets, give out condoms, and publicize free medical checks, the rehab program, and how to gain a residency permit. The Catholic NGOs do not hand out condoms, but they do provide information about rights and services women can access to help them leave prostitution.

CHAPTER 6

1. These meetings are called *"discussione casi"* (case discussion or case conference), and only discuss clinical cases. The psychologist in charge of a case usually presents the patient's story, outlines its main issues, and then listens to her colleagues' interpretations and advice.

2. This meeting took place on April 9, 2003. I tape-recorded, transcribed, and later translated it. I have maintained the sequence of the dialogues and only edited out the parts that were not pertinent to understanding this story.

3. Law 149 (2001) is the current legislation on foster care and adoption in Italy. It is based on the Law 184 (1983) that was later revised. The law is titled "Discipline of Adoption and Foster Care for Minors" (*Disciplina dell'adozione e dell'affidamento dei minori*). According to the law, if parents are unable to provide for their child's needs, social services must step in. If parents are judged incompetent, children are either put in foster care or hosted in communities. If problems with the biological parents continue, children are considered for adoption.

4. On the question of what she calls "melancholy subjectivity," Garcia (2010) asks, "What if we conceive the subject of melancholy not simply as the one who suffers but also as the recurring historical refrains through which sentiments of 'endless' suffering arise?" (75).

5. The Tribunal-appointed mental health practitioners do not know the person they have to evaluate beforehand. They usually formulate a diagnosis over the course of several therapeutic sessions.

6. I am quoting from the document drafted by the two mental health practitioners appointed by the Tribunal. Their names are withheld for confidentiality. This kind of document is usually called "Consulenza Tecnica d'Ufficio" and is followed by a case number and the names of the people involved. In this case, the children's names appeared on the cover page.

7. I was only able to read two of the many reports the ethno-psychiatrists wrote in support of Afërdita. Per conversations with them, I know that they supported her regaining custody of the children when her family situation changed and that she could count on her partner and siblings for support.

EPILOGUE

1. See Hanna Arendt's Sonning Prize acceptance speech in 1975 at http://miscellaneousmaterial.blogspot.com/2011/08/hannah-arendt-sonning-prize-acceptance.html. Emphasis added.

Bibliography

Abrams, Philip
  1988 "Notes on the Difficulty of Studying the State." *Journal of Historical Sociology* 1 (1): 58–89.
Agamben, Giorgio
  1998 *Homo Sacer: Sovereign Power and Bare Life.* Stanford: Stanford University Press.
  2000 *Remnants of Auschwitz: The Witness and the Archive.* New York: Zone Books.
Agustin, Laura M.
  2003 "Sex, Gender and Migrations: Facing Up to Ambiguous Realities." *Soundings* 23: 84–98.
  2005 "Migrants in the Mistress's House: Other Voices in the 'Trafficking' Debate." *Social Politics* 12 (1): 96–117.
  2007 *Sex at the Margins: Migration, Labour Markets and the Rescue Industry.* London: Zed Books.
Allen, Beverly, and Mary J. Russo
  1997 *Revisioning Italy: National Identity and Global Culture.* Minneapolis: University of Minnesota Press.
Althusser, Louis
  1971 "Ideology and Ideological State Apparatuses." In *Lenin and Philosophy and Other Essays,* 127–86. London: Monthly Review Books.
Ancora, Alfredo
  1997 *La dimensione transculturale della psicopatologia.* Rome: Edizioni Universitarie Romane.
André, Jacques
  2006 "The Misunderstanding (Le malentendu)." *Psychoanalytic Quarterly* 75: 557–82.

Andrijasevic, Rutvica
    2003 "The Difference Borders Make: (Il)legality, Migration, and Trafficking in Italy among Eastern European Women in Prostitution." In *Uprootings/Regroundings: Questions of Home and Migration*, ed. S. Ahmed, C. Castañeda, A.-M. Fortier, and M. Sheller, 251–73. New York: Berg.

Antonetto, Roberto
    1999 *Vedere Torino: Appunti ad uso dei forestieri in città*. Turin: Daniela Piazza Editore.

Apel, Karl-Otto
    1980 *Towards a Transformation of Philosophy*. London: Routledge and Kegan Paul.

Asad, Talal
    1986 "The Concept of Cultural Translation in British Social Anthropology." In *Writing Culture: The Poetics and Politics of Ethnography*, ed. James Clifford and George Marcus, 141–64. Berkeley: University of California Press.
    2003 *Formations of the Secular: Christianity, Islam, Modernity*. Stanford: Stanford University Press.

Austin, John L.
    1962 *How to Do Things with Words*. Cambridge, MA: Harvard University Press.

Bakhtin, Mikhail M.
    1981 *The Dialogic Imagination*. Austin: University of Texas Press.

Balibar, Étienne
    2002 *Politics and the Other Scene*. New York: Verso.

Ballinger, Pamela
    2007 "Borders of the Nation, Borders of Citizenship: Italian Repatriation and the Redefinition of National Identity after World War II." *Comparative Studies in Society and History* 49 (3): 713–41.

Banfield, Edward C
    1965 *The Moral Basis of a Backward Society*. Glencoe, IL: Free Press.

Barberi, Alessandra
    2008 "Dati e riflessioni sui progetti di protezione sociale ex art. 18 D.lgs 286/98 ed art. 13 Legge 228/2003." Segreteria tecnica della Commissione Interministeriale per il sostegno alle vittime di tratta, violenza e grave sfruttamento.

Basaglia, Franco
    1968 *L'istituzione negata*. Turin: Einaudi.
    1981 *Scritti, 1953–1968*. Turin: Einaudi.
    2005 *L'utopia della realtà*. Turin: Einaudi.

Bastian, Misty L.
    1997 "Married in the Water: Spirit Kin and Other Afflictions of Modernity in Southeastern Nigeria." *Journal of Religion in Africa* 27 (2): 116–34.

Baudrillard, Jean
    1983 *Simulations*. New York: Semiotext(e).

Belier, Irène, and Thomas Wilson, eds.

2000 *An Anthropology of the European Union: Building, Imagining, and Experiencing the New Europe.* New York: New York University Press.

Belmonte, Thomas

2005 *The Broken Fountain.* New York: Columbia University Press.

Ben-Ghiat, Ruth

2001 *Fascist Modernities: Italy, 1922–1945.* Berkeley: University of California Press.

Ben-Ghiat, Ruth, and Mia Fuller, eds.

2005 *Italian Colonialism.* London: Palgrave Macmillan.

Beneduce, Roberto

2007 *Etnopsichiatria: Sofferenza mentale e alterità fra storia, dominio e cultura.* Rome: Carocci.

2008 "Undocumented Bodies, Burned Identities: Refugees, sans papiers, harraga—When Things Fall Apart." *Social Science Information* 47 (4): 505–27.

2010 *Archeologie del trauma: Un' antropologia del sottosuolo.* Bari: Editori Laterza.

Beneduce, Roberto, ed.

2003 *L'etnopsichiatria, o la perdita dell' innocenza.* Milan: Franco Angeli Editore.

2005 *Antropologia della Cura.* Turin: Bollati Boringhieri.

Beneduce, Roberto, and Pompeo Martelli

2005 "Politics of Healing and Politics of Culture: Ethnopsychiatry, Identities and Migration." *Transcultural Psychiatry* 42 (3): 367–93.

Beneduce, Roberto, and Elisabeth Roudinesco, eds.

2005 *Etnopsicoanalisi.* Turin: Bollati Boringhieri.

Beneduce, Roberto, and Simona Taliani

2006 "Embodied Powers, Deconstructed Bodies: Spirit Possession, Sickness, and the Search for Wealth of Nigerian Immigrant Women." *Anthropos* 101 (1): 9–20.

Benjamin, Walter

1968 *Illuminations: Essays and Reflections.* Ed. and introd. Hannah Arendt. Trans. Harry Zohn. New York: Schocken Books.

2009 *The Origin of German Tragic Drama.* London: Verso.

Benslama, Fethi

2000 "Epreuves de l'étranger: Clinique de l'exile." *Cahiers Intersignes* 14–15: 9–29.

Berlant, Lauren

2007 "On the Case." *Critical Inquiry* 33 (Summer): 663–72.

Berman, Jacqueline

2003 "(Un)Popular Strangers and Crises (Un)Bounded: Discourses of Sex Trafficking, the European Political Community and the Panicked State of the Modern State." *European Journal of International Relations* 9 (1): 37–86.

Bernstein, Elizabeth
    2007a   "The Sexual Politics of the 'New Abolitionism.'" *differences: A Journal of Feminist Cultural Studies* 18 (3): 128–51.
    2007b   *Temporarily Yours: Intimacy, Authenticity, and the Commerce of Sex.* Chicago: University of Chicago Press.
Betancourt, Joseph R., Alexander R. Green, J. Emilio Carrillo, and Owusu Ananeh-Firempong
    2003   "Defining Cultural Competence: A Practical Framework for Addressing Racial/Ethnic Disparities in Health and Health Care." *Public Health Reports* 118 (4): 293–302.
Biehl, João
    2005   *Vita: Life in a Zone of Social Abandonment.* Berkeley: University of California Press.
Binswanger, Ludwig
    1958   "The Case of Ellen West." In *Existence: A New Dimension in Psychiatry and Psychology,* ed. Rollo May, Ernest Angel, and Henri F. Ellenberger, 237–364. New York: Basic Books.
Binswanger, Ludwig, and Michel Foucault
    1986   *Dreams and Existence: Studies in Existential Psychology and Psychiatry.* Atlantic Highlands, NJ: Humanities Press International.
Blanchot, Maurice, and Elizabeth Rottenberg
    1997   *Friendship.* Stanford: Stanford University Press.
Bourdieu, Pierre
    1991   *Language and Symbolic Power.* Cambridge, MA: Harvard University Press.
Bowen, John R.
    2007   *Why the French Don't Like Headscarves.* Princeton: Princeton University Press.
Brettell, Caroline
    2003   "Repatriates or Immigrants? A Commentary." In *Europe's Invisible Migrants,* ed. Andrea Smith, 95–104. Amsterdam: University of Amsterdam Press.
Brown, Wendy
    1995   *States of Injury: Power and Freedom in Late Modernity.* Princeton: Princeton University Press.
Butler, Judith
    1997   *The Psychic Life of Power: Theories in Subjection.* Stanford: Stanford University Press.
Calavita, Kitty
    2005   "Law, Citizenship, and the Construction of (Some) Immigrant 'Others.'" *Law and Social Inquiry* 30 (2): 401–20.
Callieri, Bruno
    2001   *Quando vince l'ombra: Problemi di psicopatologia clinica.* Rome: Edizioni Universtarie Romane.
Carchedi, Francesco, et al.
    2003   *Il lavoro servile e le nuove schiavitù.* Milan: Franco Angeli.

Cardamone, Giuseppe, and Pino Schirripa
  1990 "Lo scoglio e la salvezza. Un culto terapeutico in Calabria." *Daedalus* 4 (18): 127–45.
Carothers, John C. D.
  1953 *The African Mind in Health and Disease: A Study in Ethnopsychiatry.* Geneva: World Health Organization.
  1954 *The Psychology of Mau Mau.* Nairobi: Government Printer.
Carter, Donald M.
  1997 *States of Grace: Senegalese in Italy and the New European Immigration.* Minneapolis: University of Minnesota Press.
Caruth, Cathy
  1996 *Unclaimed Experience: Trauma, Narrative, and History.* Baltimore: Johns Hopkins University Press.
Certeau, Michel de
  1984 *The Practice of Everyday Life.* Berkeley: University of California Press.
  1996 *The Possession at Loudun.* Chicago: University of Chicago Press.
Chakrabarty, Dipesh
  2000 *Provincializing Europe: Postcolonial Thought and Historical Difference.* Princeton: Princeton University Press.
Chapkis, Wendy
  2003 "Trafficking, Migration, and the Law: Protecting Innocents, Punishing Migrants." *Gender and Society* 17 (9): 923–37.
Clifford, James
  1997 *Routes: Travel and Translation in the Late Twentieth Century.* Cambridge, MA: Harvard University Press.
Cohen, Lawrence
  2005 "The Kothi Wars: AIDS Cosmopolitanism and the Morality of Classification." In *Sex in Development: Science, Sexuality and Morality in Global Perspective,* ed. Vincanne Adams and Stacy Leigh Pigg, 269–303. Durham: Duke University Press.
Cole, Jeffrey
  1997 *The New Racism in Europe: A Sicilian Ethnography.* Cambridge: Cambridge University Press.
Cole, Jeffrey, and Sally Booth
  2007 *Dirty Work: Immigrants in Domestic Service, Agriculture, and Prostitution in Sicily.* Lanham, MD: Lexington Books.
Cole, Jennifer
  2001 *Forget Colonialism? Sacrifice and the Art of Memory in Madagascar.* Berkeley: University of California Press.
Collignon, René
  2002 "Pour une histoire de la psychiatrie coloniale francaise: A partir de l'example du Senagal." *L'Autre* 3 (3): 455–80.
Comaroff, Jean, and John Comaroff
  1988 "Through the Looking-Glass: Colonial Encounters of the First Kind." *Journal of Historical Sociology* 1 (1): 6–32.

Coppo, Piero
  2005 *Le ragioni del dolore.* Turin: Ballati Boringhieri.
Corin, Ellen
  1997 "Playing with Limits: Tobie Nathan's Evolving Paradigm in Ethnopsychiatry." *Transcultural Psychiatry* 34 (3): 345–58.
  2007 "The 'Other' of Culture in Psychosis: The Excentricity of the Subject." In *Subjectivity: Ethnographic Investigations,* ed. João Biehl, Byron Good, and Arthur Kleinman, 273–314. Berkeley: University of California Press.
Coronil, Fernando
  1997 *The Magical State: Nature, Money, and Modernity in Venezuela.* Chicago: University of Chicago Press.
Corso, Carla, and Sandra Landi
  2003 *Ritratto a tinte forti.* Florence: Giunti Editore.
Corso, Carla, and Ada Trifirò
  2003 *E siamo partite! Migrazione, tratta e prostituzione straniera in Italia.* Florence: Giunti Editore.
Crapanzano, Vincent
  1992 *Hermes' Dilemma and Hamlet's Desire: On the Epistemology of Interpretation.* Cambridge, MA: Harvard University Press.
Dal Lago, Alessandro
  1999 *Non-persone: L'esclusione dei migranti in una società globale.* Milan: Feltrinelli.
Danius, Sara, Stefan Jonsson, and Gayatri Chakravorty Spivak
  1993 "An Interview with Gayatri Chakravorty Spivak." *Boundaries* 2 20 (2): 24–50.
Das, Veena
  1996 "Language and Body: Transactions in the Construction of Pain." *Daedalus* 125 (1): 67–91.
  2000 "The Act of Witnessing: Violence, Poisonous Knowledge, and Subjectivity." In *Violence and Subjectivity,* ed. Veena Das, Arthur Kleinman, Mamphela Ramphele, and Pamela Reynolds, 205–25. Berkeley: University of California Press.
  2003 "Trauma and Testimony. Implications for Political Community." *Anthropological Theory* 3 (3): 293–307.
  2004 "The Signature of the State: The Paradox of Illegibility." In *Anthropology in the Margins of the State,* ed. Veena Das and Deborah Poole, 225–52. Santa Fe, NM: School for Advanced Research.
Das, Veena, and Deborah Poole, eds.
  2004 *Anthropology in the Margins of the State.* Santa Fe, NM: School of American Research Press.
Davis, Elisabeth A.
  2012 *Bad Souls: Madness and Responsibility in Modern Greece.* Durham: Duke University Press.
de la Cadena, Marisol
  2010 "Indigenous Cosmopolitics in the Andes: Conceptual Reflections beyond 'Politics.'" *Cultural Anthropology* 25 (2): 334–70.

de Martino, Ernesto
1956   "Crisi della presenza e reintegrazione religiosa." *Aut Aut* 31: 17–38.
1961   *La terra del rimorso.* Milan: Il Saggiatore.
1977   *La fine del mondo: Contributo all'analisi delle apocalissi culturali.* Turin: Einaudi.
2000 [1948]   *Il mondo magico: Prolegomeni a una storia del magismo.* Turin: Bollati Boringhieri.
Del Boca, Angelo
1992   *L'Africa nella coscienza degli Italiani.* Bari: Editori Laterza.
Derrida, Jacques, Christie V. McDonald, and Claude Levesque
1985   *The Ear of the Other: Otobiography, Transference, Translation.* New York: Schocken Books.
Desjaralis, Robert R.
2012   "Rhythms of Dying, of Living." *Harvard Divinity Bulletin* 40 (1–2). www.hds.harvard.edu/news-events/harvard-divinity-bulletin/articles/rhythms-of-dying-of-living.
Devereux, George
1978   *Ethnopsychoanalysis: Psychoanalysis and Anthropology as Complementary Frames of Reference.* Berkeley: University of California Press.
Diasio, Nicoletta
2001   *Patrie provvisorie. Roma, anni '90: Corpo, città, frontiere.* Milan: Franco Angeli.
Doezema, Jo
2010   *Sex Slaves and Discourse Masters: The Construction of Trafficking.* New York: Zed Books.
Esposito, Roberto
2002   *Immunitas: Protezione e negazione della vita.* Turin: Einaudi.
Faimberg, Haydée
2005   *The Telescoping of Generations.* London: Routledge.
Fanon, Frantz
1963   *The Wretched of the Earth: A Negro Psychoanalyst's Study of the Problems of Racism and Colonialism in the World Today.* New York: Grove Press.
1965 [1959]   *A Dying Colonialism.* New York: Grove Press.
1967 [1952]   *Black Skin, White Masks.* New York: Grove Press.
1967 [1964]   *Towards the African Revolution (Political Essays).* New York: Grove Press.
Farquhar, Judith
2013   "Knowledge in Translation: Global Science, Local Things." In *Medicine and the Politics of Knowledge,* ed. Susan Levine, 153–70. Cape Town: Human Sciences Research Council.
Fassin, Didier
2000   "Les politiques de l'ethnopsychiatrie: La psyché africaine, des colonies britanniques aux banlieues parisiennes." *L'Homme* 153: 231–50.
Fassin, Didier, and Estelle D'Halluin
2005   "The Truth from the Body: Medical Certificates as Ultimate Evidence for Asylum Seekers." *American Anthropologist* 107 (4): 597–608.

Fassin, Didier, and Richard Rechtman
   2005   "An Anthropological Hybrid: The Pragmatic Arrangement of Universalism and Culturalism in French Mental Health." *Transcultural Psychiatry* 42 (3): 347–66.
   2009   *The Empire of Trauma: An Inquiry into the Condition of Victimhood.* Princeton: Princeton University Press.
Favret-Saada, Jeanne
   1980   *Deadly Words: Witchcraft in the Bocage.* Cambridge: Cambridge University Press.
Feldman, Allen
   2004   "Memory Theatres, Virtual Witnessing, and the Trauma-Aesthetic." *Biography* 27 (1): 163–202.
Foucault, Michel
   1980   *The History of Sexuality. Volume I: An Introduction.* New York: Vintage/Random House.
   1988   *Madness and Civilization: A History of Insanity in the Age of Reason.* New York: Vintage Books.
   1991   "Governmentality." In *The Foucault Effect: Studies in Governmentality,* ed. Graham Burchell, Collin Gordon, and Peter Miller, 87–104. Chicago: University of Chicago Press.
   1994a   "The Ethics of the Concern for Self as a Practice of Freedom." In *Ethics: Subjectivity and Truth,* ed. Paul Rabinow, 281–301. New York: New Press.
   1994b   *The Order of Things: An Archeology of the Human Sciences.* New York: Vintage Books.
   1994c   "Psychiatric Power." In *Ethics: Subjectivity and Truth,* ed. Paul Rabinow, 39–50. New York: New Press.
   2003   *Abnormal: Lectures at the Collège de France, 1974–1975.* New York: Picador.
Foxen, Patricia
   2000   "Cacophony of Voices: A K'iche' Mayan Narrative of Remembrance and Forgetting." *Transcultural Psychiatry* 37 (3): 355–81.
Freud, Sigmund
   1974 [1939]   *Moses and Monotheism.* London: Hogarth Press and Institute of Psycho-analysis.
   1981 [1917]   *Mourning and Melancholia.* In *The Standard Edition of the Complete Psychological Works of Sigmund Freud,* ed. J. Strachey, 243–58. London: Hogarth Press.
   1989 [1920]   *Beyond the Pleasure Principle.* New York: Norton.
Frighi, Luigi
   1992   "Le problematiche trans-culturali in Psichiatria e in Igiene Mentale." In *Cultura malattia migrazioni: La salute degli immigrati extracomunitari in Italia ed in Campania: aspetti sociali, medici e psicologici,* ed. A. Dama, T. Esposito, and T. Arcella, 130–40. Naples: Regione Campania USL 27, Dipartimento di Salute Mentale, Pomigliano D'Arco.
Gadamer, Hans Georg
   1975   *Truth and Method.* New York: Seabury Press.

Garcia, Angela
  2010 *The Pastoral Clinic: Addiction and Dispossession along the Rio Grande.* Berkeley: University of California Press.
Gajic-Veljanoski, Olga, and Donna E. Stewart
  2007 "Women Trafficked into Prostitution: Determinants, Human Rights and Health." *Transcultural Psychiatry* 44 (3): 338–58.
Giannichedda, Maria Grazia
  2005 Introduction to Franco Basaglia, *L'utopia della realtà.* Turin: Einaudi.
Ginsborg, Paul
  1990 *A History of Contemporary Italy: Society and Politics, 1943–1988.* London: Penguin Books.
Ginzburg, Carlo
  1980 *The Cheese and the Worms: The Cosmos of a Sixteenth-Century Miller.* Baltimore: Johns Hopkins University Press.
Giordano, Cristiana
  2008 "Practices of Translation and the Making of Migrant Subjectivities in Contemporary Italy." *American Ethnologist* 35 (4): 588–606.
  2011 "Translating Fanon in the Italian Context: Rethinking the Ethics of Treatment in Psychiatry." *Transcultural Psychiatry* 48 (3): 228–56.
Glassgold, Eric
  2010 "When Theory Paints a Picture: A Clinician Reflects on Piera Aulagnier's Metapsychology." *Psychoanalytic Quarterly* 79 (3): 717–30.
Goffman, Erving
  1961 *Asylums: Essays on the Social Situation of Mental Patients and Other Inmates.* New York: Anchor Books.
Gordillo, Gastón
  2008 "The Crucible of Citizenship: ID-Paper Fetishism in the Argentinian Chaco." *American Ethnologist* 33 (2): 162–76.
Gozdziak, Elzbieta, and Elizabeth Collett
  2005 "Research on Human Trafficking in North America: A Review of Literature." *International Migration* 43 (1–2): 99–128.
Gramsci, Antonio
  1975 *Quaderni dal carcere.* Turin: Einaudi.
  1978 *Antonio Gramsci: Selection from Political Writings, 1921–1926.* London: Lawrence and Wishart.
Grosso, Leopoldo
  2003 "Quali interventi di comunità?" *Rivista Pagine 3.*
Guattari, Félix
  2007 *Chaosophy: Texts and Interviews, 1972–1977.* Los Angeles: Semiotext(e).
Habermas, Jürgen
  2000 *On the Pragmatics of Communication.* Cambridge, MA: MIT Press.
Hanks, William F.
  1996 *Language and Communicative Practice.* Boulder, CO: Westview Press.

Heeschen, Volker
2003   "Linguist and Anthropologist as Translators." In *Translation and Ethnography: The Anthropological Challenge of Intercultural Understanding*, ed. Tullio Maranhão and Bernhard Streck, 115–34. Tucson: University of Arizona Press.

Heidegger, Martin
1975   "The Anaximander Fragment." In *Early Greek Thinking: The Dawn of Western Philosophy*, 13–58. New York: HarperCollins.

Holmes, Douglas R.
1989   *Cultural Disenchantments: Worker Peasantries in Northeast Italy.* Princeton: Princeton University Press.
2000   *Integral Europe: Fast-Capitalism, Multiculturalism, Neofascism.* Princeton: Princeton University Press.
2009   "Experimental Identities (After Maastricht)." In *European Identity*, ed. Jeffrey T. Checkel and Peter J. Katzenstein, 52–80. Cambridge: Cambridge University Press.

Human Rights Watch
2009   *Pushed Back, Pushed Around: Italy's Forced Return of Boat Migrants and Asylum Seekers, Libya's Mistreatment of Migrants and Asylum Seekers.* New York: Human Rights Watch.

Inglese, Salvatore, and Cesare Peccarisi
1997   *Psichiatria oltre frontiera: Viaggio intorno alle sindromi culturalmente ordinate.* Milan: UTET Periodici.

International Organization for Migration (IOM)
2000   *Perspectives on trafficking of migrants.* Washington, DC: IOM and United Nations.

Jakobson, Roman
1966   "On Linguistic Apsects of Translation." In *On Translation*, ed. R. A. Brower, 232–39. New York: Oxford University Press.

Jaspers, Karl
1997   *General Psychopathology.* Vols. 1 and 2. Trans. J. Hoening and Marian W. Hamilton. Baltimore: Johns Hopkins University Press.

Jervis, Giovanni
1994   *La psicoanalisi come esercizio critico.* Milan: Garzanti.

Jung, Carl G., and Irving Stone
1953   *Collected Works.* New York: Pantheon Books.

Keller, Richard C.
2007   *Colonial Madness: Psychiatry in French North Africa.* Chicago: University of Chicago Press.

Kempadoo, Kamala, ed.
2005   *Trafficking and Prostitution Reconsidered: New Perspectives on Migration, Sex Work, and Human Rights.* Boulder, CO: Paradigm Publishers.

Kidron, Carol
2003   "Surviving a Distant Past: A Case Study of the Cultural Construction of Trauma Descendant Identity." *Ethos* 31 (4): 513–44.

Kirmayer, Laurence

2011 "Multicultural Medicine and the Politics of Recognition." *Journal of Medicine and Philosophy* 36 (4): 410–23.

2012 "Rethinking Cultural Competence." *Transcultural Psychiatry* 49 (2): 149–62.

Kirmayer, Laurence, Robert Lemelson, and Mark Barad, eds.

2007 *Understanding Trauma: Integrating Biological, Clinical, and Cultural Perspectives.* Cambridge: Cambridge University Press.

Kleinman, Arthur

1988 *Rethinking Psychiatry: From Cultural Category to Personal Experience.* New York: Free Press.

Kristeva, Julia

1992 *Black Sun.* New York: Columbia University Press.

Labanca, Nicola

2002 *Oltremare. Storia dell'espansione coloniale italiana.* Bologna: Il Mulino.

Leenhardt, Maurice

1979 [1947] *Do Kamo: Person and Myth in the Melanesian World.* Chicago: University of Chicago Press.

Lester, Rebecca

2005 *Jesus in Our Wombs: Embodying Modernity in a Mexican Convent.* Berkeley: University of California Press.

Lévi-Strauss, Claude

1968 *Structural Anthropology.* London: Penguin Press.

Losi, Natale

2000 *Vite altrove: Migrazione e disagio psichico.* Milan: Feltrinelli Editore.

Luhrmann, Tanya

2000 *Of Two Minds: The Growing Disorder in American Psychiatry.* New York: Vintage Books.

Mahmood, Saba

2005 *Politics of Piety: The Islamic Revival and the Feminist Subject.* Princeton: Princeton University Press.

Mai, Nicola

2002 "Myths and Moral Panics: Italian Identity and the Media Representation of Albanian Immigration." In *The Politics of Recognizing Difference. Multiculturalism Italian-Style,* ed. R. Grillo and J. Pratt, 77–94. Burlington, VT: Ashgate.

Mannoni, Octave

1990 [1950] *Prospero and Caliban: The Psychology of Colonization.* Ann Arbor: University of Michigan Press.

Maranhão, Tullio

2003 Introduction to *Translation and Ethnography: The Anthropological Challenge of Intercultural Understanding,* ed. Tullio Maranhão and Bernhard Streck, xi–xxvi. Tucson: University of Arizona Press.

Martelli, Pompeo

2009 "Working Together for Public Health." *Transcultural Psychiatry* 46 (2): 11.

Mauss, Marcel
  2000   *The Gift: The Form and Reason for Exchange in Archaic Societies.*
         New York: Norton.
Mbembe, Achille
  1997   *La naissance du Maquis dans le Sud-Cameroun (1920–1960).* Paris:
         Karthala.
  2001   *On the Postcolony.* Berkeley: University of California Press.
McCulloch, Jock
  1995   *Colonial Psychiatry and the "African Mind."* Cambridge: Cambridge
         University Press.
McKinney, Kelly
  2007   "'Breaking the Conspiracy of Silence': Testimony, Traumatic Mem-
         ory, and Psychotherapy with Survivors of Political Violence." *Ethos*
         35 (3): 265–99.
Merkell, Patchen
  2003   *Bound by Recognition.* Princeton: Princeton University Press.
Merrill, Heather
  2006   *An Alliance of Women: Immigration and the Politics of Race.* Min-
         neapolis: University of Minnesota Press.
Miller, Alice M., and Carole S. Vance
  2004   "Sexuality, Human Rights, and Health." *Health and Human Rights* 7
         (2): 10.
Minh-ha, Trinh T.
  2011   *Elsewhere, within Here: Immigration, Refugeeism, and the Boundary
         Event.* New York: Routledge.
Minkowski, Eugène
  1970   *Lived Time: Phenomenological and Psychopathological Studies.*
         Evanston, IL: Northwestern University Press.
Mossakowski, Krysia N.
  2003   "Coping with Perceived Discrimination: Does Ethnic Identity Protect
         Mental Health?" *Journal of Health and Social Behavior* 44 (3): 318–
         31.
Muehlebach, Andrea
  2012   *"The Moral Neoliberal": Welfare and Citizenship in Italy.* Chicago:
         University of Chicago Press.
Münzel, Mark
  2003   "The Patience of a Koranic School: Waiting for Light in the Jungle."
         In *Translation and Ethnography: The Anthropological Challenge of
         Intercultural Understanding,* ed. Tullio Maranhão and Bernhard
         Streck, 102–14. Tucson: University of Arizona Press.
Musto, Jennifer Lynne
  2009   "What's in a Name? Conflations and Contradictions in Contempo-
         rary U.S. Discourses of Human Trafficking." *Women's Studies Inter-
         national Forum* 32: 281–87.
Napolitano, Valentina
  2007   "On Migrant Revelations and Anthropological Awakenings." *Social
         Anthropology* 15 (1): 71–87.

Nathan, Tobie

1994 *L'influence qui guèrit*. Paris: Odile Jacob.

1996 *Principi di etnopsicoanalisi*. Turin: Bollati Boringhieri.

2001 *La folie des autres: Traité d'ethnopsychiatrie clinique*. Paris: Dunod.

2003 *Non siamo soli al mondo*. Turin: Bollati Boringhieri.

Nathan, Tobie, and Isabelle Stengers

1996 *Médecins et sorciers: Manifeste pour une psycho-pathologie scientifique*. Paris: Odile Jacob.

Nguyen, Vinh-Kim

2010 *The Republic of Therapy: Triage and Sovereignty in West Africa's Time of AIDS*. Durham: Duke University Press.

Obeyesekere, Gananath

1985 "Depression, Buddhism, and the Work of Culture in Sri Lanka." In *Culture and Depression: Studies in the Anthropology and Cross-Cultural Psychiatry of Affect and Disorder*, ed. Arthur Kleinman and Byron Good, 134–52. Berkeley: University of California Press.

1990 *The Work of Culture: Symbolic Transformation in Psychoanalysis and Anthropology*. Chicago: University of Chicago Press.

2005 *Cannibal Talk: The Man-Eating Myth and Human Sacrifice in the South Seas*. Berkeley: University of California Press.

Ong, Aihwa

2003 *Buddha Is Hiding: Refugees, Citizenship, the New America*. Berkeley: University of California Press.

Palidda, Salvatore

2000 *Polizia postmoderna: Etnografia del nuovo controllo sociale*. Milan: Feltrinelli.

Palumbo, Patrizia

2003 *A Place in the Sun: Africa in Italian Colonial Culture from Post-Unification to the Present*. Berkeley: University of California Press.

Pandolfi, Mariella

1990 "Boundaries inside the Body: Women's Sufferings in Southern Peasant Italy." *Culture, Medicine, and Psychiatry* 14 (2): 255–75.

Pandolfi, Mariella, and Gilles Bibeau

2005 "Souffrance, politique, nation: Une cartographie de l'anthropologie médicale italienne." In *Anthropologie de la santé: perspectives internationales et enjeux contemporains*, ed. F. Saillant and S. Genest, 199–232. Quebec: Presses de l'Université Laval.

Pandolfo, Stefania

1997a *Impasse of the Angels: Scenes from a Moroccan Space of Memory*. Chicago: University of Chicago Press.

1997b "Rapt de la voix: Awal." *Revue d'Etudes Berbères* 15: 31–50.

2006 "Bghit nghanni hnaya (Je veux chanter ici): Voix et témoignage en marge d'une rencontre psychiatrique." *Arabica* 53 (2): 232–80.

2008 "The Knot of the Soul: Postcolonial Modernity, Madness, and the Imagination." In *Postcolonial Disorders*, ed. Mary-Jo Del Vecchio Good, Sandra T. Hyde, Sarah Pinto, and Byron Good, 329–58. Berkeley: University of California Press.

Papps, Elaine, and Irihapeti Ramsden
    1996   "Cultural Safety in Nursing: The New Zealand Experience." *International Journal of Quality in Health Care* 8 (5): 491–97.

Peano, Irene
    2010   "Ambiguous Bonds: A Contextual Study of Nigerian Sex Labour in Italy." Department of Social Anthropology, University of Cambridge.

Peel, J.D.Y.
    2003   *Religious Encounters and the Making of the Yoruba.* Bloomington: Indiana University Press.

Petryna, Adriana
    2002   *Life Exposed: Biological Citizens after Chernobyl.* Princeton: Princeton University Press.

Piattoni, Simona
    1998   "'Virtuous Clientelism': The Southern Question Resolved?" In *Italy's "Southern Question": Orientalism in One Country,* ed. Jane Schneider, 225–44. Oxford: Berg.

Pietz, William
    1993   Introduction to *Fetishism as Cultural Discourse,* ed. Emily Apter and William Pietz. Ithaca: Cornell University Press.

Pitré, Giuseppe
    1896   *Usi e costumi, credenze e pregiudizi del popolo siciliano.* Palermo: Clausen.

Povinelli, Elizabeth A.
    2001   "Radical Worlds: The Anthropology of Incommensurability and Inconceivability." *Annual Review of Anthropology* 30: 319–34.
    2002   *The Cunning of Recognition: Indigenous Alterities and the Making of Australian Multiculturalism.* Durham: Duke University Press.
    2011   *Economies of Abandonment: Social Belonging and Endurance in Late Liberalism.* Durham: Duke University Press.

Pupavac, Vanessa
    2004   "International Therapeutic Peace and Justice in Bosnia." *Social and Legal Studies* 13 (3): 377–401.

Putman, Robert
    1993   *Making Democracy Work: Civic Traditions in Modern Italy.* Princeton: Princeton University Press.

Rancière, Jacques
    1999   *Dis-agreement: Politics and Philosophy.* Minneapolis: University of Minnesota Press.

Ramberg, Lucinda
    2014   *Given to the Goddess: South Indian Devadasis and the Sexuality of Religion.* Durham: Duke University Press.

Rechtman, Richard
    2000   "Stories of Trauma and Idioms of Distress: From Cultural Narratives to Clinical Assessment." *Transcultural Psychiatry* 37 (3): 403–15.

Reddy, Sita
    2002   "Temporarily Insane: Pathologising Cultural Difference in American Criminal Courts." *Sociology of Health and Illness* 24 (5): 667–87.

Renteln, Alison Dundes
2004   *The Cultural Defense*. New York: Oxford University Press.
Resta, Caterina
1988   *La misura della differenza*. Milan: Guerini e Associati.
Rieff, Philip
1966   *The Triumph of the Therapeutic: Uses of Faith after Freud*. New York: Harper & Row.
Risso, Michele, and Wolfang Böker
1992   *Sortilegio e delirio. Psicopatologia dell'emigrazione in prospettiva transculturale*. Naples: Liguori Editore.
Robben, Antonius
2005   "How Traumatized Societies Remember: The Aftermath of Argentina's Dirty War." *Cultural Critique* 59 (Winter): 120–64.
Rose, Nicholas and Carlos Novas
2005   "Biological Citizenship." In *Global Assemblages*, ed. A. Ong and S.J. Collier, 439–63. London: Blackwell.
Roudinesco, Elisabeth
2005   "Decolonizzare se stessi." In *Etnopsicoanalisi: Temi e protagonisti di un dialogo incompiuto*, ed. Roberto Beneduce, Bertrand Pulman, and Elisabeth Roudinesco, 129–38. Turin: Bolati Boringhieri.
Santiago-Irizarry, Vilma
2001   *Medicalizing Ethnicity: The Construction of Latino Identity in a Psychiatric Setting*. Ithaca: Cornell University Press.
Saunders, George R.
1993   "'Critical Ethnocentrism' and the Ethnology of Ernesto de Martino." *American Anthropologist* 95 (4): 875–93.
Saviano, Roberto
2009   "Il coraggio dimenticato." *La Repubblica*, May 13.
Schauer, Edward J., and Elisabeth M. Wheaton
2006   "Sex Trafficking into the United States: A Literature Review." *Criminal Justice Review* 31 (2): 146–69.
Scheper-Hughes, Nancy
1990   "Three Propositions for a Critically Applied Medical Anthropology." *Medical Anthropology Quarterly* 30 (2): 189–97.
Scheper-Hughes, Nancy, and Anne Lovell
1987   *Psychiatry Inside-Out: Selected Writings of Franco Basaglia*. New York: Columbia University Press.
Schirripa, Pino
2005   *Politiche della cura: Terapie, potere e tradizione nel Ghana contemporaneo*. Rome: Argo.
Schneider, Jane
1998   *Italy's "Southern Question": Orientalism in One Country*. Oxford: Berg.
Seppilli, Tulio
2001   "Medical Anthropology 'at Home': A Conceptual Framework and the Italian Experience." *Rivista della della Società italiana di antropologia medica* 11: 23–36.

Signorelli, Amalia
    2000   "Alcune riflessioni antropologiche sulla storia della prostituzione in Italia." *Spunti e Ricerche* 15: 13–41.
Signorelli, Assunta, and Mariangela Treppete
    2001   *Services in the Window: A Manual for Interventions in the World of Migrant Prostitution.* Trieste: Asterios Editore.
Sniderman, Paul M.
    2000   *The Outsider: Prejudice and Politics in Italy.* Princeton: Princeton University Press.
Spivak, Gayatri Chakravorty
    1993   *Outside in the Teaching Machine.* New York: Routledge.
Steinberg, Suzanne S.
    2007   *The Pinocchio Effect: On Making Italians (1860–1920).* Chicago: University of Chicago Press.
Stengers, Isabelle
    2009   "Intervento al Master di Secondo Livello 'Etnomedicina e Etnopsichiatria.'" *I Fogli di ORISS* 31–32: 25–35.
Stevenson, Lisa
    2012   "The Psychic Life of Biopolitics: Survival, Cooperation, and Inuit Community." *American Ethnologist* 39 (3): 592–613.
Strathern, Marilyn
    1999   *Property, Substance, and Effect: Anthropological Essays on Persons and Things.* London: Athlone Press.
Summerfield, Derek
    1999   "A Critique of Seven Assumptions behind Psychological Trauma Programs in War-Affected Areas." *Social Science & Medicine* 48: 1449–62.
Taliani, Simona
    2012   "Coercion, Fetishes, and Suffering in the Daily Lives of Young Nigerian Women in Italy." *Africa* 82 (4): 579–608.
Taliani, Simona, and Francesco Vacciano, eds.
    2006   *Altri corpi: Antropologia e etnopsicologia della migrazione.* Milan: Edizioni Unicopoli.
Taussig, Michael
    1997   *The Magic of the State.* New York: Routledge.
Taylor, Charles
    1994   *Multiculturalism.* Princeton: Princeton University Press.
Terranova-Cecchini, Rosalba
    2002   "Intervista a Rosalba Terranova-Cecchini: Passaggi." *Rivista Italiana di Scienze Transculturali* 2: 44–53.
Ticktin, Miriam
    2011   *Casualties of Care: Immigration and the Politics of Humanitarianism in France.* Berkeley: University of California Press.
Turner, Victor
    1967   *The Forest of Symbols: Aspects of Ndembu Ritual.* Ithaca: Cornell University Press.
    1982   *From Ritual to Theatre: The Human Seriousness of Play.* New York: PAJ Publications.

Vacchiano, Francesco
  2007 "Bruciare di desiderio: Realtà sociale e soggettività dei giovani 'harraga' marocchini." PhD diss., Università degli Studi di Torino.
van Dijk, Rijk
  2001 "'Voodoo' on the Doorstep: Young Nigerian Prostitutes and Magic Policing in the Netherlands." *Africa* 71 (4): 558–85.
Van Gennep, Arnold
  1960 *The Rites of Passage.* Chicago: University of Chicago Press.
Vaughan, Megan
  1991 *Curing Their Ills: Colonial Power and African Illness.* Cambridge: Polity Press.
Venturini, Ernesto, ed.
  1979 *Il giardino dei gelsi.* Turin: Einuadi.
Wagner, Roy
  1975 [1981] *The Invention of Culture.* Chicago: University of Chicago Press.
Welch, Rhiannon N.
  2008 "Under the Shadow of Our Flag: Race and (Re)productivity in Liberal Italy." PhD diss., University of California, Berkeley.
Winnicott, Donald W.
  1967 "The Location of Cultural Experience." *International Journal of Psychoanalysis* 48: 368–72.
  1986a "Cure." In *Home Is Where We Start From,* 112–22. New York: Norton.
  1986b "Transitional Objects and Transitional Phenomena." In *Playing and Reality,* 1–25. London: Routledge.
Winterdyk, John, and Philip Reichel
  2010 "Introduction to Special Issue: Human Trafficking: Issues and Perspectives." *European Journal of Criminology* 7 (1): 5–10.
Yanagisako, Sylvia
  2002 *Producing Culture and Capital: Family Firms in Italy.* Princeton: Princeton University Press.
Young, Allan
  1995 *The Harmony of Illusions: Inventing Post-Traumatic Stress Disorder.* Princeton: Princeton University Press.
Zanetti, Zeno
  1978 [1892] *La medicina delle nostre donne.* Città di Castello: Edizioni Clio.
Zarowsky, Christina
  2004 "Writing Trauma: Emotion, Ethnography, and the Politics of Suffering among Somali Returnees in Ethiopia." *Culture, Medicine, and Psychiatry* 28 (2): 189–209.

Index

Page numbers in italics refer to figures and tables.